THE PRICE OF FAME

THE PRICE OF FAME

THE BIOGRAPHY OF DENNIS PRICE

ELAINE PARKER
AND
GARETH OWEN

FONTHILL

I would like to dedicate this book to all the wonderful actors and actresses who helped make it possible, with a special thank you to Madeline Smith.

Also in memory of my dear friend, Charles Baugh of Cannock.

E. P.

Fonthill Media Language Policy

Fonthill Media publishes in the international English language market. One language edition is published worldwide. As there are minor differences in spelling and presentation, especially with regard to American English and British English, a policy is necessary to define which form of English to use. The Fonthill Policy is to use the form of English native to the author. Elaine Parker and Gareth Owen were born and educated in the United Kingdom; therefore, British English has been adopted in this publication.

Fonthill Media Limited
Fonthill Media LLC
www.fonthillmedia.com
office@fonthillmedia.com

First published in the United Kingdom and the United States of America 2018

British Library Cataloguing in Publication Data:
A catalogue record for this book is available from the British Library

ISBN 978-1-78155-689-4

Typeset in 10.5pt on 13pt Sabon
Printed and bound in England

Acknowledgements

Elaine Parker would like to thank the following people for their help in making this book possible:

Gareth Owen, for helping take my notes, research, and text and putting it all together.

Ian Carmichael, Michael Denison, Patrick Macnee, Joyce Carey, Ellen Pollock, Spike Milligan, Eric Sykes, Alec McCowen, Alec Guinness, Barry Took, Michael Powell, Leslie Phillips, Derek Fowlds, Mark Wynter, Hilary Bottomley, Nick Hague, Roy Boulting, David Battley, Michael Hordern, Bill Owen, Jo Scott Matthews, Mary Barclay, Peter Cushing, Ronald Fraser, Desmond Llewelyn, Sam West, Muriel Box, Katie Boyle, Moira Lister, Zena Walker, Geraldine McEwan, Virginia McKenna, Thora Hird, Margaret Lacey, Leslie Halliwell, Jan Coombe-Dreyer, Richard Murdoch, Joan Sanderson, Mary Kerridge, Freddie Jones, Dee Macdonald, Liz Fraser, Sylvia Syms, June Whitfield, Madeline Smith, Christine Pollon, Norman Rossington, Anna Palk, Irene Handl, Peggy Mount, Shaun Noble, Stuart Latham, Marcus Wootton, Richard Waring, Terence Alexander, Peter Jones, George Cole, Robin Askwith, Graham Stark, Kenneth Griffith, Charlie Drake, Margaret Lockwood, Joan Greenwood, Phyllis Calvert, Jean Kent, Wanda Ventham, Joan Craft, Paul Scofield, Thorley Walters, Raymond Huntley, Gordon Jackson, Derek Nimmo, Michael Gough, Ralph Michael, Joyce Cook, Edward Willis, Charles Wrinch, Peter Green, Irene Hannington, Heather Laughton, Tony Money, George Guille, Charles Falle, Jane Cox, Lawrence De Carteret, Sybil De Carteret, Edie Hamon, Stanley Falle, James Le Feuvre, Louis B. Frewer, Sam Kiley Worthington, Nick Hague, Patricia Dainton, Eunice Gayson, Bruce Montague, Steve Roud, Robin Goodfellow, Charles Baugh, Talking Pictures TV, Croydon

Library, Bristol library, Guernsey Library, The British Film Institute, and The Student File of Dennis Price at Worcester College Archives courtesy of The Provost and Fellows of Worcester College, Oxford.

Thanks also to Iris Harwood for her eagle-eyed input and to Massimo Moretti of Studio Canal Films Ltd for kindly allowing use of the Ealing and ABPC images from Dennis Price's various films made with those companies.

CONTENTS

Introduction

Dennis Price (1915–1973) was without doubt one of the most promising and talented newcomers to the world of theatre and film in the late 1930s, and arguably reached his screen best in the classic Ealing comedy *Kind Hearts and Coronets* (1949). Huge praise was lavished upon him and he was compared alongside theatrical contemporaries Laurence Olivier, John Gielgud, and Ralph Richardson as being destined for great things.

Many scene-stealing performances followed in such differing films as *The Dancing Years* (1950), *The Intruder* (1953), *Private's Progress* (1956), *The Naked Truth* (1957), *Tunes of Glory* (1960), *Tamahine* (1963), and *Theatre of Blood* (1973), to name but a few, proving Dennis Price could play comedy just as easily as he could turn his hand to horrific or dramatic roles. He also found himself incredibly at home in the new burgeoning medium of television, and delivered some of his finest acting on the small screen, perhaps most fondly and famously as the ever-reliable butler Jeeves in *The World of Wooster* (1965–1967).

Of his 100 or so feature films, there were admittedly some less than memorable roles, sometimes chosen out of necessity to pay the rent, out of friendship and loyalty, or because well-intentioned stories simply failed to find an audience. The problems came when Dennis chose more misfires than hits, and with leading parts on the big screen thereby proving more elusive, he was increasingly forced to take on bit-part and cameo roles, which, although he shone in them, they were far beneath his talents and for which he was much maligned over the ensuing years, both personally and professionally. Many critics took against him and reserved their harshest comments after he made *Lady Godiva Rides Again* (1951) and *Charley Moon* (1956), in which he was cast as failing actors. To him, they were just jobs, but the reviewers suggested there were parallels between the characters and his own fading leading-man career; they claimed

Dennis Price (1915–1973).

audiences were now laughing at Dennis Price, rather than laughing with him.

Sadly, his many talents never extended to financial matters, and in 1966 he found himself—and not for the first time—in hot water with the Inland Revenue, the result of which forced him to relocate to the Channel Islands in what he described as 'a strategic withdrawal'. In order to pay off the tax man, Dennis Price pretty much accepted any work that was offered, which further contributed to the downward spiral of quality parts. It was a self-perpetuating nightmare of sorts.

This book was initially researched between 1986 and 1993 as an intended tribute to Dennis Price, and I was fortunate in being able to interview and chat with many of Dennis's co-stars who have, sadly, since left us. Two things became clear to me: Dennis had very few real friends—you could probably count them on one hand—and he was a hugely private person. He was always terribly good mannered and kind, and no one had a bad word to say about him; pretty much everyone liked him, which, in showbusiness, is quite rare. Many of the people I wrote to or spoke with said they did not have much to say about him because beyond initial niceties of meeting and working together, they never actually 'knew' the real Dennis Price. They may have shared the screen or stage with him, but that was where their association ended.

My notes and research were set aside, but my interest never diminished, especially after a Channel 4 documentary in the mid-1990s performed a total character assassination on Dennis, suggesting he was an alcoholic, tax-avoiding, closet homosexual who had been blackmailed for years and had poured his career away. It was awful, and I felt the story of the actor I had been researching was at total odds with the man portrayed in this programme. Yet who would the public believe: an influential broadcaster or an aficionado turned biographer?

After some years in a drawer, I rediscovered my notes, letters, and research and realised it was time to set the record straight and tell the real story of Dennis Price, the most thrillingly talented actor of his generation who, while having personal demons and suffering tragedies, was actually a great wit who brightened any room he walked into and whose company people craved.

In the intervening years, there have been continued rumours (I say rumours because there was never any actual proof concerning his so-called secret homosexuality). Yet in tracing things back, it seems these Chinese whispers started spreading because of his unusual relationship with his manager, Marcus Wootton (1936–1993), by assuming that as several single actors of his generation were in gay relationships with their managers—including Frankie Howerd, Dirk Bogarde, and Micheál MacLiammóir—then he must have been too.

While I admit the nature of Dennis's business relationship with his manager was often puzzling, particularly as the latter was disliked pretty much everywhere he ventured and not least by Dennis's friends and co-stars, Wootton was married twice (as well as having numerous girlfriends), was the father of three children, and heterosexual in every way. Dennis Price, too, was married for many years, was the father of two daughters, and had engaged in a long-time affair with actress Margaret Lockwood, among other of his leading ladies. Far from him being, as claimed, in 'emotional turmoil over his sexuality during his marriage', he was in fact at his most promiscuous with women, which led to his wife divorcing him after she caught him 'in the act', as it were.

Dennis Price had clearly defined chapters in his career. The 1940s saw him as a romantic idol; he then moved into darkly sardonic roles in the early 1950s and then became a mainstay of comedies later in the decade; television beckoned in the 1960s; and he ended up as a star of horror films in his last few years.

While other leading men faded into obscurity, Dennis Price was a survivor and a bit of a chameleon, able to constantly change his act to fit the mood and style of the times. Even when the British film industry was in one of its periodic slumps and he was reduced to making films for the notoriously low-budget Spanish director Jesus Franco, Dennis found himself in good company as the great Christopher Lee was also a Franco regular.

Everybody has told me Dennis Price was an intensely private man. It seems what a handful of journalists and writers did not therefore know, they have either assumed or invented, and arguably much of what has been said and written has been based on speculation and rumour. I, however, have tried to leave no stone unturned in my quest to find the truth about my subject as I wanted to build a true and factual picture of him, which I hope I have succeeded in doing in the pages that follow.

I have concluded Dennis Price was an immensely talented actor and a very special human being and that, to my mind, means he deserves to be remembered with the truth ... and with some affection too.

Elaine Parker, 2017.

NB: Dates of film and TV projects in the ensuing pages refer to the year of production, and not their year of release.

1

It All Started with Goldilocks (1915–1936)

The man everyone came to know as actor Dennis Price was christened Dennistoun John Franklyn Rose-Price, having entered the world on Wednesday, 23 June 1915, at Ruscombe Lodge, Twyford in Berkshire, England.

He descended from nobility, namely the Prices of Trengwainton, Cornwall, whose lineage can be traced back to the first Baronet in 1815 and whose family motto declares 'All depends on God' with an accompanying crest depicting a dragon's head holding a severed hand in its jaws, described as 'dripping blood all proper'. Little did anyone realise just how it might pertain to some of Dennis's later horror film roles.

Both Dennis's father and grandfather were professional soldiers. His father, Thomas, was a captain in the 11th Lancers, Indian Army, and was the eldest of four children born and educated in Melbourne, Australia. In 1911, Thomas was sent to England to be *aide-de-camp* to the general officer commanding at Aldershot. Aged thirty-six, with his army career well established, Thomas became a regular face at many social functions and hunt balls with the primary aim of taking a wife. He found his perfect match in the daughter of an eminent land owner in nearby Twyford, and on 29 August that same year, he married Dorothy Patience Verey.

The wedding took place at the church of St Mary the Virgin, Twyford, with Dorothy's first cousin, the Reverend Cecil H. Verey, officiating. The happy couple moved in to the family home, Bridge House, where their first child, Robert Caradoc, was born the following May.

Dorothy was a very beautiful woman—tall, slim, and with dark hair—and Dennis certainly inherited his good looks from her and bore little, if no, resemblance to his father. Dorothy listed her favourite pastime as riding horses.

Despite the enviable size of Bridge House, which is today a nursing home, it seemed more fitting that the Prices should have a home of their

Ruscombe Lodge, in Twyford, birthplace of Dennis Price.

own, so they moved further down the road to Ruscombe Lodge, although it was more of a mansion than a lodge.

A couple of years later, at the outbreak of the Great War in July 1914, Thomas Price (whom his wife affectionately nicknamed 'Rose' as he was, after all, a 'Rose-Price') was posted to France. It was halfway through the following year that Dennis was born. His full Christian name, Dennistoun, was very unusual and was not considered a 'proper first name', though as it was the surname of his paternal grandmother, Thomas obviously felt otherwise. As for his other names, John was after his great-grandfather, while Franklyn and Rose went far back into the family's history.

Three years later, in May 1918 and during the final months of the war, Dennis and his elder brother were joined by a sister, Mary Dorothy, and the three children enjoyed a very happy childhood together.

From the word go, Dennis and his siblings had a privileged and enviable lifestyle. Part of their early schooling was spent learning the history of his forebears, their achievements and of the family seats spread around Britain—Trengwainton on their father's side, and their mother's ancestral home Dunboyne Castle in Ireland, not to mention other grand houses spread among various other relatives. The Rose-Prices were hidebound by traditions going back generations, but those customs, Dennis discovered, were soon to become tiresome obligations rather than an example he wished to follow.

Dennis spent most of his formative years in the company of his nanny and became close to her. In fact, he liked and was close to all the servants and because he was never any trouble; they in turn became very fond of him. Years later, he confessed to being in awe of the butlers and their air of authority, which to a small boy must have been quite daunting.

Aged nine, Dennis was sent to Copthorne Boy's Preparatory School in Sussex for a young gentleman's education. This is where his natural talent as an actor first manifested itself as after taking a keen interest in the school productions, Dennis was cast in his first part as 'Goldilocks', with three of his fellow classmates playing the bears. It must have taken a fair bit of courage, along with putting up with some leg-pulling, for young Dennis to don a blonde curly wig and dress—but then again, that is half the fun of acting.

Soon after turning thirteen, Dennis left Copthorne and progressed to Radley College in Berkshire, joining in January 1929. The family meanwhile relocated to Kent, where his father took the position of commandant at the Hythe wing of the Small Arms School in the High Street, and they moved into a large pre-Victorian house on the hill, which had been known as the 'Commandant's house' since the early 1800s. It remained Dennis's home during school holidays for the next three years, until his father retired and they moved to 67 Seabrook Road, or 'Madron House' as Thomas called it, after the Cornish town.

In the summer of Dennis's first year at Radley, there was an open day, and parents arrived to discuss their child's future. Dennis's mother, Dorothy, upon mentioning Dennis's interest in previous school productions was advised by his housemaster to, '... go see Charles Wrinch, he's a man who's connected with acting.' Dorothy, went straight to him and firmly announced 'My son's an actor!'—a rather blunt statement if ever there was one, which left Wrinch quite taken aback. Nevertheless, Mr. Wrinch gave Dennis the chance to show what he could do in the next school production, George Bernard Shaw's drama of turbulent life in America during the War of Independence, *The Devil's Disciple*. Dennis was cast in the very minor role of the aged and cantankerous Uncle Titus.

The following year, Wrinch conducted what he described as 'a very bold experiment' and cast Dennis as Carl Peterson, the middle aged and sinister villain, in Sapper's *Bulldog Drummond*. He gave him the part purely because he had shown such an extraordinary aptitude for playing elderly personalities, despite being only fifteen. He was 'thoroughly wicked and in his element as Peterson', Wrinch added. It was a first in the school's history, when the students (who were often made to watch a play) actually took notice and were in fact spellbound by Dennis's fine portrayal of the famous rogue. Unbeknown to Dennis, W. A. Darlington, the dramatic critic for *The Daily Telegraph* and good friend of Charles Wrinch, was also in the audience.

Dennis certainly proved his mother had been right in her judgement, and the faith placed in him by his mentor Charles Wrinch was deserved, though Wrinch also felt it fair to warn Dennis of the profession pitfalls; in an attempt to persuade him not to think of acting as being a serious career, he said, 'it could so easily lead to disaster,' while also admitting to himself that if Dennis had a mind to do so, he would stand a better chance than most.

With Dennis more enthusiastic than ever about acting, and with an advanced role under his belt, Wrinch and Darlington got together and discussed the possibility of Dennis playing a straight and very serious part in Oliver Goldsmith's *She Stoops to Conquer*. They agreed the role of young Marlow would be perfect, only Dennis absolutely hated it. It became obvious that he could not wait to return to his speciality of playing aged villains.

During the school holidays, Wrinch went down to Hythe to stay with Dennis and his family at Madron House and found, to his amazement, that Dennis had formed his own amateur dramatic society comprising mainly of elderly, retired Navy people, all much older than him, but in no time at all, he had them under his superb direction. They were actually busy preparing for a production of John Galsworthy's *Loyalties*, in which Dennis was to play the part of De Lavis, but tragedy struck when one of the cast dropped out. With only three days' notice until curtain up, Dennis wasted no time in roping in his schoolmaster to play the character and luckily for Wrinch, it was the part of the family solicitor who was seated at a desk the whole time, with the lines written out in front of him.

All of Dennis's thespian activities passed over the head of his father who, now retired, lived quietly in a world of his own, taking no interest at all in his son's endeavours. As to whether he paid any attention to Dennis's studies at Radley, we cannot be sure, but his son's poor academic achievements certainly would not have passed muster. However, Dennis did show more promise in extra-curricular activities, especially as an oarsman when he took part in the school's second rowing eight, and he also scooped the school's prizes for public speaking.

Dennis may have been the leading light of the school plays, but he was far from the only Radleyan to have ambitions of being an actor; there was Patrick Barr, a character actor with credits including *The Blue Lagoon* and *The Dam Busters*; and Desmond Llewelyn, who was to find fame playing 'Q' in the James Bond films some thirty years later. Llewelyn later described Dennis as a 'close friend while at Radley,' but the two men never acted together professionally, nor did they ever socialise in later years.

However, when Llewelyn was taken a prisoner of war in Germany during the Second World War, Dennis did keep his spirits up by writing to him. Though in truth, Dennis did not make any lasting friendships at Radley, apart from Charles Wrinch, and all the boys went their separate ways.

While in their teens, Dennis, his brother, and sister did not see all that much of each other apart from during the holidays. As the years progressed, they gradually drifted apart, meeting up again only at family functions. Robert (also known as Robin) was firmly set on a military career and looked every bit the part, with a square build and ruddy complexion—quite a contrast to Dennis. In fact, they were complete opposites in personality too as Robin certainly did not share his brother's sense of humour, but then again maybe the discipline of a strict army training at Sandhurst had not given him a lot to laugh about.

Dennis was a very likeable teenager. He was happy, friendly, and liked nothing better than playing pranks and dressing up for a show; he often took part in the social whirl during school holidays, including the horse racing events at Ascot and the Henley Royal Regatta. Though then living in Kent, he always felt more at home in Berkshire, where many of his relations resided, and often stayed at the Henley home of his grandmother, Lady Verey, his sole surviving grandparent.

Dennis certainly saw his future as an actor, but was often told—in no uncertain terms—that it was not respectable for a gentleman's son to enter such a torrid profession. The occasional play in the holidays was allowed, as it was just a pastime, a hobby, which is why Thomas Price probably paid his younger boy's theatrical activities little attention. In fact, regardless of Dennis's desires, his parents were making plans for their younger son's future in the Army. Appalled at the very thought, Dennis was able to swerve the idea thanks to his elder brother Robin being seemingly destined for great things in the military. Dennis could never compete nor live up to Robin so in 1932, their mother called a gathering of all concerned to try and work something out for the boy's future. They came from a very traditional and rather stiff-necked family who always made career decisions for their children. Attending from the Verey's side of the family were Dorothy's cousins, Lewis and Cecil, who were both Church of England clerics, and they suggested Dennis had 'all the right indications' to join the church, namely he was quiet, decent, and trustworthy. Surely, they reckoned, that was better than being an actor? So, it was decided and agreed.

To gain some experience in the theological field, Dennis spent some months at Magdalen Mission in London, which was run by Magdalen College of Oxford University. While there, he was put under the watchful eye of a very remarkable priest named Percy Maryon-Wilson, who before embracing the church had been *aide-de-camp* to the Governor General of South Africa. He was one of the missionaries of the poor and extremely Anglo-Catholic parish of St Mary Somerstown, St Pancras. Reverend Percy and his colleague Basil Jellicoe were responsible for establishing one of the first housing schemes for underprivileged people, directly opposite the church. Dennis stayed with Percy for a while and had an enjoyable time at his church, but as the weeks and months passed, he realised that he just did not have the dedication needed for the 'calling'. Even after two years of trying to submerge himself into all things religious, and still not feeling the 'call', Dennis's family insisted he must persist to avoid being 'plunged into acting' at any cost. Reluctantly but dutifully, Dennis agreed to study theology at university.

'I tried to get into Morton but couldn't pass the entrance exam' he said, though after sitting a second, token, exam in 1933, Dennis left for his second choice of Worcester College, Oxford.

It was not long before he reverted to his first love as during his holidays, and once more observed by Charles Wrinch, Dennis was back at Hythe organising a play, *Payment Deferred* (based on the novel of the same name by C. S. Forester), in which Charles Laughton had scored a huge success in London. The play was about psychology and in watching Dennis perform, Wrinch realised for the first time he was now able to express sympathy and pathos in his characterisations. This was clearly not a young man just indulging himself in a youthful pastime, he was showing a great depth of feeling in what was essentially a very unattractive leading role.

At Worcester College, Dennis quickly became a member of the Oxford University Dramatic Society (OUDS) and became so involved with college productions that he sorely neglected his studies and narrowly missed being expelled. 'After that', said Dennis, 'I gave up acting temporarily to become secretary of the OUDS, and pacified tutorial tempers.'

So much so he appeared in only one play, in June 1935, the Worcester Buskin's version of *The Merchant of Venice* in which he played Gratiano—a small part for an actor of his potential, opposite a young woman named Barbara, who later became Mrs Wrinch.

Dennis left Worcester College for the summer holidays in July 1936. On 15 August, he wrote:

> Dear Mr Provost,
>
> Since last seeing you I have finally realised, that for the moment, I do not feel sufficiently convinced to go on with plans for my ordination, as I had originally intended. It may be that later I shall want to go into the church and shall feel then more thoroughly determined about it. Therefore I have had to turn towards something else, and having been

> always deeply interested in the stage, I'm arranging very shortly to join a London acting school and try my luck from there. For such a career, a degree would be of no advantage—so further expense which would be involved in securing one, seems only to be wasted....

On 17 August, the Provost replied:

> My dear Price,
>
> I am sorry to hear of your change of plans though I am not altogether surprised, and sorry also that your course here is not to be finished by your graduating. It is unsatisfactory whatever you do subsequently that it should come to an end without a degree. I hope you will be successful in what you propose ...

In later years, Dennis offered the diplomatic explanation, 'You see, I wasn't very good at my books' as to why he left the college, whenever he was asked.

Having won his mother round to his way of thinking, and with her no doubt seeing his absolute determination, Dennis applied to and was accepted by The Embassy Theatre School, Swiss Cottage, London. Their carefully worked-out budget allowed for some young student actors who had shown great promise to be given a free place, while the other hopefuls were expected to pay a £100 fee per term for their tuition—a huge amount of money back then. Dennis was one of the lucky ones who was honoured with free membership, which meant he did not have to ask his family to pay his way. Together with another recipient of a free place, William Devlin, Dennis and the paying students studied acting under Eileen Thorndike (sister of Sybil) and Ronald Adam, where, as he put it, he had 'all the fundamentals rammed into me'. For a while during the mid-1930s, it was, without comparison, the best drama school in the country with a superb team of actors adept at passing on their skills in a practical and straight forward fashion. There was not any self-indulgent or 'method' acting allowed.

William Devlin was one of Dennis's few friends at the school who also showed great promise and was soon after praised by James Agate for his performance of King Lear. Devlin was frequently seen on television and in films during the 1950s and 1960s, but never quite made the grade as a leading man and had to satisfy himself with a series of supporting roles in low-budget horror films such as *The Shuttered Room* and *Blood of the Vampire* with Sir Donald Wolfit.

Eileen Thorndike was described as 'being more of a motherly figure rather than a teacher' and her brother, Russell, was deemed 'a loveable old brigand'. Incidentally, he was the first man to play Peer Gynt in England and perhaps more famously wrote the *Doctor Syn* series of books, which were made into several films, most notably by Disney and starring Patrick McGoohan (*The Scarecrow of Romney Marsh* in 1963). Russell occasionally took some 'enlightening' classes when the fancy took him. Both Eileen and Russell Thorndike obviously saw something in Dennis, as despite having only amateur stage plays behind him, right from the start, Dennis was offered the starring roles, the most outstanding performance of which he gave at The Embassy as 'Noah' in a translation of the play by Andre Obey. His handling of the role was said to be 'sheer brilliance' and 'very memorable'. In fact, when reflecting on his career later, Dennis said that playing 'Noah' was one of his all-time favourite stage parts.

Among the budding young actresses training at The Embassy was Irene Handl, who demonstrated early signs of skill as a comedienne with a brilliant ability to play any character role put her way, which she much preferred to the leading parts. In later life, though they had been contemporaries, Ms Handl had no recall of Dennis being in any plays with her and when they were both cast in the film *Watch It, Sailor!* (1961), she thought she was meeting Dennis for the first time. She soon appreciated his natural ability and seemed impressed by him 'swinging from light to sombre moods at the drop of a hat'. Dennis thoroughly enjoyed his time among other actors and despite all the discouragement and arguments with his family, he felt he had finally won the right to do what his heart was set on, and it was clear he was going to go far. Though no matter how hard he tried and proved himself, his family were not the slightest bit interested in his new career and regarded him as a rebel, the black sheep of the family who challenged their very ideals. There was certainly a snobbery in the close-knit community of the Rose-Prices and their society friends, who frowned that Dennis should mingle with people from other walks of life, but Dennis could see no reason why having money and breeding should set him apart from the rest of the human race.

Having won one battle, Dennis found himself about to face another as his family's attitudes concerning marriage were about to be laid down to him—the men married for property, titles, and social status rather than for passion. It was important, they said, any wife of Dennis's had her own income and knew how to conduct herself as the hostess at important functions. Dennis was aghast at yet more interference to come in his life.

2

Learning the Ropes (1937–1940)

After spending almost a year at drama school, Dennis travelled the provinces with a touring theatre company without much effect, and next became a member of the Croydon Repertory Company for whom he made his first stage appearance on 12 April 1937, playing Duggie Dent in *Behind your Back*, a comedy by Charles Landstone set in the bar of a West End theatre. The part was small but gave him scope to try out his talents. It was at Croydon he first met fellow young actor John Le Mesurier, who was also in the play in an uncredited role, although he was then known as John Halliley.

Nicholas Hannen, an established actor of stage and screen and a personal friend of the family for some years, had obviously been drafted in to try and encourage Dennis to take a more suitable career path, as he proclaimed 'It's a starving job, my boy. If you are lucky, you may jump over some of the others to find fame and fortune—never imagine you're there for long.' To a less headstrong individual, it may well have done the trick, but not Dennis.

Around this time and possibly even spurred on by his family's continued interference, Dennis made a strike for independence. He left the family home in Hythe and moved into his own bachelor flat at 49 Maybury Mansions, London (an address that no longer exists). After *Behind your Back*, he broke away from the Croydon company for a while on the recommendation of Tyrone Guthrie, the famous Shakespearian producer, who arranged an interview for Dennis with John Gielgud, who was about to embark on his 1937 season of plays at the Queen's Theatre, London. Dennis debuted in the West End on 6 September as Green and Exton's servant in *Richard II*, under the direction of Gielgud.

While in the company, Dennis became acquainted with Alec Guinness and they got on well together, though never became close friends, as Sir

Croydon Repertory Theatre, Dennis Price with John Le Mesurier, 1938. Reproduced with permission of Croydon Central Library.

Alec was fast to admit in what seemed to be a common trait in Dennis's life and career.

It was highly unusual that Gielgud's company were allowed the luxury of seven to nine weeks in which to rehearse their parts—usually it was far less, if even half that time—and each play ran for a minimum of eight weeks and a maximum of ten. The season opened with *Richard II*, followed by Sheridan's *The School for Scandal*, Chekov's *Three Sisters*, and ended with Shakespeare's *The Merchant of Venice*.

Following his West End run, Dennis's next stage part was as Marcellus in *Hamlet* at the Arts Theatre during January 1938; he returned to Croydon in June to become a regular player, joining established members Richard Wattis and Erik Chitty. The Repertory Theatre was very small, seating some 300-odd, and rather barn like in appearance. The stage was around 18–20 feet wide and 10–12 feet deep with no flying facilities. All the plays produced there were beautifully directed, notably by the late Michael Barry (a future head of the BBC Drama Department) and many of them were produced by Edmund Bailey, who also worked hard as an actor.

When he was not acting himself, Dennis always took an avid interest in every new production and especially rated Ivor Novello's *The Dancing Years*, which he went to see a total of eighteen times. The company presented a season of well-known and contemporary plays of the time, both comedy and drama. In another production, Dennis played Mark in *Autumn* by Margaret Kennedy. In the local newspaper, *The Advertiser*, their theatrical critic wrote:

> *Autumn* is a tragedy of a middle-aged woman, who through her own scheming, finds her lover losing his passion for her and falling in love with her step-daughter. Susan Richards plays with rare understanding of Catherine's agonising attempt to give Mark up and her difficulty in appearing restrained. Dennis Price in the part, is restrained. He makes the man a charming person ...

Next followed a short season at Hull with the company and then the annual summer vacation period after which the Croydon Repertory theatre unveiled its seventh season. First up, Dennis was seen in *Housemaster*, a popular comedy on school life by Ian Hay which had just finished a long run in the West End.

The Advertiser reviewed it thus:

> *Housemaster* is every bit as funny as any of its predecessors, which means it abounds in laughs. The characters are well defined. Other members of the school staff are thoroughly well done by Sidney Monckton as Hastings and Dennis Price as the diffident music master.

Dennis then appeared in *Whiteoaks* and J. B. Priestley's *I Have Been Here Before* prior to leaving the company during October 1938, to star at the Arts and Haymarket Theatre, as Michael Firbanks in *A Party for Christmas*, though Dennis was back at Croydon in November to play Detective Raines in *I Killed the Count*.

Undoubtedly, Dennis's best role that year was Croydon's lavish production of *1066 and All That*, a musical with lyrics by Reginald Arkell that opened on Boxing Day. The company had been working hard for months organising and promoting the play and it resulted in a very high attendance. The musical consisted of three acts, each depicting a different chapter in ancient history, and all hilariously sent up. In Act 1, entitled 'Alfred the Grate', Dennis played Alfred, William the Conqueror, and a devilish Baron at the court of King John. In Act 2, he really went to town as a padded and grumpy looking Henry VIII, sitting on his throne while his six wives played a game of musical chairs. He then reappeared on stage as a dandy and in the third and final act, the play approached the time of 'William and Mary' with Dennis cast as Marlborough and in scene ten, the big finale, the full company came on stage to perform a big musical number.

> It is almost impossible to single out scenes, let alone performances, stated the local news review. There is a good array of monarchs, beginning with Alfred involved in a nightmarish pantomime and progressing to William the Conqueror, both played by Dennis Price. This actor's best piece of work during the revue, is his impersonation of Mr Charles Laughton as Henry VIII.

Having enjoyed a fleeting Christmas and New Year holiday, Dennis's first project of 1939 was to star as a very elegant Robert Browning in *The Barratts of Wimpole Street*, to Marion Holmes's Elizabeth; it was a role made for him. Joining the cast as Bella Hedley was a twenty-three-year-old aspiring actress named Joan Schofield, the daughter of Major General Arthur C. Temperley, who had taken her aunt's name for the stage. As soon as she met Dennis, there was an instant rapport and they quickly became good friends. They acted together again, when Dennis repeated his portrayal of Michael Firbanks in *A Party for Christmas*, with Joan taking the role of Pamela Sutton.

> Marion Holme supplies a delightful portrait of a lovesick maiden, while Richard Wattis as her brother exhibits amusingly the characteristics of romantic but inexperienced youth. Dennis Price and Joan Schofield are the effective exponents of young love ...

So proclaimed the review, which was in fact closer to the truth than they might have realised. Yet Dennis found making close and lasting friendships difficult, as although he was often outgoing with his jokes and impersonations, he was also a very shy and private man, so it was not exactly a whirlwind love affair as more a slow burning attraction.

Dennis next starred in Richard Llewelyn's *Poison Pen* in Croydon, a drama set in the vestry of an old church, and again he shared the bill with Richard Wattis and Joan. In *Gentleman Unknown* by A. A. Milne, Dennis proved ideal casting in the part of 'that unorthodox salesman of hosiery', Geoffrey Fontanelle. 'He reconciles charm of personality with very human weakness in such a way as never to lose sympathy. Every line entrusted to him is given full effect.'

Dennis's most outstanding performance during the year however was playing Laurent, lover of French adulteress Theresa Raquin (Marion Holme) in the English version of Emil Zola's powerful story of a murderous couple *Thou Shalt Not*. Edmund Bailey was cast as the ill-fated husband Camille and the much-acclaimed stage actress Nancy Price as Theresa's suspicious mother-in-law. The company were quite honoured to have such a celebrated lady of the theatre joining them. However, Miss Price's meeting with her namesake Dennis led to an embarrassing incident during the rehearsal; at one point in the play, he has to grab her, whereupon he is rebuffed with the words 'Mind my breasts, dear boy!' and for once Dennis was left speechless and blushing.

After another production and a short break, Dennis portrayed Adrian Blenderbland in George Bernard Shaw's comedy *The Millionairess*. Then there was *Claudius and the Bee*; just as the name suggests, it was a peculiar comedy about a hive of bees with the players dressed accordingly. Dennis and fellow actors Stafford Byrne and Richard Wattis capered about outside the nest on a sunny afternoon, or so the plot went. *Service* by Dodie Smith featured Dennis in the lead part of Geoffrey Fielding, with Joan as Isobel Service and Paul Scofield, a student with the company, was given the minor part of Mr Tressit, in a story set in the slump of 1932–33. Scofield, as a young actor just starting out, was in awe of the established players such as Dennis but his shy nature prevented him entering into conversations with the 'stars' of the show. Though he did observe that, 'As a young man, Dennis was most kind and friendly to the rest of the company, but could be tense with a submerged emotional quality.' While Joan Schofield on the other hand, 'Displayed a calmness and radiance which seemed impressive

After Dr Bland makes a fatal faux pas about the millionairess's father, she throws him in the river. Dennis is seen here with Sophia Loren in the film *The Millionairess*.

to the other, less confident actors'. Many people thought Paul Scofield was the younger brother of Joan, unaware of their different name spellings and that she had changed her name by deed poll.

It is a fact that a lot of couples have differing personalities, which attract them to one another, as they each have something the other does not possess. It was partly these contrasting qualities in Joan that attracted Dennis, but he was a quiet, unassuming man and did not share his feelings very often, least of all with his fellow actors. After watching a performance of *The Dancing Years* in the company of Joan, he artfully used the romance of the occasion to propose marriage and she gladly accepted. He and Joan left the company on 19 June to prepare for their forthcoming wedding and in announcing their plans surprised everyone; the other actors were not even aware that there had been a romance going on between them, and understandably so, as the players worked at such a pace there was little time left over for socialising especially as there was always a mad dash to catch a train at East Croydon back to London after the performance. Whether Dennis and Joan's sudden engagement was the result of a whirlwind romance or the snap decision of a single man giving in to the pressures of 'finding a nice girl and settling down' remains uncertain, especially as there had been no outward signs of their feelings for one another, no longing looks or whispered messages, or no extra depth to their love scenes on stage. Yet there was no denying Joan Schofield had captured her beau's heart with her striking good looks, dyed blonde hair (which she always wore short and usually in rigid curls), and along with her beautiful and rounded oval face, her most outstanding feature, her eyes, which looked especially large when she opened them wide—so much so she often used them to great effect when needing to appear soulful and appealing. Joan had a soft and well-spoken voice, a slim physique and was said to never put on any weight. She was also rather petite at 5 feet 3 inches tall. Although seldom seen to smile, she was said to have 'an angelic appearance'.

Underneath, Joan was a very strong-willed, ambitious person, boasting lots of self-confidence. Coming from an affluent background, acting began for her out of more of an interest than a career. Yet Joan never regarded her work as a pastime, and her greatest wish was to one day be as famous as Joan Crawford or Margaret Lockwood, who were then dominating the cinemas. If determination and ambition were all that was needed for success, she was already there.

Dennis had come under pressure from his relatives to find a good match and thankfully, in the family's estimation and that of their social circle, Joan was the perfect partner in every respect—she was elegant, genteel, good looking, and had her own income. Charles Wrinch said,

'Dennis made a very good marriage. Joan came from a good background and family. Her father was military—a Major General, I believe. Yes, an excellent choice of partner'.

Although engaged, marriage was not Dennis's first priority. More important to him was making a success of his career and to prove to his relatives that he was not a failure. Acting in the 1930s carried the stigma of being 'not respectable', an attitude left over from the Victorian era, when many travelling actresses were regarded as no better than prostitutes, and male actors were most famous for frequently skipping their lodgings without paying the rent.

Quite how actors in the burgeoning medium of television were regarded is not so clear, but on 13 March 1939, Dennis made his first TV appearance in a BBC drama broadcast live from Alexandra Palace (the first television production of Patrick Hamilton's *Rope*) as one of the two students who strangle a youth to test a theory. Dennis became more certain than ever that acting was to be his life's career. Yet with war looming, Dennis's hand was forced, and arrangements for the wedding went ahead straight away, cutting the couple's courtship period short, which undoubtedly led to strains on the relationship later.

Dennis's last play at Croydon was *The Queen was in the Parlour*, a comedy by Noël Coward. He was certainly missed by the company in the coming months as they had all got on very well together and there was a pleasant atmosphere; some of their friendships were more enduring than others and of his colleagues, Dennis kept in touch with Stafford Byrne and Richard Wattis; the latter remained a close friend of the couple and later became godfather to their daughter, Susan.

Many actors who made their debuts at the Croydon Repertory later became household names, most notably Dennis, Paul Scofield, John Le Mesurier, Richard Wattis, and Erik Chitty (of *Please Sir!* fame) to name but a few. Others diversified into various branches of the business and became writers and directors, including Stafford Byrne who penned a children's story *Willie the Squouse* about an animal that was half-mouse, half-squirrel. The BBC thought so highly of it that they broadcast the story on the radio.

Sadly, many of the other artistes from Croydon were not so lucky and struggled on with bit parts, or faded into complete obscurity. In 1941, at the height of the Second World War, the repertory theatre was bombed, thankfully when it was empty. Gradually, all the old theatres in the area disappeared and were eventually replaced with one large concrete complex 'The Fairfield Halls', sadly indicative of the post-war ugly buildings that make modern Croydon such an eyesore.

Meanwhile, on 29 June 1939, six days after his twenty-fourth birthday, Dennis was married to Joan at St Paul's Church, Knightsbridge, London, by his mother's cousin, Reverend Cecil Verey, assisted by the Reverend E. K. C. Hamilton. Dennis's brother, then serving in the Welsh Guards, was best man. His bride, wearing an empire-style dress of white slipper satin and carrying a bouquet of white roses and lilies of the valley, was given away by her cousin, Henry Whitehead. Dennis, elegant as ever, wore his best morning suit. Nicholas Murray Leslie was their page, dressed in a Gainsborough suit of white satin to echo Joan's ensemble. The reception afterwards was organised by Joan's aunt, Mrs Christopher Schofield, and was held at 23 Knightsbridge. The couple honeymooned in the South of France.

The (second) love of Dennis's life, as ever, was his acting and he was not away from the stage for long. That following October, he returned to tread the boards in a season at The Playhouse Theatre in Beaumont Street, Oxford. He took the lead in a variety of different productions and scored a hit in *String Quartette*, a very topical anti-Nazi drama by Gerald Savory. It was due to run in the West End with Dennis in the lead, but the Blitz saw plans cancelled. Oxford was a city that held many nostalgic memories for Dennis and he was thrilled to return as a professional actor just three years after his theology studies. He wrote:

> My very happy memories of the Playhouse go back to undergraduate days at Worcester College, when it was one's particular pleasure to lure Stanford Holme [Playhouse's producer] out to dinner, see him arrive in a weird horse and cart contraption, listen to the inconsequential talk and later to watch, in the old Playhouse, an extremely efficient and exciting production which was his own.
>
> Later in the year and very early in the war, before one's enlistment and at the New Playhouse, it was my great privilege to act for Eric Dance [founder of the New Playhouse] and his colleagues. James Agate was in the city for a while then and kept us all highly enlightened and instructed after the shows, in one or other of the pubs we all frequented during that 1940 phoney-war winter. Eric Dance's generosity and good fun will long be remembered by many.
>
> It fell to my lot to play Sir Percy Blakeney in *The Scarlet Pimpernel* and for the opening scene when Sir Percy as a revolutionary hag approaches the Paris barricades with refugees, the stage management had chosen a nag to draw the cart, whose particular dislike of lights, theatres and the excitement of the scene had obviously never been realised. Sometimes I would leap in terror from the whirling cart, only to reveal the hag's outfit on top and Sir Percy's ballroom clothes below or else retreat in confusion to the wings, hoping that the ghosts of Fred Terry and Julia Neilson wouldn't gasp with indignation and despair.

> It will always be a great delight to return to The Playhouse as audience or actor and to wander home down Beaumont Street with very happy memories.

Returning to London and their comfortable rented flat in the West End, from 6 February 1940, Dennis appeared as Roderick McArdin in the play *September Rain*, a comedy by H. D. Barr, which was set in Scotland and staged at the Chanticleer, a small theatre within the old Webber-Douglas School of Acting in South Kensington. The other players pretty much faded into history, except for his co-star, Andrew Cruickshank, who famously portrayed Dr Cameron in the long-running BBC television series *Dr. Finlay's Casebook*. The theatre itself was not around much longer as shortly after the run ended, the building was bombed out of existence by the Luftwaffe. The War Office ordered places of entertainment, such as theatres, to close to avoid mass casualties during such bombing raids. Dennis had to give up acting for a while, which depressed him more than the blackouts, the Blitz, and rationing put together.

3

The Army Game (1940–1942)

Rather than waiting to be called up, Dennis enlisted into the armed services in March 1940 and was accordingly able to choose to be a gunner with the Royal Artillery; the division proved a popular choice with young men signing-up and was soon fully subscribed, though from day one, Dennis hated the Army and the dull daily routine he felt subjected to, and was very vocal about it to anyone in earshot. He could not wait to get back to acting, and envied his contemporaries who were making films as part of the war effort. Dennis had no desire to follow other Rose-Prices in a military career, and in fact wished he had not even passed his Army medical. Fed up and deflated, he was adamant military life would not turn him into a dullard.

Fortunately, he fell in with some like-minded comrades, some of whom were fellow actors, and they formed a close circle of chums to help relieve the daily monotony of Army duties. By most soldiers' standards, Dennis had a very comfortable war spending most of his time at barracks, including Northolt Aerodrome, Hayes in Middlesex, and those on the south and east coasts of England. When he was moved to Sevenoaks in Kent, he discovered half the enlisted acting fraternity were there too. It became a very laid-back battery, and when Alec Guinness visited (with a view to joining up himself), he found, to his dismay, the officer in charge was knitting. Dennis talked to Guinness enthusiastically about his fellow thespians Hughie and Sebastian, and what fun they had larking around. That sealed it for Guinness; he went off and joined the Navy.

Word soon got around about the slack regime at Sevenoaks, and having been deemed shambolic, the unit was broken up and sent to other artillery batteries around the country. Dennis had been deemed a bad influence, and with him treating the Army as a bit of a joke and a place where he just dressed up as a soldier, much as he would in a play, it was felt he needed to be taught a lesson. His attitude and carefree approach needed to be addressed, so Dennis was transferred to the east coast to another artillery battery. On arriving, he found his reputation had preceded him when his new commanding officer gave him a pep talk in which it was made quite clear that Dennis could not expect any special treatment because of his family background and there would be 'no nonsense tolerated'. The talk went on about the seriousness of war and the danger posed by Hitler, poised just across the English Channel. Dennis shut off and thought of other things.

On arriving at his billet, Dennis's first priority was to find some common ground with the other men; in glancing around, he surveyed the faces of his comrades and his heart sank as there were clearly no other like-minded sorts within the ranks. As he unpacked his kit, a rough voice said, 'Cheer up mate, it might never happen'. A man introduced himself as Alf and the ice was broken. After that, Dennis got to know the others fairly quickly, but realised they were all working class men and prior to call up had been builders, labourers and factory workers; there certainly were not any actors among their ranks. In fact, their backgrounds could not have been more different. Dennis had never done a day's manual work in his life, felt he had nothing in common with these working-class men, and felt at a loss as to how he would converse with them on a daily level, let alone get into any discussion of his passions, such as acting. The other soldiers soon picked up on Dennis's public-school accent and started to impersonate him, using exaggerated upper-class phrases such as, 'Don't mind if I do dear boy', 'I say, you chaps', and 'Frightfully good of you.' Dennis appeared to be amused by their jokes at first, but soon longed to be back among his chums.

While Dennis served his country, his wife Joan discovered she was pregnant. Once she was well on the way to having their first child, she moved to a nursing home in a town nearby Dennis's billet. One night, a German plane flew over and looked as though it was going to drop a bomb directly on the nursing home, but fortunately, its payload passed out to sea. Joan was left very shaken and it only served to make Dennis more intent to leave the services.

During authorised leave, Dennis and Joan travelled to London. It was there on 7 July that Joan gave birth to their first daughter in their first floor flat at 8 Sloane Street, Knightsbridge. She was christened Susan Joan Rose the following month, at the church of St Paul's, where her parents had been married just a year before. Dennis was every bit the proud father and felt on top of the world. Being in the heart of the West End and above a line of busy shops, the flat was far from an ideal place to bring up a child but before Dennis could turn his thoughts to moving, he had to return to camp. His leave had only served to remind him how much he hated the rigours of army life and a burning resentment set in; it was only going to be a matter of time before there was trouble.

Dennis's return to his unit was remembered by Charles Baugh, who was on guard duty that night. When a tall figure emerged from the darkness and approached him, Baugh uttered the classic line, 'Halt! Who goes there?'. Dennis remained silent—as if in defiance—and much to his surprise was marched away to see the commanding officer. He protested that it was 'quite ridiculous' for the squaddie to ask 'who goes there?' when he quite clearly recognised him. When asked why he did not respond, Dennis offered the excuse of being 'lost in thought' in his new role as a father, and the responsibilities were weighing heavily on his mind. He promised to be more careful in the future, and thought that was that. However, his CO told him that he was not the only father serving in the forces and he was extremely lucky to be in a position to make a home visit, as the men fighting overseas certainly could not nor did they have any regular contact with their loved ones. The CO ordered Dennis be sent to the Glasshouse (military prison) for a month, to reflect on the error of his ways.

Charles Baugh, in later years, was asked for his side of the story, and said:

> Dennis Price was very grand because he was an actor. He thought he was better than the rest of us. When he refused to answer me, I realised it was out of contempt and he needed to be taken down a peg or two and that's why I took him to the CO.
>
> His face was a picture when he was put on a charge, he couldn't believe what hit him. Putting him in prison certainly gave him something to think about. I later saw some of his films and used to love thinking of how he was back then—put behind bars in a holding cell. I hope he remembered me?
>
> What really rubbed it in for me was when he did those war films like *A Canterbury Tale*. He never went anywhere near the front line. While I was risking my life in the desert, he was capering around on a film set. Those people in the audience watching their hero should have known what he was really like. I enjoyed telling people about him.

Dennis was of course mortified to receive such a harsh punishment for what he regarded as an inconsequential act. He wondered if they had it in for him because he was an actor. Did they envy his lifestyle? His head was swimming as he was led away. He dreaded the thought of being locked up with types rougher than the usual squaddies he had encountered and so thought as only an actor might—he would play a part, a part that would mean he would adapt to their level of character. He would be 'one of the boys'. That was the only way he could see himself getting through the 'dreadful experience' ahead. He was correct in his assumptions as his fellow inmates were coarse, vulgar, rough, and totally lacking in any good graces. They soon started ribbing him with jokes about his upper-class accent, so in character, Dennis would reply in whatever regional accent they spoke with—cockney, Brummie, Yorkshire and so on. He actually took them by surprise and had them in fits of laughter; he was soon accepted as one of the lads.

Life in the Glasshouse was all about punishment, and as such, inmates were tasked with menial duties and faced long periods of boredom and confinement. Dennis found some more approachable than others and though they were types he had never ordinarily meet, let alone befriend, their class barriers had been temporarily lifted, though Dennis was selective in his companions insomuch as he always sought out the brighter men as he had always been attracted to intelligent conversation and never suffered fools. He actually learned a lot from their streetwise cunning and became aware some inmates were there solely to avoid the war and coming face-to-face with the enemy. Some would say they were cowards, yet Dennis listened to their stories and empathised and ultimately identified with them. In turn, he confided in the men about his own family's demands and expectations, and how he had hated army life.

One day, to relieve the boredom, the inmates suggested they play the 'anagram game'. Dennis had never heard of it, so it was explained as being very similar to Scrabble, where a jumble of letters had to be used to make up words. Instead of taking letter tiles from a bag, a phrase or sentence was chosen—be it a line from a poem, the title of a film, or a catchphrase—and the letters were written down in block capitals and then cut out and mixed up. The aim was to scramble the letters and make new words until they formed a sentence. There were no rules, as long as the words were spelt correctly. Sentences with the longest words, sentences that were prophetic, and sentences that were as vulgar and crude as possible were the three main goals; providing there was an 'F' and a 'C', it generally worked out. Dennis had been brought up to believe swear words were 'the language of the gutter', but he gave it a try, if only to please his companions. In debating what the first phrase would be, they asked Dennis what his full name was. When he told them it was Dennistoun John Franklyn Rose-Price, they all roared with laughter and decided this was just the phrase needed to get things underway. Between them, they produced many outstanding phrases, such as the following crude examples:

JOAN KINDLY OPENS HER CUNT FOR SINNER
JOAN FUCKS HORRID, STERN LENNY IN OPEN

DRY JOKES IN PINNER AFTER NOON'S LUNCH
SORRY, JOKER DENNIS CANNOT HELP IN FUN
THIN JOAN FUCKED LENNY'S PRISONER, RON
FUNNY CORNISH JOKER DENNIS TORE PLAN
SORRY! SINNER CANNOT HELP IN JOKE FUND
JOAN LETS DENNIS FUCK PENNY IN HORROR
INTERNALISED JOHNNY FUCKS PRONE RON
JOHNNY FOUND RON'S PRANK IN LEICESTER

Dennis appeared bowled over by the endless stream of profundities that could be created from his name, and surprised himself by the dark nature of what had emerged. It made him realise, if nothing else, now aged twenty-five, he had lived a pretty sheltered and blameless life, but the dark side to his nature was just waiting to be released under the right set of circumstances. Perhaps these Army experiences were prophetic. Even his name 'Dennis' could be rearranged as 'sinned'.

When he eventually emerged from the Glasshouse, Dennis resumed his normal duties though maintained his friendship with his new-found acquaintances. On his next spell of leave, he was invited to join one of these chums on a tour of London, as seen from the 'wrong side of the river'. Dennis was promised an unforgettable experience that would really open his eyes—visiting the seediest pubs, race tracks, dog tracks, gambling dens, card parties and night clubs. He was also introduced to some of the murkiest of East-End characters.

With war still raging, the subdued lighting and undercover nature of these dens gave it all an added dimension which thrilled Dennis. It was this introduction to a world Dennis had not previously known that proved to be both exciting and alluring; sadly, it also marked the beginning of his addictions—an addiction to liquor, such as whiskey, rum, and the strong beer Guinness; a fascination for gambling; and an urge to frequent East End pubs ('magical places' he called them) and mix with some rather questionable personalities. There was no doubt the rather green Dennis was taken advantage of, but he did not seem to mind as indulging in his new-found vices proved more exciting, and he was soon hooked. The addictions were to plague him throughout the rest of his life, and eventually cut it short.

Back at camp, feeling towards Dennis was divided. Some of the men resented him for not taking the war seriously, as they were risking their lives after all—or were at least prepared to—whereas Dennis never would.

He was next transferred to Hayes in Middlesex, where many soldiers' records were kept. Dennis worked in the office dealing with the non-commissioned officers. He described himself as 'the office boy' though, again, he did not particularly show any interest or enthusiasm. The one saving grace was that Joan and the baby lived nearby, and he was certainly fond of showing off Susan to all and everyone.

Dennis had three senior officers at Hayes and delighted in doing impersonations of them, making mimicking them a fine art. In fact, he rather perfected his technique as an impersonator and comedian in the army and might have easily gone on to star in post-war revue shows, of which there were many, but he yearned to break away and return to serious acting, and it was this thought of soon being able to tread the boards again that got him through the days. That day of breaking away came rather sooner than Dennis thought, as in June 1942, he was rushed to hospital, suffering with acute appendicitis. It marked the end of his army career, and despite the pressure piled on him by his military family, Dennis had not risen beyond the lowly ranks of gunner, while his brother was doing very nicely for himself as an officer working for Army Intelligence. Dennis continued to disappoint his family, but he did not seem to care.

Following formal discharge in July 1942, Dennis was soon well enough to appear on stage in one of the lead roles in *The Springtime of Others* at the Arts Theatre. His performance was witnessed by film director Michael Powell who had been searching for 'just the right actor to play Sergeant Peter Gibbs' in his upcoming film of *A Canterbury Tale*. It is rather ironic that having hated his time in the army, Dennis was about to make his mark in the film world playing a soldier. Powell had said he had found 'beautiful young men with good manners and excellent training hard to come by'. He was so impressed with Dennis's performance and striking good looks that he immediately offered him the part.

4

An Instant Success (1942–1946)

A big opportunity came Dennis's way in September 1942, when he joined Noël Coward's company and toured the provinces taking small parts in *Blithe Spirit*, *This Happy Breed*, and *Present Laughter*. Dennis said:

> Then Noël fell ill one day ... Not very seriously, so there's no need to say I was sorry. Quite honestly I wasn't. It was my chance. I took Noël's parts. But I'm not only grateful to Noël for his jaundice. Not by any means. I learnt more from that tour with him than I can ever hope to learn from anyone. How to deliver dialogue, how to concentrate on saying your lines; Coward taught me everything. He even taught me to do as I'm told. You know, there was one actor who went to Noël and said he didn't think one line sounded convincing. Couldn't he say so-and-so instead? Noël replied icily, "All I ask of you is to repeat my lines in the right order—nothing else". I learnt the lesson of discipline.'

Dennis had stepped in to play the lead at both Exeter and Bournemouth.

Meanwhile, to escape war-torn London, Dennis, Joan, and their two-year-old daughter decided to move to 22 York Avenue, Clewer on the outskirts of Windsor—a very peaceful part of the town. They became popular with the locals, especially Dennis with his amusing turn of phrase and gracious manners.

They were much happier in Windsor than they had been during the start of their marriage, which admittedly was overshadowed by the nightly bombing raids; this was their first real family home, where they lived quite contentedly for the next six years. The house was elegant, built in the 1930s, detached, roomy, and situated in a quiet back road. It was to be the best time they had together.

22 York Avenue, Windsor, where the Price family lived between 1942 and 1948.

When not working, Dennis used to exercise and indulge in his favourite pastime, riding regularly in Windsor Great Park, often with friends or family. The couple became close friends of John Counsell and his actress wife, Mary Kerridge, who ran the Theatre Royal Repertory Company. Miss Kerridge's impression was of Dennis was of, 'An amusing, witty and civilized man, with a great talent as an actor and the ability to play himself with tremendous poise and style, something that a lot of actors find very difficult.'

Dennis also took an interest in the local theatre, yet commitments elsewhere prevented him from being a regular player in their productions. His one and only appearance at the Theatre Royal was in the spring of 1943, for five days, in a controversial new play by David Wehl entitled *Torn Banner*. It was produced, for the second year, by Mary Kerridge, who also co-starred. The story had caused quite a stir the first time around because it concerned a family living in occupied Czechoslovakia who had to make up their minds whether to support the new Nazi regime or oppose it. The author had made the local German gauleiter a human character and the German's Nazi beliefs were offset by his kind and pleasant nature—an odd mixture indeed. Despite the theme, it was very well received by the audience as it had been extremely well written and acted on both occasions. Dennis played Jaroslav, the elder son of the

Skramlik family, who together with his sister Anicka (Enid Hewit) worked secretly for the Czech underground movement. Just before the end of the play, he delivered a dramatic speech about the indomitable human spirit that somehow survives oppression, 'Like the little blades of grass that push their way up through the cracks in an asphalt path.' Dennis played this scene with tremendous effect that famed director Tyrone Guthrie, who had come along to watch the performance, was so impressed he chose Dennis to play the same role when he later staged it himself in Liverpool.

Dennis had also scored such a success in the three Coward plays that in July 1943 that he was offered the chance to perform in the West End, as Morris Dixon in *Present Laughter* and as Sam Leadbitter in *This Happy Breed* at the Theatre Royal Haymarket. Yet it was during August that Dennis came into his own, playing Charles Condomine in *Blithe Spirit* at the Duchess Theatre, taking over from Cecil Parker who was on a badly needed vacation. Coward's dry wit suited Dennis and the role of Condomine—the man who's driven to despair by a wife and a ghostly former wife—became his personal favourite. During the time in the company, Dennis became a personal friend of 'The Master' and was one of the many celebrities to visit Coward's Jamaican retreat. In a letter Coward wrote, he recalled, 'Dennis Price approved of everything, right down to the plumbing, which shows that kind hearts are better than coronets any day of the week.' They remained friends, but seldom had the chance of working together in subsequent years.

Some of the best advice Dennis ever received came from actor Leslie Howard, of whom Dennis was an earnest admirer. He told Dennis never to refuse the offer of a part for the simple reason he considered he was not suited for it. 'Never throw a script out of the window. If you do, you may be sure someone else will pick it up', he also added, 'never be rude to anyone on the floor, unless you're certain you're right—and even then don't say it!' Being ever mindful of those words earned Dennis a deep respect in the profession and he was greatly loved by virtually everyone who came into contact with him, from the lowliest of floor runners through to studio management. His quiet effectiveness and dramatic understatement made people compare Dennis to Leslie Howard, and it was a great tragedy Howard died that very same year, before he could see Dennis's career really take off.

In September 1943, Dennis filmed his part in *A Canterbury Tale* by the Archers, Michael Powell and Emeric Pressburger, who along with directing also produced and wrote the screenplay. The storyline was certainly out of the ordinary and Powell saw great hopes for his film, with its message to the youth of the time, with the actors portraying modern day pilgrims—Dennis being an English sergeant, Peter Gibbs; Sheila Sim was cast as a land girl; and real-life American soldier and newcomer to acting John Sweet played a visiting G.I. Each character has a problem that is solved thanks to a trip to Canterbury Cathedral and an eccentric lecturer and magistrate, played by Eric Portman. Its message was that the beauty, greatness, and heritage of Britain had not changed since Chaucer's day and we should spend time to appreciate it.

Though the beautiful Kentish countryside was delightfully photographed (shots of nine different villages were used to produce one), the most outstanding feature of the film was Canterbury Cathedral itself, but the film-makers were not actually allowed inside, so a set was constructed at Denham Studios. Not all the critics cared for the 'strange storyline' and its tame conclusion, but Dennis and the other players were praised all round.

This first film role set Dennis on the road to international stardom and adding to his good fortune, on 30 October, his wife gave birth to their second daughter, Tessa Alexandra, at Windsor's Princess Christian Hospital. He ended the year by going on stage at The New Theatre, London, to play Horatio, with Robert Helpmann taking the lead role in his own production of *Hamlet* for the Old Vic Company, which ran until February 1944. Then, as a direct result of Michael Powell and Emeric Pressburger's film, Dennis was put on casting directors' short list and his future in films seemed secure.

Dennis Price as Sgt Peter Gibbs in *A Canterbury Tale*, with Eric Portman, John Sweet, and Sheila Sim.

At 6 feet 1 inch tall, he was certainly one of the tallest actors on the screen at that time, with a slim figure to match, weighing 11.5 stone. His clear, distinguished voice and extremely handsome face were qualities that would take him to the very top as a romantic lead at a time when audiences queued around the block to see movies. Dennis had thick and very dark brown hair, usually waved, and grey eyes that could convey all kinds of looks, one minute mischievous like a naughty schoolboy, and the next showing great sensitivity and feeling, or be cold when playing a villain, depending on the requirements of his role. The impact he had on audiences was instantaneous and lasting.

Dennis was, inevitably, offered a contract by the J. Arthur Rank Organisation and went to work for Sydney Box at their subsidiary company, Gainsborough Productions. His first picture there, filmed during July 1944, was *A Place of One's Own*, a dramatisation of Osbert Sitwell's creepy ghost story set at the turn of the century. Dennis played a dashing young Harley Street doctor, Dr Selbie, and his leading lady was Margaret Lockwood, who was already well established in films, having made her debut in 1934. In *A Place of One's Own*, Dennis looked purposely lean and hungry as if he had been living on bread and water for a month, and while his performance was full of charm, he had the rawness of an actor new to films. The location chosen for filming was a lovely house at Esher in Surrey, which reportedly really did have a ghost, as a lady in white was seen to walk around the lake in the grounds on certain nights.

Nearly all of the critical acclaim went to male lead James Mason, who literally bent over backwards to look old and stiff jointed as a retired merchant, but Dennis did not go unnoticed and the foundations establishing him as a rising star and leading man were laid. Dennis was not overly keen on pursuing successive similar roles with sugary romantic storylines; in fact, he would have preferred playing Mason's older-man part as it was a type of character he felt he could get to grips with. Unfortunately, however, there were to be many more such 'romantic' roles before Dennis was to have the chance of the more serious, intelligent parts he longed for.

Next up, Dennis was offered a secondary role in the British National produced film *The Echo Murders*, which was the latest addition to their series of Sexton Blake thrillers, starring David Farrar as the famous detective. It was never intended to be a big box office hit, but rather more a 'boy's own stuff' B-movie, which, sadly, has now been relegated to the archives to gather dust. This, incidentally, was Dennis's first colour picture.

In October 1945, Dennis appeared as Major Henry Grantley opposite Dorothy Hyson (the wife of Anthony Quayle) at the Lyric Theatre and then at Wyndham's in *A Scandal at Barchester*, a Trollopian dramatisation. In March 1946, he switched to the Duchess Theatre for another run of *Blithe*

A scene from *A Place of One's Own* with a heavily made-up James Mason on the right.

Spirit and he went on to play in it intermittently well into the mid-1950s. For one such performance in Dublin, Noël Coward himself directed with Dennis and Kay Kendall in the lead. Dennis's friend Jan Coombe-Dreyer remembers the Dublin tour:

> Dennis Price really loved Kay Kendall, and I think maybe he was in love with her but at that time she had other romantic interests. The reason they got on so well was because they had a shared sense of humour and were always laughing and joking together. Their chemistry made their performances sparkle.

Going back to the end of the Duchess run, Maurice Ostrer of Gainsborough Pictures extended Dennis's initial film contract to a longer-term and exclusive one, which prohibited him from working on the stage. Dennis could not quite believe his luck at being propelled so suddenly into the cinematic limelight but he took it all with good grace.

He soon became a firm favourite with the public as was reflected by the fan mail he received and the box office takings of his films. His next production was one that he enjoyed making very much, as he was cast as an out-and-out stinker in *Caravan*. It must have been one of the silliest pictures ever produced at Gainsborough—a pure slice of romantic nonsense. As the villain of the piece, Dennis was given lots of scope to revel in being wicked, just as he had done as Carl Peterson at Radley, opposite his leading lady Anne Crawford. Making up the other duo in the foursome involved in a complex love affair were Jean Kent and Stewart Granger. Adding to the comedy, egg-eyed Robert Helpmann was employed as Dennis's sidekick, an obsequious servant with a shady past. Jean Kent, incidentally, made her screen debut in the film and played a lovelorn gypsy girl, who was charmed by Dennis's manners and gentle good humour throughout rehearsals and production. The rugged terrain and quagmire that looked so convincing in the film was, in fact, filmed on location in nowhere more exotic than Wales during October.

Caravan may not have been as great a film, yet out of all his movies as a Rank star, Dennis chose it as his favourite. Journalist Ruth Miller asked Dennis how he rated the success of a film: 'Of course a film musn't be bad or it will be a flop,' Dennis told her. When she dared to then question the 'success' of it, he exclaimed: 'I beg your pardon! It made £400,000. Who is to be the judge of quality? In the last resort, it's what comes in to the till that counts. You can't be choosy. Who am I to refuse a part? Fans are mobbing you one day and the next day they've forgotten you!'

Subsequently, Dennis started work on *The Magic Bow*, a mainly fictitious account of the life of violinist Paganini and his rise to fame. Little was known about Paganini's story and so the plot was largely contrived by writer Manuel Komroff and laden with romantic and clichéd characters. Paganini was played by Stewart Granger, who was merely a decorative front for the talents of virtuoso Yehudi Menuhin. Like *Caravan*, there are four central characters, as portrayed by Dennis, Granger, Jean Kent, and Phyllis Calvert who were all involved in a tangled cross love affair. Dennis loved Phyllis Calvert's character, who was in turn in love with Granger's, who was loved by Jean Kent. *The Magic Bow* had its moments, but is basically very silly and the irritating characters and their dialogue stretch credibility a bit too far. Dennis played the spurned suitor well, with black looks and rude remarks of the sort he was to use again in many other films.

Not unsurprisingly, the film received a roasting from the critics for its 'weak and insipid storyline' and Stewart Granger, they said, failed to bring out the personality of Paganini.

Dennis may have played second fiddle, if you will forgive the pun, to Granger (just as he had done in *Caravan*) but made up for it by stealing every scene they were together in with effortless ease. In Stewart Granger's autobiography *Sparks Fly Upwards*, there is not even a passing mention of Dennis, which perhaps suggests the star was a little envious of being upstaged.

The exciting climax to *Caravan* sees Dennis, as Sir Francis, menace his rival for the love of Anne Crawford's Oriana.

The exciting duel scene from *The Magic Bow*, with co-star Stewart Granger.

A devilishly handsome Dennis in *The Magic Bow*.

Christmas that year was particularly special for Dennis and the family as not only was it the first since the end of the war, but it marked the beginning of his life as a movie star. Suddenly, everyone he passed on his way to the pub or walking in the park recognised him. He gained a large female following overnight, though he said he was not aware of it at the time; all he could feel was the immense pleasure at becoming famous, but fame can be a double-edged sword, and it was destined to change Dennis's life and relationship with his family, though not necessarily for the better.

As Dennis's popularity grew, he regarded the Windsor home as 'unsuitable for a star', so he proposed they should return to London where he would be among other film actors. While filming *Caravan* and *The Magic Bow*, Stewart Granger had invited Dennis and his family to his home for dinner; it was a vast mansion that, he said, had once belonged to Leslie Howard. Howard had in turn bought the house as a secondary home to install his mistress, Violette. Some years later in an interview, Granger described how he found Howard's love letters and poems to Violette tucked away in a drawer and promptly gave them to Howard's widow. The Price's modest home was in stark contrast to Granger's, but that was largely due to the fact Dennis had not saved any money to put towards buying the kind of house he thought befitted his status, as no sooner did he earn it, he spent it.

5

Riding High (1946–1947)

The Rank Organisation was keen to promote Dennis as their new young star and by the summer of 1946, his services were so much in demand that he found himself contracted to do three films at once, at three different studios spread far apart. *Hungry Hill* was based at Denham Studios, *The Master of Bankdam* was at Walton-on-Thames, and *Dear Murderer* was at Gainsborough in Islington, North London. Fortunately, he was able to juggle everything and despite huge amounts of concentration and calm needed to carry off three entirely different characters, not to mention memorising long stretches of dialogue, it proved Dennis was a consummate professional. I would challenge anyone who watches these three very different films to have guessed he had been rushed off his feet.

Hungry Hill was one of the best films from his melodrama period, about two stubborn Irish families feuding over a copper mine and land in Victorian times. Margaret Lockwood starred opposite Dennis as his flirtatious sweetheart and a host of other top British actors featured, including Cecil Parker, Michael Denison, and Dermot Walsh. Dennis could easily have become big-headed over his new stardom, but he was and remained very modest—a likeable quality that was not always beneficial to a career in which pushing and selfishness are often needed.

Away from the studio, he invited all the other actors to visit his home for extravagant social gatherings, which began a lifelong drain on his income as he felt it was expected he should always be the generous host.

Dennis was meanwhile causing a sensation with audiences countrywide and received sacks full of fan mail. The authors of those letters imagined Dennis having all kinds of romantic encounters; their fantasies encouraged by larger than life articles in film magazines. He left a strong impression on everyone he met, yet it was often behind the scenes people, the ones

Above left: A dramatic scene in *Dear Murderer* with Eric Portman, which is rather prophetic as it resembles Dennis's own suicide attempt seven years later.

Above right: With Margaret Lockwood in a scene from *Hungry Hill*; the pair were to become lovers in real life.

who shared those moments on the set but were never on camera, who remember him best.

One such studio employee was a young Irene Hannington who had started work at Denham as tea lady. She was in awe of the big names and recalled every moment with clarity:

> I remember Dennis Price very well indeed from when he was making *Hungry Hill*. He would always make a point of coming over—however busy—to give me sweets. He would always spare some time for me—I wasn't a beauty or anything like that. I would arrive at the studio in the morning and we had a little room where I went to make the teas, then take them to the stars—whether they were on the sets or in their dressing rooms. If Dennis wasn't in his dressing room, I knew he'd be in make-up.
>
> I'd knock on his door and he'd announce 'Come in' in that gorgeous voice of his. I'd enter and say 'Good morning, Mr. Price'—all fingers and

thumbs—and he'd say 'Calm down, calm down' as he moved things to make a space for his tea. Then he'd ask 'Now, what have you been doing?' so I'd say, 'Nothing much—just helping my mother with this and that'. He'd tell me 'When you get to be a big girl, that will help you to raise children of your own and know how to wash up and run a house' and I used to think, 'Well, it's alright for you to speak—you don't have to do it!'

I realised much later, that he was just being very kind as only he could be. I used to watch him through the window as he looked in the mirror and fiddled with his hair (he was very proud of his dark curls) then looking up at me, he'd say 'You know, when you grow up you'll be a beautiful lady'.

There was another occasion, when I upset some tea and somebody sat on it and they were quite annoyed, but Dennis, in a calm voice, standing tall, upright and elegant, said 'Anybody could have done that—I jogged her arm', and one of the big directors apologised to me! That was fantastic.

Dennis was just as polite outside the studio too, as Irene recalls:

At Morden, South London, the studios held a garden party where all the top stars went and you could mingle freely amongst them. For 2/6', you could have your photo taken with them and they'd sign autographs. They each did an act in turn—if they couldn't sing, they would recite poetry and the like. Then someone remarked, 'Oh look, there's Dennis Price!' and I looked up at a platform to see Dennis performing a butler scene with an actress. He caught my gaze and when he'd finished his act, he walked over to me and said, 'What on earth are you doing all this way from home?' So I replied, 'I've come to see you!' and he said, 'Don't you see enough of me all the week?' I told him 'No' and we talked about the studio. When he returned to the stage, the people around me were amazed and asked 'How do you come to know him?' I told them he was my brother.

Later on, when people were posing for photographs, I looked in all the different tents and found Mr. Price. He turned round and said, 'Not you again! You're like a little white mouse!' After that, the nickname stuck and I became 'the mouse'. At the party, he asked me 'Have you eaten?'. I said 'Yes' but my stomach was rumbling. He said, 'There you are' and gave me ten shillings, which was a lot of money, as I was only earning one pound and ten shillings a week. 'You mustn't spend it on photos—go and have something to eat'. I went into a big tent and was eating from a plate of buns, when Dennis tapped me on the shoulder and said 'Just making sure you're getting something to eat.'

Come Monday morning and time to serve him tea in his dressing room, I found Dennis had gone to Ireland to finish *Hungry Hill* There

> was a big box of chocolates for me and a five pound note, from him as a thank you. I was thrilled to have such a lot of money and kept the £5 note for a long, long time, until eventually I was desperate for a new coat and had to use the money—a very sad moment for me. I'd love to have kept the note forever.

Many people who came into contact with Dennis said much the same, and there are certainly no recorded incidents of his being rude, short, or dismissive with anyone for he knew the importance of keeping his admirers happy.

Three quarters of the way through *Hungry Hill*, Dennis's character contracts typhoid. For the sequence, Dennis considered it necessary to see his doctor straight away.

'Where do you feel the pain, Mr. Price?', the doctor asked.

'In my neck', he replied, 'but never mind that—I want to know how to die of typhoid. I've got to do it in a film and I want to get the symptoms right.'

His doctor was pleased to give him his professional advice, saying he had not yet seen a believable typhoid case at the cinema. The supposed sufferers invariably always over-acted by writhing as if in a frenzy, whereas in reality, they would be too weak to lift a finger. It could be compared to falling asleep.

'That seemed to be lacking in dramatic value, so we had to compromise a little,' said Dennis. He was satisfied the end result rated among his best achievements to date, and this was only his sixth film.

This was Dennis's second film with Margaret Lockwood as his sweetheart, and the couple fell in love in real life despite the fact that they were both married with children. Margaret was a great beauty and seduced Dennis with her quiet charm before they embarked on a passionate affair that was to last throughout the 1940s and conducted under the noses of their respective spouses. Like Dennis, Margaret had a young daughter, named Julia, and her husband, Rupert Leon, was very much overshadowed by her movie star status, which eventually led to their divorce.

When the Prices were living in Windsor, Margaret became a regular visitor and young Julia would play with Susan and Tessa. Since they were conducting an affair, it was very audacious and not to mention in rather poor taste, but the couple used great skill of acting and ingenuity to conceal their affair from Joan and from the ever-inquisitive journalists of the day. Their acting abilities paid off, and the affair did not become common knowledge until long after Margaret's death (in 1990). However, six years prior, in 1984, Margaret stated in an interview: 'We were both married with small children, so we decided to call it off'. Yet it would seem not many people heard or were aware of this interview.

Hungry Hill was given a favourable write-up in the daily papers and in his article entitled 'Dennis Price leaps to the top', Jympson Harman wrote:

> The surprise of this picture is Dennis Price. He considers himself best suited by character to villainous parts, but his grace and charm as sensitive John Brodrick lifts him to the top romantic class at a bound. I now look forward to his next leading part in *The Crowthers of Bankdam.*

Having leaped to the top of his profession, the real art was staying there and Dennis knew his competition was both fierce and abundant. Michael Denison played Dennis's brother in *Hungry Hill* and in real life, Dennis and Michael were often mistaken for one another, being much the same age and build and even having similarities in their names. Dennis once rang up Denison to apologise after one such mistake occurred at a function he had attended. A north country mayor had introduced Dennis as 'Michael Denison', then asked roguishly why his 'lovely little wife Dulcie Gray' was not with him, and what he thought she was up to while he was there. He quickly came back with, 'Probably in bed with Dennis Price', much to the amusement of the audience and the great surprise of the mayor.

For his role in *The Master of Bankdam*, Dennis had to adopt a North Country accent as Joshua Crowther, the hard-working son of a Yorkshire mill owner. The tale was the rags to riches story of the Crowther family, spanning nearly a century, itself an adaptation of Thomas Armstrong's novel, full of moodiness and passion. After capturing initial shots of Yorkshire's rural views and the mills, the rest of the picture was filmed almost entirely within the confines of Nettlefold Studios. The characters were typical of a Victorian family (the canny father, autocratic mother, bickering sons, one good, one bad), along with depicting the social attitudes of the day. Tom Walls played the father, Stephen Murray, and Dennis one of the sons, Joshua, while Nancy Price, whom he had not worked with since the Croydon plays, played Dennis's mother. Anne Crawford was again cast as his screen wife.

His interpretation of the sensitive, fun-loving Joshua gives an insight into his own personality, though at times, the script was much too flowery and the ideals and morals of another age now appear quite ludicrous, even creating moments of unintentional laughter.

Dennis felt somewhat hampered by the necessity of sounding like a Yorkshire man. Interestingly, the studios thought better of burdening him with an accent again for many years, and then only in a comical capacity.

The finale, featuring a collapsing mill, was equally disturbing for actors and audience alike. Dennis recalled:

With Anne Crawford in *The Master of Bankdam.*

Brotherly love—well, not quite in this instance. Dennis and Stephen Murray play siblings who seem at constant odds with one another in *The Master of Bankdam.*

> And that was one of my most uncomfortable deaths. There was no fake about that wreckage. The bricks were real and so was the timber. Of course, it was constructed in such a way that I could crawl in from underneath, but I had the feeling that any moment, something might slip. Nor did it help my peace of mind to have prop men showering me with handfuls of plaster!

In mentioning 'deaths', it soon became clear Dennis was getting tired of dying in his films, but he did not fare any better as young solicitor Richard Fenton in his next film *Dear Murderer* when he fell foul of a jealous husband, portrayed with typical nastiness by Eric Portman, and was killed off within the first fifteen minutes.

To make his screen death look as realistic as possible, Dennis had once again asked for medical advice—in this case, on the after effects of gas poisoning. 'They were too gruesome to repeat, let alone show on the screen. I came away from the consulting room that night feeling really sick'.

During the post-war years, Dennis gave many interviews for film magazines which offered a greater insight into his psyche than ever before. In one for *Film Reel*, he expressed some personal views about fashion and clothes, of all things:

> Although Dennis Price says it is hard for him to pass judgement on women's clothes because he suspects women dress entirely to please themselves, he has some interesting comments to make. The first feature of a dress that catches his attention is the colour. He likes the clothes to be as colourful as possible and does not mind the colours being mixed. He thinks black is smart, but tires of it easily. He feels it's a camouflage colour—a safety first. In summer, he prefers flowered prints worn with gay hats, and woollens in glowing shades on winter days.
>
> 'They make me feel more cheerful just looking at them.'
>
> As for a 'new look', Dennis feels that it will take some time for men to get used to this, so he asks fashionable women to gradually adapt the masculine eye to the new styles. Men are creatures of habit. Don't buy an outfit different in outline from everything we have seen for ages. They demand applause—you won't get it, because the shock will have been too sudden.
>
> I do like crazy hats. I thoroughly enjoy noting a frothy little number worn with an air on a sleek head. The more flowers, fruit, veils and ribbons, the more I like it—so long as the colours are right for the outfit. I am also very partial to large, romantic hats with roses in a strategic position—on the right girl.

Dennis was always immaculately turned-out himself and paid great attention to his appearance even down to his hair, which had a natural widow's peak but tended to be straight normally. To produce the waves known to millions, he would crimp his hair using electrically heated tongs. On one occasion, while staying in the country with a friend, he went to plug in for his perm and the fuse went bang; he put out the lights in the house and the whole of the village.

Dennis was at his professional peak during the late 1940s and, physically, was in great shape too. He had everything going for him and seemed set for a long and prosperous future. In private, however, his family life and marriage were under great strain. He had been working continually since his first film and work was beginning to take over his entire life; he had been so engrossed in perfecting his numerous parts that he had neglected his wife. Joan craved fame even more than he did,and yearned to receive the adulation that Dennis was enjoying, instead of just being 'Mrs Price'. Joan had sacrificed her career to raise their two young daughters, and that was the reason she was absent from cinema screens, or so she told their friends. The truth is slightly different in that she had a regular nanny to cater for the children, so her time should have been her own had she wished to pursue offers. Yet no such offers had been forthcoming, perhaps causing her to begin resenting Dennis's success.

Dennis had come far since his days at Croydon with effortless ease and had become a very big name, while Joan's progress had been slow to say the least. As the many publicity articles went to press headlining Dennis, the gap between the couple widened. Despite her adequate experience, Joan was constantly passed over when the plum film parts were casting, and during this period, she was offered only one small part in an obscure film called *The Angel with the Trumpet* with Basil Sydney starring; she played a governess.

Dennis now became mindful of the cracks forming in his marriage and did his utmost to alleviate his wife's frustration by giving more publicity interviews, in which he gave her all the credit for backing him. Joan wholly agreed with his graciousness and even told a family friend that he would never have got anywhere in acting if it had not been for her guidance. Additionally, she told actor friend Richard Wattis that she had 'made' Dennis in his career by ensuring he arrived on time, went to the right places, and met the right people, those who could influence his career; Dennis seemed content to go along with her taking credit—anything for a quiet life.

Joan's boasts were certainly exaggerated, as Dennis had shown great promise going back to his college days and was always on time for everything. Joan was not instrumental in giving Noël Coward the jaundice that led to Dennis stepping in to the leads in his plays, nor did she arrange for Michael Powell to give him the lead in *A Canterbury Tale*, yet she would have happily claimed otherwise. It was hard for her to accept that Dennis's rise to fame had very little to do with her input.

Dennis had a wonderful chance to be a cad again when offered the starring part in Muriel and Sydney Box's production *Holiday Camp*. Godfrey Winn's story was of a varied group of 1940s British stereotypes whose lives intermingle when they each spend a week's vacation at the Silver Sands holiday camp, which was loosely based on a Butlin's holiday camp at Filey. Director Ken Annakin remembered Winn 'put together a very good story but Sydney and Muriel Box decided we should add extra elements' and he suggested producer Muriel Box was inspired by the then headlining Heath Murders, and suggested her assistant Peter Rogers (later producer of the *Carry On* films) that they introduce the Dennis Price character as a murderer. Neville Heath incidentally became notorious for carving his initial 'N' on his female victims with a knife.

So among the romances and jolly old knees-ups of the holidaymakers, Dennis played a sinister charmer posing as Squadron Leader Binkie Hardwicke, who was in fact a sex killer, hiding out in the camp and looking for fresh victims. It fell to little Esma Cannon to be his first victim and a sequence was filmed in which Dennis's character strangled her on the cliffs.

As *Holiday Camp* and the characters in it were chiefly comical or romantic, the killer character seemed totally out of place with everything else on first viewing of the edited film, so the murder sequence was drastically cut as were other scenes featuring the murderous Hardwicke, ahead of its cinema release. The film presented audiences with a rich slice of post-war life and there is much to enjoy in the many whimsical touches, a lot of which were provided by Dennis.

It was not the most pleasant of filming locations though as much was shot inside the grounds of Butlin's holiday camp at Filey, Yorkshire, in the winter months in very cold conditions which caused great discomfort for the many actors concerned, especially Hazel Court and Yvonne Owen who had to wear bathing costumes. Dennis, however, was always smartly attired, complete with silk scarf.

Ahead of receiving the script, when Dennis heard that he was to be starring in a picture about a holiday camp, he thought it would make a refreshing change from the films he had been in of late as he had pretty much always been killed off. That was before he found out the murderer he plays is eventually caught and taken away to be tried and hanged.

Jassy was another costume melodrama he made at Gainsborough Studios for Sydney Box and Dennis groaned when he read the script. Once

Esma Cannon innocently and unwittingly takes morning PE alongside the murderous Hardwicke in *Holiday Camp*.

It does not look as though it is going to be a happy ending for at least one of the couple.

again, his character was to be killed, this time in the first twenty minutes. It was the third occasion when he co-starred with Margaret Lockwood, except in this case for a change, she saved her affections for his adult son (played by Dermot Walsh) who looked more like he could be Dennis's younger brother.

Dennis's role in *Jassy* could well have been written about him had he lived in 1830. Christopher Hatton, the character he portrayed, was a wealthy and privileged gambler who staked all he owned on the single throw of a dice. Reduced to poverty when he lost, he tried to win back his estate in subsequent games but when he resorted to cheating, he was humiliated in front of old friends, and committed suicide. Dennis too liked to gamble and he was not very good at it either, frequently losing large sums of money, though he kept his gambling habit, much like his taste for drink, very much to himself and his public were blissfully unaware.

Another romantic weepie was to follow, with a part in *The White Unicorn*, filmed at Nettlefold Studios, and once again with Margaret Lockwood.

Based on the novel by Flora Sandstrom, the story, though set in modern times, is full of Victorian sentiment about love and marriage, especially marrying beneath one's own class. What the film lacked in style, Dennis strived to make up for in substance, but had his work cut out with this one. He was cast as a suave beau who sweeps Miss Lockwood off her feet. Margaret's own daughter, 'Toots', featured in the role of her screen child. Dennis's character was again killed, though this time made it until nearly the end of the movie when, in a foolish accident caused by his sweetheart, he is swept away by the rushing waters of a Finnish ice hole on his honeymoon—very original.

The scene at the ice hole was the high spot of the film; the ear-piercing screams, as Margaret has to let go of her 'husband' sound particularly convincing. Miss Lockwood stated she almost lost her voice because she was yelling so hard. It stayed in Dennis's memory for a different reason; it was the only occasion when he actually enjoyed dying on the screen:

> I was drowned on honeymoon in Finland, you know. Well, we filmed that scene in the middle of a summer heat wave amid studio snow and ice. Even the technicians in their short sleeves were a bit hot and bothered. So you can imagine that poor Margaret and I, in heavy furs, found it difficult to look frozen. Death, as you might say, lost its sting.

Despite his busy filmmaking schedule, Dennis still managed to broadcast a couple of times on radio; firstly, on Bob Monkhouse's show *Starstruck* as guest of the week, and then in *Navy Mixture* in July 1947. Whenever he

Tragedy in *The White Unicorn* when Dick (Dennis Price) drowns on honeymoon.

Times and tastes were very different in 1947, as the censor insisted the honeymooning couple must have separate beds.

had any time to spare, which was quite rare, Dennis liked nothing better than rowing down a quiet stretch of river, or riding across Windsor Great Park, accompanied by his friend and fellow actor Stewart Granger.

Around this time, Dennis was to meet a man who would have a huge impact on his life. During the 1940s, film director Michael Powell organised lavish showbiz parties for the actors of his films, and in mingling with the guests on one such occasion, Dennis's eye was caught by a man with an intense gaze who stood out from the assembled crowd. His name was Shaun Noble, an Irish actor based in London, who had been a bit part player in *Black Narcissus* (1947). Noble's scenes with Deborah Kerr are short and shown in flashback as he plays the boyfriend she used to have before becoming a nun. Dennis struck up a conversation with Noble and they soon established a rapport, fast becoming firm friends and vowing to stay in touch. Dennis subsequently found out Noble had a flat in Chelsea and went around to visit him for drinks and conversation. The drink flowed freely and Dennis found himself confiding in Noble about his affair with Margaret Lockwood.

As it turned out, Noble was himself something of a lady's man, saying he totally understood Dennis's predicament and made the outrageous suggestion that Dennis could use his flat for sexual liaisons as it would make for a discreet meeting place. Dennis was taken aback momentarily, but then considered it a very good idea. Under the pretext of visiting his friend, he could entertain the ladies in style, well away from his family home. So, with Noble's help, Dennis embarked on a series of affairs, all conducted in relative secrecy. His choice of partner was always a married woman because they would not be able to go to the press, having as much to lose as he did; the law courts took a very dim view of women who committed adultery in those days. Also, he did not want any of his conquests trying to oust Joan and become the next Mrs Price, for in a strange paradox to this behaviour, he happened to love Joan and his daughters.

Noble had his own philosophy about women and said they were 'like wild horses who have to be broken in by an experienced rider.'

Author Elaine Parker met Shaun Noble in 1989 in Chelsea, when aged twenty-one, and Noble was in his sixties. He said, 'Dennis Price won't fuck you, because he is dead, but I am very much alive and available! Why don't you come and stay with me in my Chelsea flat—stay as long as you like?' Needless to say, the offer was not taken up. Sometime later, I phoned Noble to talk about Dennis Price again and realised he was very drunk. Through sobs, he said in his posh voice, 'I'm such a failure!' I found it quite amusing for someone so cocksure to make such an admission.

Noble had always considered that Dennis, with his very handsome looks, was 'purely wasted on just one woman' and so in late 1947, Dennis

Dennis's friend and confidant during the 1940s, Shaun Noble (pictured in 1989).

started casting around. He was attracted to the most beautiful women and with his good looks and charm, he found he could have his pick of them.

Noble was a corrupting influence, similar to the character of Lord Henry Wootton with the young Dorian Gray. Through the Irishman, Dennis got to meet some rather strange and undesirable people and when you consider Noble told Dennis of his friendship with the nephew of Adolf Hitler, who was living under the name William Stuart-Houston in Long Island, America, and encouraged Dennis to accompany him on a trip there, you do have to wonder. Noble persuaded Dennis that Stuart-Houston and other friends including the birth control campaigner Margaret Sanger would be worth meeting and Dennis seemed all for it, so they arranged a holiday. On 17 August 1947, they left London airport for a fortnight in the USA.

Sanger was a controversial figure and in 1932 had written the following:

> Keep the doors of immigration closed to the entrance of certain aliens whose condition is known to be detrimental to the stamina of the race, such as the feebleminded, idiots, morons, insane, syphilitic, epileptic, criminal, professional prostitutes and others in the class barred by the immigration laws of 1924. Apply a stern and rigid policy of sterilization and segregation to that grade of population whose progeny is already tainted or whose inheritance is such that objectionable traits may be transmitted to offspring.

Such views were in keeping with Adolf Hitler's dream of creating a master race, by eliminating what he considered to be undesirable types, and would surely be deeply worrying to any sane minded individual.

Just ahead of departing for America, Dennis was asked by Sydney Box to play Lord Byron in his ambitious new film about the life of the notorious poet, whose love affairs were just as famous as his poetry. This opportunity meant more to Dennis than all his previous romantic leads as he had a personal admiration for Byron, coupled with the fact that portraying an historical figure was a more rewarding prospect. Dennis spent the eighteen-hour flight scrutinising no fewer than five biographies of Byron, trying to get the feel of his complex personality.

What Dennis thought of the various individuals Noble introduced him to was not recorded, yet curiously, the duo kept well away from Hollywood during their time in the USA, which seemed very unusual for people in their profession. When later asked about Hollywood, Dennis said: 'Any British star who leaves Rank now is foolish. Give me Shepherd's Bush every time.... Hollywood doesn't attract me, and the columnists—I'm all for publicity, but not that kind. I want my private life to myself.'

Dennis did not realise it at the time, but he was heading for the end of his contract with Gainsborough Pictures and a break in American films would have given a dramatic boost to his career; he was to need it.

When he returned to England, Dennis started work on the Byron film at Gainsborough Studios, where most of the interior scenes were shot. To give the picture an authentic flavour, during October 1947, Box took his film unit over to Venice where Dennis was to retrace Byron's steps. While they were filming in Moncenego Palace on the Grand Canal, where the poet had lived, they could hear a mysterious voice singing in English. They questioned the wealthy family who were living in the palace and were casually told that the voice was that of Byron's ghost who had often been seen by the family and their employees. Some 14,000 feet of film was put in the can, showing Dennis on his travels around Venice and other parts of Italy and Greece. On the island of San Lazaro, he visited the Armenian monastery where he was filmed with monks in the cloisters and ascending the library stairs where Lord Byron once studied the Armenian language every day. Other scenes included a coach ride through the streets of Este near Padua, swimming in the lagoon, and joining in a carnival. Then, the J. Arthur Rank Organisation, which was going through one of its several rough patches in the business, ordered a cut in expenditure and said no film cost should exceed £200,000, so the rest had to be made on home ground using budgeted sets. Dennis certainly looked the picture of Georgian elegance in the part, with slim, well cut trousers, and crisp white shirt.

Due to restrictions of the film's running time, not all of Byron's many lovers were featured in the movie, but Dennis had his hands pretty full with Joan Greenwood as Caroline Lamb, Mai Zetterling as Theresa Guiccioli, Linden Travers as his sister Augusta, and Sonia Holm as Lady Byron. So very much hard work went into making *The Bad Lord Byron*, as Sydney Box named it, that it was halfway through the following year before the final scenes were completed.

The news that Dennis was to play Byron caused much excitement among his followers and critics, and everyone expected it to be the high spot of his career. His fans could not get enough of him; neither could the studios who did not give him a moment's rest and before *Byron* was finished, three other films were being lined up with him as the star.

Muriel and Sydney Box's joint production *Easy Money* told the stories of four separate people who each win on the football pools and how it affects their lives. He hardly had time to draw breath before he was rehearsing for the lead in *Snowbound* (based on Hammond Innes' book *The Lonely Skier*); audiences saw Dennis cast as a hero, in the form of a young film extra who is chosen by his boss and former British intelligence officer, as played by Robert Newton, to go on a mission to the Alps. There, he falls foul of a sinister man, portrayed by Herbert Lom, searching for Nazi gold buried beneath a ski lodge. It was a routine story, more 'boy's own stuff' than first rate excitement, and not very convincing. For all its action, *Snowbound* is strangely dull, with shallow characters that do not have enough to do. Mila Parely, the leading lady, was new to British films and resembled a young Marlene Dietrich. For Dennis, it signified time he was given something better than romantic leads. It is interesting to note that between snatches of dialogue, he is seen to smoke one cigarette after another (a total of ten) as if the director David Macdonald did not know what else to do with the character.

There was a great atmosphere on the set and Dennis got on particularly well with Robert Newton, who became a friend and, apart from their mutual liking for drink, Newton could be very entertaining company when he rendered forth with his fund of showbiz anecdotes. Newton sadly died prematurely at the age of fifty-one in 1956. In his tribute book about Dennis Price, the author Elliot J. Huntley recounts a most bizarre story passed around about Newton and how when he died and was cremated, his ashes were entrusted to Dennis's safekeeping as one of his closest friends. Later, he says, Dennis hosted a party where one of his drunken guests proceeded to flush Newton's ashes down the toilet, 'Giving him a proper send-off'.

In actual fact, Newton died while out in America and was buried in Westwood Memorial Park Cemetery, Los Angeles, California. What is especially moving is that his wife Vera died in 2000, some forty-four years later and is buried with her husband. They may have been separated a long time, but she never stopped loving him.

Above: Dennis enjoys a joke with director David MacDonald on the set of *Snowbound*.

Below left: Adding to the fun atmosphere on *Snowbound* was the brilliant comedy actor Stanley Holloway.

Below right: Dennis and his nightclub singer girlfriend (Greta Gynt) in a send-up of Rita Hayworth's *Gilda*, seen here in a dramatic scene in *Easy Money*.

After *Snowbound*, the next film on Dennis's agenda was a drama called *Good Time Girl* on which he worked alongside Flora Robson. She was given the part of a magistrate called Miss Thorpe, and was required to memorise a lot of dialogue. Arriving at the studios, she found Dennis was word perfect and they worked together very smoothly, with timing in harmony. As a result, they finished their scenes within a day and a half rather than a week, which saved the production a considerable amount of money and helped earn Dennis a reputation for being very reliable.

Good Time Girl was based on Arthur La Bern's novel *Night Darkens the Street*, about the true-life case of a teenage delinquent who was convicted of complicity in a murder. A far cry from Dennis's usual romantic films, there is nothing soft and gentle about *Good Time Girl*. Despite his frequent protests, it was yet another film in which he was killed, as in this one he played the innocent victim of the teenager.

Despite tightened budgets in some quarters, Dennis felt the British film industry was going places and expressed the foresight that films should be made with women in mind as it was women who comprised the greater section of the cinema-going audience.

Anyone and everyone who happened to meet Dennis during this high spot in his career found him to be charming and noticed his complete lack of pretentiousness. He was very casual about being a prominent British film star, considering an actor to be the same as anyone who works for a living; his job was to entertain and he just got on with it, but he always knew the value of his public and was never too grand to appreciate them. 'In the end', he said, 'I imagine we all do much the same and behave the same off duty as the man next door'.

One of his last engagements that year was to appear on a radio show called *Alhambra of the Air*, a variety show. Also on the bill was Margaret Lockwood. The past few years had been fantastic, but Dennis's good fortune was soon to hit a rough patch. When the film industry faced a post-war slump in 1947, due to a dollar drain and an ill-thought-out Government austerity programme that heavily taxed Hollywood films, it cast a dark shadow over the industry, which had until then looked so promising. Dennis was by no means the least to be affected and his fat contracted salary of £25,000 a year quickly diminished.

Dennis Price had been a man who had everything—looks, fame, money, and a family. What could happen to spoil it? The next few years would reveal all.

6

Byron (1948–1949)

Dennis had earlier expressed a desire to move from Windsor to London, but did not have the financial means to make it happen. However, in early 1948, his Uncle Franklyn, who had spent most of his life in South Africa, decided to pass his London town house over to Dennis. Moving from their Berkshire home where they had been content and happy for six years, Dennis and the family made 15 Mallord Street, Chelsea their new base. Convenient for both studios and the West End, the Price's elegant new residence also became the ideal setting for many a lavish party.

Dennis loved to entertain in true Regency style, sitting at the head of the dining table where he and his guests would eat by candlelight, and the drink always flowed with abundance. He certainly did not believe in doing things by halves and always gave his visitors the very best of everything. Dennis's witty and intelligent conversation ensured an evening spent in his company was never dull and coupled with his generous hospitality he quickly earned himself an enviable reputation. Sadly, it also led to the home being targeted by every nimble-fingered burglar in London, with three robberies taking place in the course of their first year there.

During the third break-in, the artful villains scaled a drainpipe to gain entry, and took items worth £1,000. By September 1948, Joan was thoroughly tired of her jewellery being stolen and said she felt like putting a sign outside advertising the fact she had 'no more left.' She said, 'I'm sick of burglars. I haven't a necklace or bracelet left to wear. I think it's about time they kept away from me.'

Dennis's life seemed to be one long social round. At the 1948 British Film Festival, he was well to the fore and loved the glittering occasion and the praise it lavished upon him; for all his fame, accolades still meant a lot to him. The gathering also gave Dennis the chance to catch up on all the

Above: Mr and Mrs Dennis Price at their Chelsea home. There seems to be a sadness in Joan's eyes, and it was not long afterwards their marriage was wrecked by Dennis's infidelities.

Left: The loving father—Dennis with daughters Susan (kissing him on cheek) and Tessa, taken in 1948.

industry gossip, of which there was plenty. During the festival, clips from many outstanding films of the previous year were shown, and then the big news came—the completion of *The Bad Lord Byron* was announced. Dennis was very excited about its potential as a future classic of the cinema and could hardly wait for the public's reaction.

Byron was a sulky, petulant man and facial expressions played a key part in portraying him, which Dennis had developed brilliantly, pouting his lips petulantly whenever provoked by an enemy or rebuffed by a woman. As he grew older, Dennis's lips became softer and more elastic than ever and he was able to drop his lower lip without contorting the rest of his face; his flexible features and high, arched eyebrows were a great asset in portraying this particular role.

Eileen Griffiths of Gainsborough's research department was responsible for giving Dennis all the details the studio could gather on the poet's private life and personal habits, so he could completely get into the part, which was undoubtedly the most important element of the whole project. Dennis observed that Byron had a fondness for biting his nails, though Dennis preferred not to emulate that particular characteristic. Nor did Dennis appreciate the idea of appearing on the screen wearing curl papers in his hair that were the fashion in Byron's day. To emulate his personality, it was important that Dennis projected the 'supercilious aloofness' that Byron was known for since his schooldays—a combination of natural vanity and a lordly awareness of his position in society.

Five writers were engaged to work on the script and it certainly proved a case of too many cooks spoiling the broth. Instead of using an overall narration to explain events, they came up with the idea of having Byron put on trial in a heavenly courtroom, to determine if he was 'a great poet or a seducer and libertine'.

In between the courtroom deliberations, viewers were offered a series of scenarios between Byron and his various amours, notably the mentally unstable Caroline Lamb. Leslie Dwyer appeared throughout as his invaluable manservant, Fletcher, and Raymond Lovell was memorable in the role of Byron's friend, John Hobhouse. With the talents involved, it should have been a successful combination, but the inane format proved to be the film's undoing. Far too much time was devoted to the heavy courtroom debates and not enough on Byron's exciting escapades.

Certainly, they could not have chosen anyone better than Dennis, with his perfect combination of looks and style, to play the amorous poet and admittedly, the film contained several outstanding scenes, including Byron's verses. Yet with the enforced budget cuts by Rank, equally several outstanding scenes looked cheap, not least when Dennis was filmed against a beautiful Mediterranean background (unfortunately black and

During the filming of *The Bad Lord Byron*, Dennis arranged to have his portrait painted by James Proudfoot; it features in the finished film.

white) while his penetrating voice uttered the immortal line 'So, we'll go no more a roving'—the very phrase that was to be Dennis's own epitaph.

Just prior to the Rank accountants stepping in, Sydney Box and his team had gone to extraordinary lengths to immerse Dennis in all things Byron. For example, some of the furniture used in the shots of Byron's home had actually belonged to him, which the company hired at considerable expense from museums and private collections; these included a goblet made out of the top half of a human skull. The rest was crafted by experts, using traditional methods.

Then, it was off to Venice where Dennis was filmed surrounded by a flock of pigeons carefully lured to settle around him with offers of nuts from property men in a one-hour period when the square was roped off by police. When filming had finished, the unit was pestered by postcard sellers complaining angrily that they had lost an hour's trade and so wanted compensation.

Dennis next spent the day at a lunatic asylum on the shores of the lagoon to film a swimming sequence. His changing room was a cell, kept locked by the warder until he was ready to plunge into the lagoon for his take.

The wardrobe department studied pictures of Byron and his followers so the costumes were exact replicas right down to the last button. In order to imitate the poet's famous limp, Dennis was supplied with a pair of specially made shoes, though when he came to change into his own clothes after a day in front of the cameras, he had grown so used to walking with a limp that he had to really concentrate to try and walk normally again.

As there were a few weeks after the unit's return from Italy before studio work commenced, Dennis and a publicity team were sent up to Byron's old home (Newstead Abbey) to take some publicity stills of him in costume in the historic setting, but because Box had chosen to call his film *The Bad Lord Byron*, permission to take cameras into the Abbey was refused by the Nottingham Corporation. The national press got hold of the story and had a field day. For a time, it seemed unlikely they would be able to shoot there at all before a simple solution was found; Dennis, accompanied by a few technicians, walked up to the gates of the Abbey, paid over their sixpences as members of the public, went inside and the pictures were taken.

At the height of the press 'controversy' surrounding the choice of title, Dennis wrote to Sydney Box telling him that he was being challenged by members of the public over the matter. Here is an extract from Mr. Box's letter of reply:

> I was frankly delighted to hear that you are being attacked about the title of the Byron picture. This is exactly what we anticipated—in fact, exactly what we planned. The important thing about a title is that people should talk about it. *Inter alia*, they talk about the picture. Do you remember *The Seventh Veil*? I was begged a hundred times by very influential people to change that title and refused to do so because I believed it would bring the people in on Monday night. I am convinced that it did so—and I am equally convinced that *The Bad Lord Byron* will do the same. All we have to do, is to make a sufficiently good picture, so that people will continue to come in on Tuesday, Wednesday, Thursday, Friday and Saturday. If we can do that, we shall have nothing to fear!

The finished picture, centred in the heavenly courtroom, showed Byron's life through the eyes of each mistress in turn, with the idea of building a giant 'jigsaw'. Yet it was decided some characters and places were not really essential to the plot, so should be left out, not least because of budgetary reasons. The film-makers discarded some of their best ideas while saving the dross. Some of the cut scenes included those in a monastery, walking the streets of Venice, joining in a carnival, swimming in the lagoon, and sequences that would have explained Byron's moodiness. A wordy courtroom debate punctuated by black and white flashbacks was not the stuff of great epics and with so little of

Drinking from Byron's own goblet, as fashioned out of a human skull. The sequence was not featured in the final cut of the film, perhaps being viewed as being too decadent.

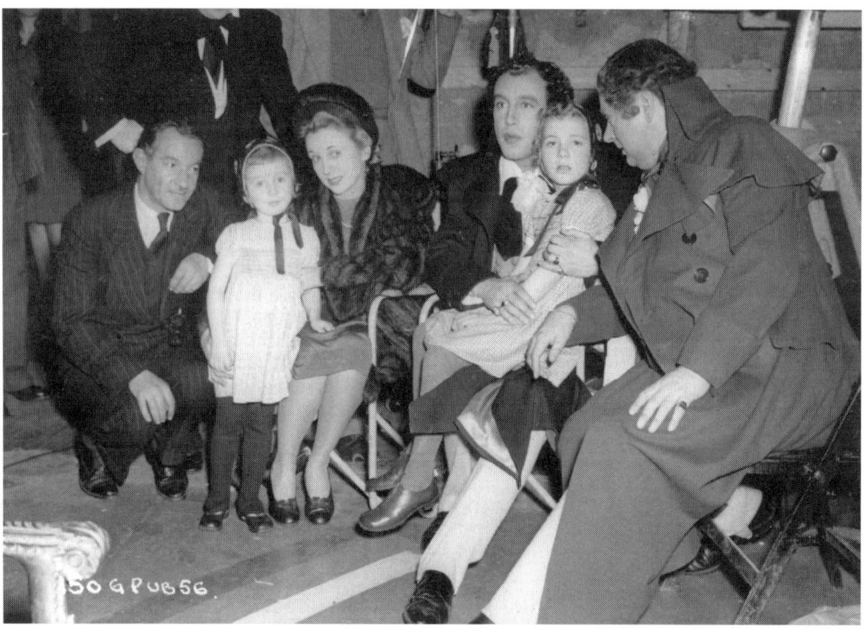

On the set of *The Bad Lord Byron* in 1948. Dennis sits next to his wife Joan, with daughter Tessa (aged five) standing and Susan (aged eight) sitting on his lap. Raymond Lovell is to the right.

Venice on screen, the scenes could have easily been filmed on the Thames. As for the borrowed furniture, it went unnoticed.

Sadly, and despite everyone's best efforts, the film suffered from a disjointed script and bad editorial choices. Dennis, modest and self-effacing as usual, summed up his own feelings:

> Well, at any rate, it will always be possible for actors much more talented than I to play Lord Byron on the screen again. His life and times provide a vast canvas which our film would never hope to cover. I am not (thank goodness) a producer, but if I were, I'd be most grateful to his lordship for a host of real life entertainment stories which the scribblings of modern fiction can scarce begin to rival. Had I started on the Byron subject ... I would have retired in confusion very early on! There was and always will be, only one George Gordon Byron of Newstead and I hope he will forgive us for encroaching on the reality and brilliance which he gave to the world of his time. I feel he would have acknowledged this picture's reception, good or bad, with an appropriate gesture.

The film could and should have been a great success. Sadly, it became a box office disaster.

Leslie Dwyer and Mai Zetterling share a scene in *The Bad Lord Byron*.

While Dennis was preoccupied with this one film, Joan was feeling increasingly out of things and restless to return to acting. She resumed her stage career but said, because the children were 'so young', she had to decline numerous offers of parts in plays that were to be tested in the provinces before being brought in to London. Whenever she could, she appeared in 'purely London-based shows'; those included productions of *Great Day* and *The Country Wife*. Joan claimed she intended to make 'a full comeback' once the girls were of an age to look after themselves.

On his rare days off, Dennis enjoyed being with his family and listed his favourite leisure activities as the company of his children, reading biographies, rowing, listening to light music, and riding in Hyde Park with Joan and their eldest daughter; on two such occasions, he was accompanied by actor Michael Gough, who observed 'what a fine horseman Dennis was'.

Films also fascinated him; when away from the studios, Dennis watched at least two a day and explained it was not only because he loved movies but because seeing as many as he could was an essential part of his work. His personal favourite was the original version of *Mayerling* with Charles Boyer, filmed in 1939 with French dialogue. The tragic love story moved Dennis more than any other as, at heart, he was a very sensitive and romantic man.

There were some things he did not care for, such as cats, sweet foods, milk puddings, and beef. Dennis always ate sparingly, preferring a pub snack washed down with a glass of Guinness to a three-course meal, and this was probably the reason he stayed so thin. This was the public image he liked to portray while keeping his other great passions of heavy drinking and gambling secret. He treated money as no object and took wealth for granted.

With a string of hit feature films behind him, Dennis was becoming immensely popular and as a box office attraction was equal with Stewart Granger, John Mills, and Michael Wilding. He also received more fan mail than Hollywood giants Gary Cooper and Humphrey Bogart. Dennis's annual income had reached £25,000—a huge amount—but he frittered away large amounts on entertaining and playing the tables in the London casinos. In efforts to maintain his film star image, the Prices were often seen out together at film premieres along with all the other top names of the 1940s, while at home, a nanny was employed to look after the children. As they grew older, Susan and Tessa happily joined their father and mother in many a group photo session for the newspapers and film magazines, and soon came to love the limelight. Always dressed in pretty clothes, sometimes with bonnets and usually in matching outfits, the girls attended one of the very best London schools where they also learned the basic steps of ballet. Dennis was particularly proud of the progress of his two fair-haired, blue-eyed daughters in this field.

In the many interviews Dennis gave when any of his films was released, journalists always hoped for an interesting angle, though Dennis—outwardly modest to the last—put on a show of utter amazement whenever praised. 'Who me, dear chap, a star?' he would say, in answer to questions such as 'To what do you attribute your success, Mr. Price?' 'I'm just a fellow who does what he's told around the place. Acting is a job to me, a way of keeping my wife and family. I just do what the director tells me.'

The columnists found his candour fascinating at first, though were never quite sure if he did not care about publicity or whether he was having a little game with them. He claimed he wanted 'to play as many character parts as possible', yet he was always hugely modest about his acting ability, though his 'I'm too modest' approach turned sour when one journalist commented on a scene Dennis played in *The Bad Lord Byron*, remarking how difficult it was bringing Byron to life; Dennis replied with a defeated air:

> But of course, in fact I shouldn't be playing this part at all. It's a role for Laurence Olivier or Eric Portman—they could make a wonderful job of it. But you know what things are like in the film business these days. Costs are being cut and all that. And you see, old man, I'm cheap.

It was always difficult to compliment Dennis on any of his work, as whenever praise came his way, he would brush it aside, seeming content just to have any parts that were going, provided it was a character he could do something with. 'Just give me a job and tell me how to do it and though I may not do an Olivier for you, I'll never let you down.'

Every year, he made more films than the one previous, though gave credit for their success to his fellow actors. For all his casual talk, he had a certain amount of ambition and it was his portrayal of Byron that he really hoped would be considered his greatest achievement—hopes that were sadly dashed—but with his continued self-effacing attitude, Dennis did himself and his career more harm than good. If you say something often enough, people will believe it, and that was just what the film companies did by giving the parts he 'wasn't worthy of' to other actors. It was the ones who blew their own trumpet, had no doubts, and proclaimed their great abilities who stayed at the top in the business as Dennis was soon to realise to his great regret.

In December, Joan Schofield took to the stage again as one of the prominent characters in a play called *I Walk Unseen*, which was being produced for a fortnight at the Q Theatre on the outskirts of London. Also in the cast, in a minor role, was the young Ian Carmichael. Fresh from his Army service and with a wife and infant daughter to support, he was working hard and keen to make a name for himself. He was aware 'Dennis was a very big star indeed', though as a struggling young actor, he had not had the opportunity to meet him before. During the play, he got to know Joan fairly well and was in awe when she announced, 'Dennis will be in front tonight'.

Afterwards, in the dressing room, 'the great man' and Ian Carmichael were introduced. Being wealthy people, Dennis and Joan had their own cars (his was a beautiful red Packard), a luxury Ian could hardly afford on his modest income, but as he lived only a short distance from their home in Mallord Street, Joan offered to drive Carmichael to and from the theatre each night—a kindness he forever remembered.

On one occasion, Carmichael was invited in for drinks and was impressed by the Price's luxurious furnishings and elegant taste. The living room was situated on the first floor of the house and overlooked the street, with large bay windows; there were deep easy chairs and long, low bookshelves at each side of the broad fireplace to accommodate (among other works) Dennis's biography collection, and he was particularly proud of his glass collection too. The young actor recalled 'everything seemed fresh and airy in the house, in particular the girls' day nursery which was on the ground floor where Dennis always made a point of calling in on arriving home from the studios'.

The trappings of wealth seemed a great contrast to Ian Carmichael's own sparse attic rooms on the fifth floor of a house off the Fulham Road. It was to be some years until he and Dennis met again, with roles virtually reversed.

After a day filming, Dennis always made a point of heading straight home to his daughters' bedroom to tell them a story and tuck them in.

15 Mallord Street—Dennis's home between 1948 and 1950.

The Price family in the first floor living room of their Chelsea house, admiring a photo of Dennis in *Caravan*.

7

Kind Hearts (1949)

As 1948 neared its end, Dennis was offered a contract with Ealing Studios—whose output was distributed by The Rank Organisation—to star in a black comedy called *Kind Hearts and Coronets*.

It was a big step from straight parts to comedy and if all went well, Dennis knew his place at the top would be secure once again. He also hoped that this time he would see the picture through without being killed off, as he told a reporter:

> I made a new year resolution—to abolish the death sentence. I mean the one passed on me by the film industry. Look at it this way, in nine out of my last dozen or so pictures, I've either been killed or succumbed to some awful disease. In fact, I'm beginning to wonder whether there is any life left in me.

Even *Byron* was no exception, as the poet is finally stricken by a fever and dies. It was not the actual process of dying that was the problem, but the impression the audience would have; 'if I go on this way,' he said, 'I'm afraid people will come to associate my name with gloomy subjects. And who wants gloom today?'

His primary ambition had always been more comedy. 'Yes, not falling into buckets of whitewash, but light, frothy stuff with witty dialogue and amusing situations. One of my favourite stage parts, for instance, was *Blithe Spirit*.'

Filming on *Kind Hearts and Coronets* started in January 1949; meanwhile, *The Bad Lord Byron* was to be released.

Not quite realising the size of the turkey they had on their hands, Gainsborough sent Dennis out—in what was to be his last series of publicity for the company—to make more personal appearances than ever before.

Yet these were hampered when his anxiety came into play and he would sometimes have to rush away to be sick. For just such an occurrence, he carried a supply of pills and medicines in a little bag. Meeting his admirers without preparing beforehand worried him and affected his system, though it never occurred to him that his fans were just as nervous about meeting him.

Dennis's assured and positive publicity ahead of the film's release was further displayed with in-depth articles in all the major film journals. In one of these, he observed:

> It would be interesting to know the feelings of the public. But I always believe the sight of Maggie Lockwood or Pat Roc, dressed up to kill and talking charmingly from the stage, can't bring anything but pleasure to the people who have admired their actual films.
>
> Perhaps us men in our dreary old black dinner jackets aren't much of a catch.... and there's a lot of truth in the plaintive cry from the male section of the audience, 'Well, what's he got that I haven't?'

In another, quite telling, article for *Hollywood-London Film Parade*, Dennis gave this detailed insight into his psyche.

> I like to think of myself as an average fellow—tolerant, with a sense of humour and understanding. I try to appreciate the other person's point of view, but I don't always succeed. To be honest, I have to admit that like most people, I have my pet hates. Generally speaking, they all concern trivial things, but it's usually the trivial things that are most irritating. Perhaps the one thing I hate more than anything else is being described as 'That actor who always gets killed or dies before the end of his pictures'.
>
> I've come to a sticky end in nine films and I don't like constantly being reminded of it. It happened in *The White Unicorn* and in *The Bad Lord Byron*. Perhaps one day I'll live throughout an entire picture?
>
> My premature deaths on screen are really my prize hate, but a close runner up, believe it or not, is tea. I used to love tea and welcomed a 'cuppa' at almost any hour of the day or night. That was before I encountered the studio brew. That's a peculiar and rather incredible concoction which would make even a sergeant major squirm. Studio life has cured me of buns and sweets. With rations what they are, my wife seems to think there is a lot to be said in favour of studios.
>
> As I'm writing this in my studio dressing room, it is appropriate to refer to some hates that are brought about by working in a film studio. There are several factors that go in the making of a successful picture. A good story, then a director who is sympathetic and knows his job and an enthusiastic and experienced cast. All these are important but

are of no avail, unless there is team work from all those engaged in the production. Realising that, can you imagine anything more irritating than the actor who comes on the set without knowing his lines? Not only is it intensely irritating for the people with whom he is appearing, but holding up production is very costly and a waste of money which would be better employed in the making of more and better pictures. With a little thought, there's no need for these complaints. Can you wonder that I put this high up among my list of pet hates?

While I am on the subject of films, I ought to mention the arty crafty continental films about psychoanalysis American style. I find them remote from real life and cannot see anything entertaining in them. They bore me.

My next hate is one which is by no means exclusive to myself, and fellow sufferers will be most sympathetic. It concerns late arrivals in a theatre or cinema and probably all of you have been victims of this menace. You know the sort of people I mean. They arrive just as the curtain is going up, or worse, when the play or film has begun. Inevitably, they have trouble with their tickets, can't find the right seats and talk in a loud whisper to one another. Mostly the offenders are habitual late comers who consider it 'the thing' to make their entrance as the lights go down. They pay little regard to the intense irritation caused to people they disturb and are oblivious of the discourtesy to the actors.

In the same category are the people who leave before the show is over. There are times when it is unavoidable. In such cases, the early departure is excusable, but those who walk out for effect cannot be forgiven. Before I leave the theatre, I ought to mention those actors and actresses who are completely inaudible. How intensely annoying to find, after paying good money to see a play, that it is impossible to hear a word uttered by some of the cast. It ruins the evening, causes bad tempers and reduces what might have been a first class show to a meaningless mumble.

I abhor 'canned music'. It's just one of those things I can't stand at any price and I avoid it like the plague. I think it's very unlikely that many of you will share my next hate. I ought to break this one gently and tell you in a whisper—that I hate staying in bed late on Sundays. I know that most of my friends who work in films like to spend their day off resting, but I find I have so little spare time, that I want to make the most of my free moments. I am far happier spending a Sunday without constant interruption, than I would be lazing away in bed. I ought to know, as I've tried them both!

My last two hates both concern the English climate. Nobody could be more enthusiastic about a seaside holiday, but oh how I hate bathing in England. Even on a hot summer's day, I need an awful lot of coaxing and persuasion before I can be made to venture into the water. And then

> there is the fog. Well, friends, I think that about covers my pet hates. I wonder how many of them are the same as yours?

This was one of the few occasions he gave such an account of his personal views, as in the coming decades, he disappeared from the film magazines, to be replaced by the up-and-coming leading men.

For all his efforts, the film Dennis most wanted to succeed was a flop. All the critics were unanimous in laying the blame for its failure squarely at the door of its ill-thought-out format. For example, *The Daily Worker* commented:

> Bad is an unfortunate adjective to have used in the title, because bad it is. Sometimes it is boringly bad, occasionally funny bad, but most of the time, it is so torturingly bad, that I wanted to rise from my seat and scream.

With a bad script, bad format, and bad editing, it must have been extremely embarrassing for all those involved in *The Bad Lord Byron* following such confident publicity. Dennis felt more deflated than a burst balloon over his first bad reviews and found the repercussions lasted for years to come and his future in the industry seemed very uncertain for a while.

The one and probably only saving grace was James Proudfoot immortalising Dennis's role by completing a lifelike painting of him as Byron, which appears in the opening scene. Afterwards, the painting went on display for a time at an exhibition of The Royal Society of Portrait Painters.

Dennis's spirits were given a lift, when in June, *Kind Hearts and Coronets* was released. It was chiefly the work of Robert Hamer, who both directed and wrote the brilliant screenplay, adapted from a novel by Roy Horniman, called *Noblesse Oblige* (also the title the film went under when released in France). Hamer found adapting the screenplay very heavy going, but the end result was inspired, giving Dennis his first real opportunity to display a unique talent for comedy to a wide range of people.

Playing Louis D'Ascoyne Mazzini (the half-Italian distant heir to a dukedom), Dennis murders his noble relatives one by one in revenge for their cruel treatment of his mother. For this reason alone, you cannot help sympathising with the character. Narrating the story as it unfolds, in flashback from a prison cell, Dennis begins by playing his 'father' with the addition of a moustache and has only had time to sing Mozart's '*Il mio tesoro intanto*', before dying of a heart attack at his son's birth. The antics that follow are hilarious as Louis proceeds to kill his relations, all eight of whom are played by Alec Guinness.

Reading the script of *Kind Hearts and Coronets* had been like reading his own life story because every one of the characters had an uncanny resemblance

'I think I'll have a small developer,' says Louis D'Ascoyne to his intended victim, Henry, in a scene from the classic *Kind Hearts and Coronets.*

to his own family circle, and several of his own relations had themselves died in similar circumstances or prematurely. The similarities go as follows:

Reverend D'Ascoyne—A pompous old windbag who talks rubbish from the pulpit. Dennis's first cousin once removed, Reverend Cecil Verey, married his parents in 1911 and Dennis in 1939. Died as an old man in 1960.

The banker—A kindly old man who employs Louis in the banking firm, unbeknown to him after Louis has murdered his son! Says Louis he's 'Glad [he doesn't] have to kill the old man.' As the head of the family, Dennis's father Thomas Rose-Price would be 'the banker'. He died suddenly of a heart attack aged seventy-four in 1949.

The banker's son—An arrogant young man, responsible for getting Louis fired from his job as a draper's assistant. Louis murders him by untying his boat and sending it drifting over a weir. Dennis's elder brother Robin, a strong person, not known for his sense of humour.

Young Henry D'Ascoyne—A likeable young man who is blown up when igniting chemicals in his potting shed, converted into a photographer's dark room. Dennis's young cousin, Thomas (son of uncle Franklyn) who got killed towards the end of the Second World War, in 1945.

The 7th Duke of Chalfont, Ethelred D'Ascoyne—The last of the family to be murdered by Louis, in order for him to succeed to the title and claim the family estate. Baronet Rose-Price, Dennis's distant cousin and title holder of the family seat, Trengwainton manor in Cornwall.

Lady Agatha D'Ascoyne—A suffragette who gets shot down by an arrow which punctures the hot air balloon she is travelling in over London. Dennis's aunt, Mary Rose-Price, died in 1925.

Navy Commander Horatio D'Ascoyne—not murdered, but dies when he goes down with his ship. Dennis's uncle, Vivian Rose-Price, sank with his ship HMS *Europa* in 1915.

Colonel Rufus D'Ascoyne—blown up by a bomb, concealed inside a jar of caviar. An old bore who talks endlessly about old army campaigns. Dennis's grandfather, Thomas Caradoc Rose-Price, served in many military campaigns and his whole life consisted of army duties. Died in 1911.

Edith D'Ascoyne—Wife of murdered young Henry. Louis makes her his wife, because she is 'tall and slender as a lily and just as beautiful', but 'what a prig she was', disapproving of alcohol consumption. Dennis's wife, Joan Schofield, disapproved of his drinking.

Sybella—Louis's mistress, who also happens to be a married woman. Dennis had a married lover, Margaret Lockwood.

Lionel—Sybella's husband who commits suicide. Margaret Lockwood's own husband, Rupert Leon, later divorced her.

It was very surprising that a sharp-eyed journalist of the day did not pick up on the parallels between the D'Ascoynes and the Rose-Prices and the fact that Dennis himself was related to a baronet. That would have made wonderful publicity but perhaps because he was so private, Dennis did not want his public to know. He liked to keep the punchline of the joke to himself—his thorough enjoyment in killing off his relatives on screen, almost rubbing their noses in it.

Kind Hearts and Coronets was a tremendous success with cinemagoers, and a triumph for Ealing Studios. It became Dennis's all-time favourite film and admirable compensation for the disaster of *The Bad Lord Byron*. In fact, it is a film he would forever be remembered for and certainly so by his co-star Joan Greenwood, who thought he was 'a darling man, charming, witty and generous.'

An actor is lucky to find one role in his career that is absolutely made for him. Dennis Price found it as Louis D'Ascoyne, and few people could ever disagree that his performance was brilliant. Dennis proved he had the most important element needed in comedy—timing. His approach was relaxed and natural, uttering words that could have applied to him and his family, giving his performance added depth and verve, with his eyes

The dramatic concluding scene in *Kinds Hearts and Coronets* when Louis realises he may have just incriminated himself in his memoirs, carelessly left behind in his cell. A young Arthur Lowe is on the left.

sparkling with wicked amusement. No one else could have played Louis and given the character such realism.

Some critics claimed he was the kingpin of the film, while others pointed out he was in the shadow of Alec Guinness with his clever adoption of eight contrasting characters. This eternal argument as to who gave the greater performance only defeats the end purpose—to enjoy an excellent comedy.

After his Ealing success, Dennis was offered the lead in Gainsborough Pictures' *The Lost People*. It was one of the last films made at their Shepherd's Bush studios and his last for Rank under contract. The company's final few films were transferred to Rank's main studio, Pinewood, ahead of it closing down completely with significant losses. In the film, Dennis played Captain Ridley, who was in charge of a dispersal centre for displaced persons in Germany at the end of the Second World War. The story was based on a successful play of the day called *Cockpit* by Bridget Boland (the cockpit referring to all the scrapping and in-fighting among the foreign refugees, of which there was plenty during the film). Dennis embodied the role with all the qualities he was known for—sensitivity and feeling for the subject. It made a nice change from Gainsborough's period romances.

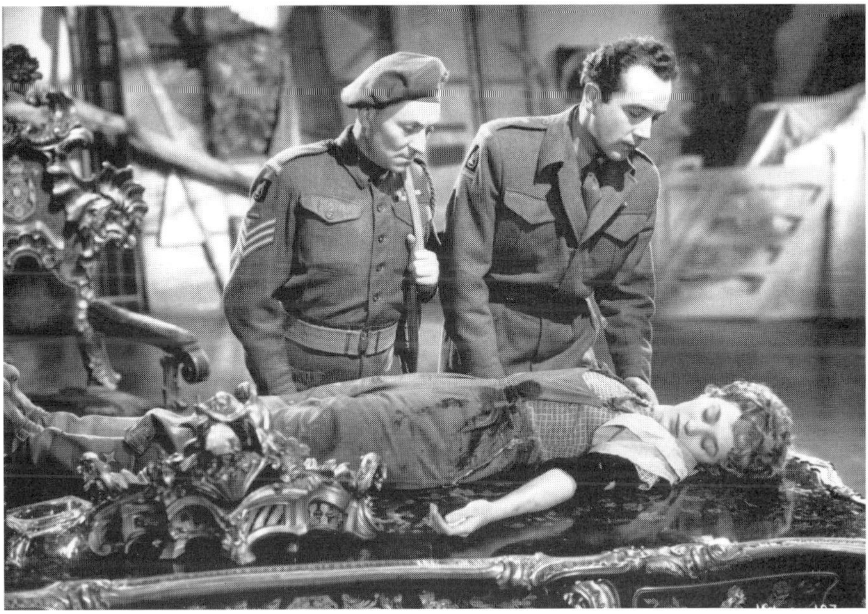

Mai Zetterling co-starred with Dennis on his next film, *The Lost People*, seen here alongside TV's first Dr Who, William Hartnell.

Dennis played one of two British soldiers holding a disparate and hostile band of refugees in a theatre, prior to returning them to their homelands after the Second World War.

He was also seen in a crazy slapstick comedy called *Helter Skelter*; in fact, it was some footage of him as Byron, lasting only a few seconds, and a load of mixed-up rubbish it was, only serving to further contribute to the death knell sounding for Gainsborough.

Gainsborough Pictures, and its parent company Rank, had suffered significant financial losses with the failure of *The Bad Lord Byron* (along with a few other recent misfiring films such as *Helter Skelter*) and the company was all but shut down in 1950; along with it, many contracts were terminated, Dennis's being one.

Offscreen, Dennis's seemingly happy home life was about to come to a dramatic end. In August 1949, his wife came home unexpectedly one evening and caught him in bed with another woman at their Chelsea home. This blow came as the final straw in what had become a very rocky marriage ever since they had moved back to London from Windsor. Joan may or may not have been aware of his previous infidelities, but this was intolerable—taking place inside their home and in their marital bed. Joan had tolerated his drinking and gambling, but brazen adultery was another matter.

Joan continued loving Dennis very much, as was apparent by their enduring friendship, which was to last for the next twenty-three years, but while she was a gracious and dignified woman who tried her best to maintain the public image of a united family, this proved to be her biggest challenge, as Dennis had, quite frankly, broken her heart.

Then, on 21 October 1949, Dennis's father died suddenly in London at the age of seventy-four. Due to work commitments, Dennis was unable to attend the memorial service, held for the Brigadier at Wellington Barracks the following week, though feelings for his father were always mixed as they never had the close relationship they should have enjoyed.

News of his adultery was not made public until 1950, when Joan filed for divorce. Those worst affected were their two daughters—Susan, aged nine, and Tessa, only five.

Up until the divorce announcement, Dennis continued to attend numerous film premieres with his wife in an attempt to keep up the image of a happy couple for the sake of his career. The family's move from Windsor to Chelsea had proved to be an unfortunate decision and now the only thing in Dennis's favour was a prestigious address, enabling him to mingle more conveniently with important contacts.

While heading for the divorce courts, Dennis's passion for gambling, coupled with his expensive lifestyle, did not help matters; he and Joan's careers were at very different levels and unlike other acting couples (Olivier and Leigh or Taylor and Burton), Joan never appeared in any of Dennis's films. As his work became increasingly prolific, it brought more social obligations, which were hard for her to avoid.

Joan remained a very attractive and, in her own right, wealthy woman, yet she did not marry again until after Dennis's death many years later.

After *The Lost People*, Dennis played the leading role of Rudi Kleber in Ivor Novello's musical *The Dancing Years* for the Associated British Picture Company. Following its huge stage success, it was made under Novello's own guidance and several of his original stage cast were used in supporting roles—Grey Blake, Olive Gilbert, Anthony Nichols, and a young, up-and-coming actress, Patricia Dainton:

> I was 17 at the time of being cast in the film and really quite nervous ... I remember Dennis Price being very kind, charming and welcoming to all the young actors in the company. He was very helpful towards me and when I had my first scene with him coming up he sensed I was worried about it, so came over and said 'I tell you what, let's rehearse this together now and that'll put you at your ease when we come to do it in front of the camera'. It was so kind of him.
>
> I didn't really mingle with Dennis off set, but do recall when we travelled to Austria for the location work he seemed very unhappy if perhaps a little depressed, and he carried a medicine chest with him everywhere but had no idea why, or what was in it [it was his anti-anxiety medication].
>
> Whilst the main place for gossip was the make-up room at the studio, I never heard anything untoward about Dennis nor did we realise at the time that his marriage was coming to an end. He kept his private life very much to himself.
>
> Incidentally, I first met Ivor Novello when I was 15 and auditioned for a part in the stage version of *The Dancing Years*. He laughed and said I was too young but kindly suggested I come in as a dancer and understudy. He was so charming and had such a terrific presence that had he been in a room and walked out before you entered, you'd instinctively know he'd been in there. I remember when we were on tour in Wimbledon the actress playing Maria fell ill and understudy Ruby Newell went on – what a voice! Ivor was called to the theatre, and we knew he was in to hear Ruby, and when he saw her on stage a star was born. She changed her name to Vanessa Lee and went on to great things, and Ivor helped her all the way including paying for surgery on her nose to help her breath more easily.
>
> When the film premiered, Ivor naturally came and there was a dinner afterwards where I sat on his table. He was not at all pleased with the film and despite six months of rehearsal and shooting, felt it just didn't work. On stage yes, it was terrific, but on film it just wasn't the same. I watched it again recently and can see Dennis Price wasn't right for the part—he was miscast. I thought he seemed awkward in his scenes.

Taken during a break on *The Dancing Years*, this photograph shows Dennis with Giselle Preville and Ivor Novello (centre). Novello approved all the casting and supervised the production.

Dennis shares a scene with Patricia Dainton in *The Dancing Years*.

> It was however a wonderful experience with such a wonderful crew and cast. I don't regret a moment of it, I'm just sad it never quite worked as a film.

Painstaking lengths were taken to make the settings as authentic as possible and the film unit went over to Austria, where many of the outdoor scenes were shot in the actual locale of Novello's story.

During breaks between filming, Dennis amused himself by captaining a cricket team, to try and teach the game to their Austrian assistants. Not having the right equipment, they made do with rolled-up tape for the ball and a strange looking object from the props department serving as a bat. On several occasions, the 'ball' landed up in the local post office. The residents of the town, St Wolfgang, were surprised at hearing shouts of 'Well bowled, sir' in the air, but just put it down to 'the mad English film-makers' up to their antics again.

Back at Elstree, some of the biggest sets ever constructed in a British studio were built with the most outstanding being a model of the huge Ander Wien Opera House. Dennis said he had been especially pleased to accept the role of Rudi because it brought back nostalgic memories of when he had seen the musical years before: in fact, having seen it so often he was virtually word perfect from the start and was really keen to re-create Novello's part on screen. The story followed the original stage version closely in every respect and Novello personally approved of all the cast. However, as Patricia Dainton stated, in spite of the high production values, the glowing colour photography of the Austrian Alps and a striking performance from Dennis (an admitted Novello fan), the film received poor reviews. When Novello devotees watched it, they were outraged and stated Dennis's portrayal of Rudi was 'sacrilege'. No one else but their darling Ivor, they said, could hope to put the right amount of expression and feeling into the part. One important fact escaped them—in 1949, Ivor Novello was fifty-six years old and Dennis was thirty-four, and much more the studio's and cinemagoers' image of an attractive young leading man. Novello had also approved of Dennis taking his part, so his admirers should have maybe taken this into account before pulling his performance to pieces. 'Dennis Price as Novello is no Novello' was one critic's comment, which pretty well summed up the general feeling.

The failure of *The Dancing Years*, another venture that Dennis had held great hopes for, just about put the lid on his romantic film roles. Dennis meanwhile hoped that film companies would now consider him for more worthwhile roles, such as in *Kind Hearts and Coronets*.

In December 1949, he took to the stage again and played Mr Manningham, the leading character in *Gaslight*, opposite Rosamund

Rudi and his lover Maria (Giselle Preville) toast the success of his first operetta in *The Dancing Years*.

John as the wife he systematically attempts to drive mad. The production reached the Vaudeville Theatre in London the following June, but Dennis's role was taken by Robert Newton. Also in December, on the penultimate day of the year in fact, fans huddled around radios to hear Dennis broadcast as one of the lads who enjoys himself having *A Night out with the Boys*, though Dennis's exceptional good looks and charm were wasted on radio, and this was one of the few broadcasts he made in the 1940s.

With a new year ahead, Dennis was on the threshold of a dramatic change in his life, both privately and career wise. He knew it was time to take stock or he would soon be treading the path walked by so many romantic leads whose services were no longer required; he had just faced his toughest criticism since his career began and his future in films would depend on his next batch of work. He had certainly reached a crucial turning point.

8

The 'B's and the Blues (1950–1953)

Compounding the failure of both *The Bad Lord Byron* and *The Dancing Years*, the mood in the cinema was changing; people were tired of silly, unreal, romantic melodramas and preferred to see films that had some bearing on reality, or just out and out comedy (to entertain). Having proved, in *Kind Hearts and Coronets*, that he was more than just a pretty face, Dennis naturally expected to continue in some really good diverse parts, but changing tastes also meant a change in leading men. Many established actors, Dennis included, quickly became associated with the 'old style' of films and Dennis had a tough time convincing the powers that be that he could tackle serious, solid roles. He had to start fighting for them all over again.

Murder Without Crime was director J. Lee Thompson's first film, based on a West End stage play he had written. Dennis was cast as the lead, but it was a venture that almost resulted in a hospital spell as on 26 February 1950, while driving to Welwyn Studios for a day's filming, Dennis had a near miss when his car collided with a lorry on the Barnet bypass near Hatfield, resulting in serious damage to the car. Luckily, he escaped without serious injury and was able to return to work soon after. Dennis replaced his shattered vehicle with a black Packard HP27.

The format of *Murder Without Crime* used so few locations and characters that it appeared unable to shake off its stage origins. Thompson was later responsible for many big films, including *Tiger Bay* (1959) and *The Guns of Navarone* (1961), and did not wish to be reminded of this early career attempt.

Dennis starred as an embittered landlord, whose love of wine, fine dining, and gambling have forced him into renting his sprawling West End house to a struggling author. As Matthew, Dennis was sardonic and menacing, traipsing around in a brocade dressing gown (left over from

Stephen realises Matthew has switched the wine glasses and has drunk the poison meant for him—the dramatic concluding scene in *Murder Without Crime*, with Derek Farr.

the wardrobe department for *The Bad Lord Byron*, no doubt). He put a great deal of effort into his character and tried to make the film exciting, but he was let down by the gimmicky idea of having a brash American narrator explaining the story, cutting in, and interrupting the flow of the film throughout with inane remarks that would have been better left unsaid. Any sparks of suspense there may have been in this routine thriller were all irreparably dampened. Despite the recent protest he had made, Dennis's character came to yet another nasty end, but at least he got to live through the picture this time.

Next was an assignment on director David MacDonald's *The Adventurers*, set in the South African veldt during the Victorian era. Dennis's family had strong connections with the country as his grandfather Thomas had won his laurels there, fighting for the Orange Free State at the battle of Veltevreden, before forming his own rifle club. His uncle Franklyn lived in Johannesburg too. As most of the action in the film took place outdoors, the company had little option but to send the film crew on location. The realism and scenery are very pleasing, though it would have been better realised had the budget stretched to colour photography.

In search of diamonds in South Africa, Dennis played the appropriately named Clive Hunter.

Dennis flew out to film his role as Clive Hunter, a disgraced British officer, morose gambler, and heavy drinker who is in for a rough ride when he becomes associated with tough Boer commando Pieter Brandt (Jack Hawkins). Brandt was an unusual role for Hawkins and saw him growing a rugged beard and being the bad guy for a change, though his many ardent fans were not used to seeing him as anything but an English gentleman, and he soon returned to more righteous roles.

Packed with action, *The Adventurers* was an exciting film that lived up to its name and though definitely aimed at men, there is also something for the ladies; the blazing hot African sun presented a rare opportunity for the fans to go wild over Dennis's hairy chest.

The actors and crew spent eight weeks filming, and encountered 'the worst weather for eighty years'. Some of the most gruelling scenes were shot on the mountainsides and at the plateaux summit of the Drakensberg Mountains. Whenever one of these mountain shots was called for, it entailed a major operation and took all the crew's energy to haul themselves up, not to mention carrying the camera, sound recording equipment, and numerous props before starting a day's shooting. Commenting on the somewhat rough travel arrangements in the Drakensberg Mountains,

Dennis said 'I have never taken much to oxen, but my admiration went out to the eight solid beasts who dragged us back and forth.'

There was a lovely atmosphere on this set and Dennis found himself among friends old and new, namely Aubrey Baring, Jack Hawkins, Bernard Lee, and Grégoire Aslan. They felt at ease together and had a mutual admiration for each other's performances.

Having rehearsed the all-night poker game sequence numerous times, Dennis and Grégoire almost believed the high stakes they had set were real, but they were not so keen to recall their real-life bets. While in South Africa, they both placed a modest pound each way on L'Amiral in the Derby. The most exciting bet Grégoire had had up to then was on a trip to Brazil when, left with his last chip in a roulette casino, he put it all on a single number; as the wheel spun, he walked away, thinking he had lost. Yet he had chosen a winning number and was rewarded with £50 for just one spin. 'That was exciting enough,' he said, 'but my gambling with Dennis in the film had me more shaky, even though we were acting!'

It was quite a comedown for the actors to return to England and finish the picture in the homely surroundings of Pinewood Studios.

When Grégoire Aslan's wife, Denise Noel came to England for the first time during production, Dennis acted as their guide. Among other places, he took them to see Windsor, Eton Chapel, and Westminster—Dennis's old stomping grounds.

Though his film work was going well, all was not well in his private life and his marriage to Joan Schofield was at an end. There was no trust nor spark left in their relationship and therefore no point remaining together when they could start life afresh. On 24 October 1950, Joan brought a divorce petition against her husband on the grounds that he had committed adultery in August the year before. Dennis was content to let her go ahead with the claim and after due deliberation by Judge Sir Henry Braund, Joan was granted a decree nisi with costs and was given custody of their daughters. In addition, Dennis was ordered to make Joan regular maintenance payments, despite her own substantial reserves, for as long as she remained unmarried.

Both Dennis and Joan found it very difficult adapting to being divorced. For the sake of their two daughters, and in reaching a middle ground for themselves, it was decided they would keep in close contact via the telephone, if not in person. Joan would only ever be a phone call away and could come around and see Dennis if necessary. Joan had been quite a dominant figure in his life and her complete physical absence was not something Dennis could cope with. It was almost as though they were in a love/hate relationship; they hated being apart and Dennis relied on Joan's support, yet peculiarly he vowed never to marry anyone else who might encroach on his free spirit.

That same year, Dennis's lover Margaret Lockwood was divorced from her husband Rupert Leon after a sixteen-year marriage. It left both Dennis and Margaret free to get together and be a proper couple, but with both hurting from their marriage break-ups, they instead decided to go their separate ways, with Lockwood declaring: 'I would never stick my head into that noose again.' She did, however, live for many years with the actor, John Stone, whom she met when they appeared together in the 1959 stage comedy, *And Suddenly It's Spring*. Although Dennis was to enjoy many close relationships with women, he too remained single for the rest of his life.

Dennis's return to the state of single blessedness was in the humble surroundings of a basement flat at 15 Egerton Gardens, a guest house in South Kensington. The charge of adultery had a negative effect on his image and career in what were much more conservative times, with the once proudly photographed family man now publicly separated from his children, which added further to his fall in popularity and made the next few months hard to bear. He became very despondent.

Trying to counteract his depression, Dennis plunged himself into work, any work he could get, and he went on the stage on 11 December, appearing as Maxim De Wynter, in a run of *Rebecca* at The Playhouse Theatre, Oxford. Portraying his timid little mouse of a wife was Christine Pollon.

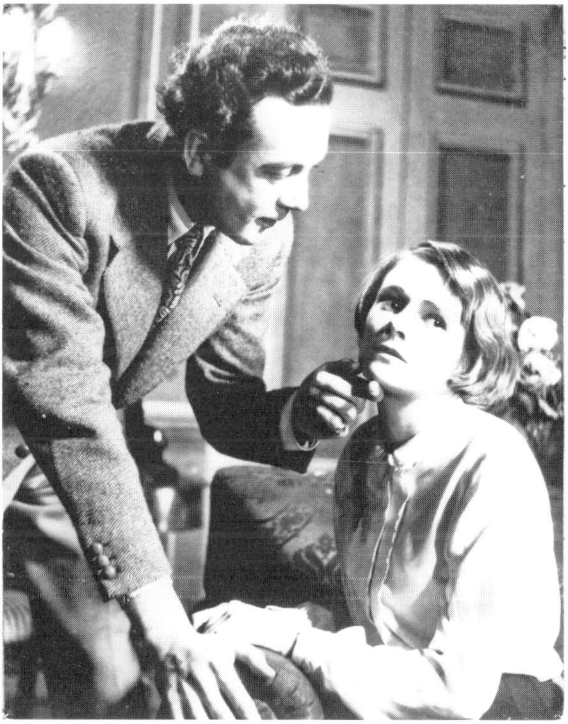

Dennis with Christine Pollon in *Rebecca* at the Playhouse Theatre in Oxford, December 1950. (*Kenny Parker*)

During the play, the second Mrs De Wynter appears at the top of the stairs, in a dress identical to one worn by Rebecca, and Maxim (who was sitting playing the piano) is meant to stop in shocked surprise when he sees her. Unfortunately, Dennis could not play the piano so he mimed to a record off stage and on one night, the stage manager forgot to stop the record, much to the delight of the audience—there was Miss Pollon stuck at the top of the stairs, unable to move until Maxim stopped playing but poor Dennis had to keep on playing until someone offstage realised what was happening.

As usual, Dennis got on famously with his fellow actors and although they sensed he was unhappy at this sad time in his life, they still enjoyed some very jolly evenings together at The Bear pub in nearby Woodstock. The play finished its run on 23 December and somewhat surprisingly, Joan Schofield went along to see him perform, as did his Radley tutor Charles Wrinch, who had been watching his progress with great interest. Wrinch was disappointed to discover the Prices had gone as far as divorcing, because he had always considered Joan to be a most suitable partner. That same month, the divorce was finalised.

In 1951, Dennis was recruited, along with fifty-nine other famous faces, to appear in John Boulting's lavish colour production *The Magic Box*, which centred on the life of William Friese-Greene (played by Robert Donat). This was the film industry's contribution to 'The Festival of Britain'. With such a multitude of stars ranging from Richard Attenborough to Laurence Olivier, Marius Goring, Joyce Grenfell, Kathleen Harrison, Glynis Johns, Michael Hordern, and Cecil Parker, it was hardly surprising that Dennis was given precious little to do. Having had his hair permed and been kitted out as an Edwardian gent, he had only one line to say as Friese-Greene's assistant at his Bond Street studio. If you blinked, you would have missed him.

The House in the Square came next, a period fantasy combining American and English actors with a contrast of black and white photography for the scenes showing the present, and the main sequences representing the eighteenth century filmed in Technicolor. Dennis had a prominent role as Tom Pettigrew, a Regency dandy and good-for-nothing indulging in the pastimes of the day, like snuff-taking and gambling. Here, for the first time, Dennis found himself taking a part of secondary importance to Tyrone Power's leading man. Those close to Dennis realised his self-effacing nature was working against him and if he did not assert himself soon, he would never be as important again. This routine storyline was in fact a remake of the older *Berkeley Square*, which was also a tried and tested stage play, meaning the film held few surprises for the audience and critics. Dennis came out of it very well, as reviewer Richard Winnington noted: 'Of the English cast, which includes Michael Rennie, Beatrice Campbell, Raymond Huntley and Irene Browne, only Dennis Price fits the costume.'

Above left: Many top names featured in cameo roles for the festival of Britain feature film offering, *The Magic Box*, Dennis being one of them.

Above right: Dennis in his regal splendour for *The House in the Square*.

Still keen to throw himself into work to avoid time dwelling on his private life, one film Dennis should have been advised to avoid was the comedy *Lady Godiva Rides Again*, a starring vehicle for Diana Dors. He was cast as Simon Abott, a leading man and movie idol, and Pauline Stroud (a total newcomer to acting) played a young girl who is an ardent fan of his and wins a beauty competition by accident, when Abott is one of the judges on the panel. The prize is a fur coat and a film contract working alongside her idol. Abott invites Marjorie on his houseboat, where he proceeds to woo her using lines straight out of one of his romantic films, though when Marjorie completes the lines he's feeding her, Abott turns cold and hostile, declaring he cannot abide fans who, 'dote on every word and gesture.' Then, her boyfriend Johnny (George Cole) arrives and, together with her father (Stanley Holloway), he launches into a fight with Abott, with the result the actor is pushed overboard into the river. At that

Dennis certainly did his career more harm than good by accepting the part of Simon Abott in *Lady Godiva Rides Again*.

precise moment, a pleasure boat comes along and one of the passengers took a photograph of Abott floundering in the water, bald; his wig has floated off down river.

The film was notable for one of the contestants of the beauty contest, in the line-up with Diana Dors, being Ruth Ellis, the last person to hang in the UK. Ironically, Dors later played her in the film *Yield to the Night* (1956).

Although Dennis had excellent billing in the film, the part of Simon Abott (a leading man in decline) was far too close to home and was generally viewed as being self-parody. By taking the part, Dennis held himself up to ridicule and wide open to criticism. 'If he did not take his own career seriously, how could he expect to be taken seriously by the studios?' they asked.

The damage was done, and for the next couple of years, Dennis found himself relegated to a succession of 'B' movies while the top film roles went elsewhere. It also marked his sudden disappearance from the pages of all the film magazines, as if he was no longer worthy of any publicity. He had done himself and his career a lot of harm.

One of the 'B' films he appeared in was *Song of Paris*, a romantic comedy originally entitled 'Clementine', which was a British attempt at making a saucy French farce. Additional gags were from Frank Muir and Denis Norden, then at the height of their success as a comedy writing duo. Leading the cast and shedding the label 'sophisticated man about town', Dennis played a timid young businessman who was seduced by a French cabaret star, Anne Vernon, despite the fact that she was already spoken for by Mischa Auer as a phoney count. Fast and furious acting by all parties ensured the audience had little time to consider the far-fetched antics, though *Song of Paris* never pretended to be anything more than a light-hearted romp. With glamour and music provided by Anne Vernon (who sang four French songs) and an ingenious character interpretation by Dennis, there was something to appeal to everyone. It was the perfect combination and the critics praised it. It proved yet again that he was very adept at comedy.

However, his next choice did nothing to build on his comedy skills as he opted for a low budget melodrama, *Tall Headlines*, about a respectable family whose ordered life disintegrates when one of their twin sons is hanged for a sex murder. Dennis had a featured role as boyfriend of the executed man's sister, though the characters are such an unpleasant bunch that there is little to choose between any of them. Fortunately, fine actors Flora Robson and Michael Denison made it at least enjoyable for Dennis.

In December 1951, marking a whole year since his divorce, Dennis did his annual stint on the stage, though this time leaving for America, where he had been invited to play Shepherd Henderson, the leading character in John Van Druten's sparkling comedy, *Bell, Book and Candle*. It was to be an extensive tour from coast to coast, taking in the major cities (nineteen in all). His leading lady was the lovely Rosalind Russell until they reached Chicago, and then Joan Bennett replaced her. Van Druten's witty narrative concerns a coven of modern day witches living in Manhattan, and it marked Dennis's American stage debut. The audiences were very appreciative and he scored great personal success. The stage was in fact to prove a saviour for Dennis in the years ahead as with good parts in films becoming scarcer, Dennis found himself turning more and more to the boards for his income; there, at least, he would always find a prominent position.

When Dennis returned home in 1952, he found the offers of film work were less than scintillating, and a sad step down for him. There were days when he felt very low and needed someone close to reassure him that he was still needed; that was when he started missing Joan, furthering his despair.

In *Noose for a Lady*, Dennis assumed the identity of Simon Gale, an amateur sleuth who solves a village murder and saves his accused cousin from the hangman's rope. It was as good as you could expect of a low budget, black and white thriller to be—a pale version of an Agatha Christie.

Song of Paris was also known as *Bachelor in Paris* in some countries, and alongside Anne Vernon, Dennis returned to romantic-comedy form.

Tall Headlines featured an all-star British cast and dealt with the effects of a family seeing their son go to the gallows for murder.

The lack of quality parts coming Dennis's way were compounded by the studios starting to make films with an accent on realism, the sort of stories where Jack Hawkins played sturdy detectives and officers, epitomising the English warrior spirit and tough guy dramas about robbers, from which emerged Stanley Baker. Casting directors were constantly on the lookout for that fresh face with something new to offer, like the young man whose bovine brown-eyed appeal was fast winning the fans; his name was Dirk Bogarde. In the wake of these and other new discoveries, Dennis's place on casting wish lists was threatened hugely.

Dennis realised he should have chosen his roles better and reflecting to a journalist on the days when he had made as many as nine films in just eighteen months, said: 'It was too much, I realise now. Too much for me, far too much for the cinema public.' Now, the best he could hope was for a decent part in an important film among the many second-rate stars.

Fortunately, Dennis found a part in a new play, a comedy entitled *Husbands Don't Count*, which provided him with a great boost and brought him face-to-face with the public once more. For several weeks, he travelled around the country before the production came to London, on 1 October, for a West End run at the Winter Gardens Theatre. As a French lawyer in matrimonial trouble, Dennis was handling a situation bordering on farce, and had co-star Betty Paul, a very experienced actress, to aid him. Dennis said optimistically, 'Perhaps this job may prove the road back to the studios too, if the producers—and the public—recognise my name.

Rona Anderson starred alongside Dennis in the race-against-time drama *Noose for A Lady*.

There is one tentative offer already, not for a big picture, but I may accept it, even though it would mean working all day and night. After all this time, I feel cinema goers should have a gentle reminder of my existence.'

That film offer materialised early the following year, when he starred as Inspector Peter Lawton in the thriller *Murder at 3am*. The plot concerned identical twins, one of whom was a serial killer, and was as corny as a harvest festival and passed by virtually unnoticed at the cinemas.

Dennis was to come into his own on television when he was offered the chance to emulate the legendary Noël Coward as part of the entertainment for Easter Monday. The BBC screened an extravagant two-hour production about showman Charles B. Cochran entitled *The Passing Show*, and the script was written by Cochran's friend, actress Diana Morgan. Frank Lawton played Cochran and Dennis was cast as his friend Coward. By all accounts, he was astonishingly so like the man himself in voice and mannerisms that Coward, on seeing the show, was amused, impressed, and a little intrigued at seeing his former 'student' taking him off. It was hardly surprising that Dennis was so good because it was a routine he had perfected when entertaining at his many parties.

The programme concentrated on Cochran's revues, which had featured such other names as Jessie Matthews, Clifton Webb, and Ernest Thesiger plus a host of songs, including Coward's 'Mad Dogs and Englishmen'.

In April 1952, Dennis made a live guest appearance on popular radio show *Forces All-Star Bill*, which featured Tony Hancock, then in his ascent as a comedian. Supporting Hancock each week were Graham Stark and Geraldine McEwan as the girl they are all vying for.

Graham Stark recalled:

> I have one anecdote which I remember with delight. The very first time I ever met Dennis was on a broadcast of the radio show, written by Galton & Simpson and starring Tony Hancock, myself and lots of guests. Dennis, then at the height of his powers as the-man-you-love-to-hate sex symbol of British movies, went out with me to have a cup of tea during a rehearsal break. We used to do the show live at The Garrick Theatre and next door was a very modest little cafe. Looking frightfully smart and devastatingly handsome, Dennis sat at the table. The little waitress didn't react to me, but took one look at Dennis and almost swooned with delight. He ordered my tea, but then in a manner straight out of some Regency film, said 'But I m'dear, will have a double strength Bovril'. The stress on the word 'double' made it seem as if he was ordering the most dissolute and depraved aphrodisiac. Breathlessly the waitress took his order, obviously convinced that this was the dangerous way all film stars lived. Yes, a much missed member of our profession and the most

> delightful person. Very professional, lots of funny stories and the sort of actor one was always pleased to know was on the cast list. Well, I did a film with him in Ireland, *Rocket to the Moon* and I can remember the glass of dark brown liquid [Guinness] did seem to be quite often in his hand.

Dennis went on to make his best and most memorable film for that year, *The Intruder* based on Robin Maugham's (nephew of W. Somerset Maugham) book *Line on Ginger*. It was finely directed by Guy Hamilton and starred his old friend Jack Hawkins. Dennis was given the kind of part he loved, a solid, real character he could really bring to life—in this case, Leonard Pirry, the cowardly captain of a wartime tank corps. The story, told in a series of flashbacks, concentrated on the exploits of one particular trooper, Ginger (Michael Medwin) who has the misfortune to be serving with Pirry's outfit. As Pirry, he displayed some very convincing emotions as a man without a conscience, one who knows 'which side his toast is caviared' and has the ability to turn any situation to his advantage, usually on the efforts of others. He was hopeful, on this showing, that some good meaty scripts would be coming his way.

The Intruder was director Guy Hamilton's first film, and arguably one of his finest. In this scene, Dennis appears alongside Jack Hawkins.

When this film, hailed as one of the best British efforts in post-war years, was released during the second week in October, Dennis, wearing an old mac and hoping not to be recognised, hung about outside the Empire in Leicester Square, where it was being shown. As he mixed with the crowd waiting outside, he was spotted by a journalist who was curious as to why he was there. 'I want to see the big brass come out of the premiere,' he explained. How did he feel about frequently being cast as the rat in the pack? Dennis replied, 'I'm quite happy to be a villain. I could play in light comedy until I dropped, but weak characters are the strongest to play.' Then with a mischievous smile, he added, 'I wish George Sanders would drop dead. Then I would get all his parts.'

Many of his contemporary cads had already gone to America, drawn by lucrative offers from Hollywood. 'So why hadn't he?' thought the journalists. He was simply one of those people who preferred the British way of life, and his loyalties got in the way of good business sense. It was a decision he would bitterly regret.

Just prior to *The Intruder*'s premiere, Dennis had been appearing at The Grand Theatre, Blackpool as Cyrus Armstrong in *The Man Upstairs*. Next, he was back in the West End at St Martins, playing Dr Frank Chevasse in *Blind Man's Buff*, an Irish murder trial drama new to the theatre. However, it was fated as the day before it opened, Dennis broke his collarbone and the run was curtailed. Bad luck followed Dennis to Munich where he caught the flu and was ill for so long that he had to turn down a part in another West End play that ran during the Christmas holiday.

It was only now, when he was down on his luck, that Dennis realised what an absolute fool he had been by not trying his chances in Hollywood. Scores of other British actors had packed their bags years ago without hesitation (Ray Milland, Stewart Granger, David Niven, and James Mason to name a few) and all without a backward glance. Instead of soaking up the Californian sunshine, he downed pints in his basement flat and worried about his uncertain future.

Dennis had a procession of different actor flatmates who should have cheered him up, but they were too preoccupied with their own ventures to see that he was on the brink. Dennis had always been a good listener and problem solver, but no one seemed to be able to spare the time to help with his. When he was not wallowing in self-pity and drink, he would steel himself to make the short journey to the corner of Brompton Road where the dubious delights of the tiled Hour Glass pub awaited him. There, surrounded by a bunch of attentive cronies and hangers on, he would hold court. He actually wanted their support and reassurance, but never received it.

The only bright patches Dennis enjoyed during these miserable times were the weekends when he would lavish affection on his two daughters during his all too fleeting visits. The girls found it hard to adjust to their parents being divided and the moments they shared with their father were precious, though with long spells away at school they soon learned to stand on their own feet. To Dennis, these brief meetings only drove home how much he had given up and the depression over his failing career coupled with the guilt of his broken marriage certainly clouded his judgement and good sense. On the surface, taking into account all the work he had been doing, Dennis was doing well financially, but no sooner did he earn money than he spent it all and was totally unprepared when tax demands came flopping onto his door mat. In fact, he was unable to pay the tax due, and so Revenue seized most of his earnings at source, leaving him with just enough to live on. As a result, he had to economise, and one of the first things to go was his car.

Just around the corner from the offices of film mogul Sir Alexander Korda was a pub called The Rose and Crown. Actors often gathered there to have a quiet drink before going to lunch in a posh Mayfair restaurant; Dennis, however, remained behind in the pub, and economised with sausage and mash and one glass of Guinness. He began to refuse social invitations as he could not return them.

This went on for a year until he had repaid several thousand pounds to the Inland Revenue. He had actually been very near to bankruptcy, but remained determined to pay what was owed.

9

Melancholia (1954–1955)

With the advent of a new year came plenty of work, but Dennis was still disappointed that the big films were thinning out as far as offers to him were concerned at least.

Terry-Thomas had devised a new series for radio called *Top of the Town* in which a different celebrity would reminisce each week about the town in which they were born, with additional comedy and music. In January 1954, Dennis was featured, discussing the days he had spent in Twyford, some thirty years before. He could claim, by way of his grandfather being the majority land owner, that he owned Twyford. Also on the bill were Joan Sims and Leslie Mitchell.

In February, Dennis was seen again on television with Yvonne Mitchell in a production of *The Jewels* (based on a short story by Guy de Maupassant), an acerbic, sparkling play in which he and Miss Mitchell played a young French couple. Their life seemed too good to be true; he was a clerk in the civil service and she was a model wife. However, there was a twist in the tale as in the introduction, Maupassant (played by Denis Shaw) says 'Marriage is a lottery of a rather special kind in which the woman loses and the loser wins.'

In every performance he gave, Dennis was always suave and sophisticated. Yet privately, he was suffering from increasing depression over his tax troubles and career, and he so hated living in a basement flat. He nevertheless forged ahead and played a villain in the film *Time Is My Enemy*, opposite Renée Asherson. As usual, he delighted in this above average, if low budget, thriller. Being sardonic, he scored with the critics and public alike.

Then, a black cloud descended. There came a point when, for the first time ever, his depression began to affect his work. Dennis was due to appear in a play called *We Must Kill Toni* with Michael Denison and

Dulcie Gray, but feeling unhappy and unsure of himself, he withdrew from the production during rehearsals, much to the regret of his co-stars. Everyone was aware he had troubles weighing on his mind, but he was too proud and private to share his problems, even with his family.

Though he had been pleased to shake off his romantic film image, the leads he had been playing in low budget films caused journalists to suggest he had been resting on his laurels. In truth, he had been working all the time and their criticism otherwise did nothing to help his flagging spirit.

During April 1954, Dennis was engaged at Elstree Studios on the film version of Arthur Watkyn's play *For Better, For Worse*, taking the part of Peter Debenham alongside love-struck newlyweds played by Dirk Bogarde and Susan Stephen. It was a British farce about the problems of early married life in a pokey bedsit and actually featured a strong role for Dennis, but he was second on the bill to Bogarde who had suddenly become the new leading man in films; his star was rising while Dennis's was slipping. Bogarde was ambitious, very determined, and worked hard to maintain a public persona of a straight leading man, which was ironically at complete odds with his personal life. Once his name appeared above the title, he was not willing to accept any role that was less than the starring part. No doubt Dennis's seeming willingness to accept pretty much any job offered puzzled Bogarde, and maybe even forewarned him about how important it was to meticulously control every element of his career and film choices; it was not surprising that they did not become friends. In Bogarde's autobiography *Snakes and Ladders*, he refers to Dennis as a 'lipsticked and Brylcreamed god'—the only mention he is given.

Dennis was very much aware it was only the top films that counted, as smaller features passed pretty much unnoticed, but how to get a good part in a top firm was an altogether different proposition. He was no longer earning the big salaries that went with being a leading man either, but he tried to remain the generous host, finding it almost impossible to economise; he would often ignore the fact he was running up debts and tax bills.

Before he had finished filming his part in *For Better, For Worse*, Dennis was involved in a real-life drama that was both desperate and foolish. On Easter Monday, 1954, Dennis got up early and turned on the gas in the kitchen oven, without lighting it. He put some cushions on the floor so he could rest his head, and lay down in front of the open stove door, breathing in the deadly fumes.

At 8 a.m., his housekeeper Mrs. Edna Lamb, a kindly Irish woman, went down as usual to the basement but on trying the kitchen door found it jammed and realised there was a strong smell of gas in the air. Without further ado, she rushed away to phone for the police. When the officers arrived, they broke open the door and found Dennis lying unconscious on the floor near the stove. They dragged him out of the room and applied artificial respiration; luckily, they brought him round and said had it been ten minutes later, it would have been too late.

Dennis was rushed to St George's Hospital, Hyde Park, for immediate attention. On regaining consciousness, he found himself the centre of a blaze of publicity—the sort he had not enjoyed for years. Typical of his sense of humour, he said to one of the doctors 'What glory, Price!'

The first person to come to his aid on hearing the news was his ex-wife, Joan. She informed the reporters, who were hungry for news: 'I shall make it my business to look after him till he is well. My only concern is that he will get fit and strong as quickly as possible. To do that, it is important he feels he is not neglected.' When asked about their divorce, she continued, 'our marriage was dissolved three and a half years ago after many years of happiness. We are good friends and always have been.' With regards to their daughters, Joan confirmed, 'I have kept the news from them'.

Joan spent most of that day by Dennis's bedside, giving him the moral support he so badly needed. Dennis's friends were shocked when they learned of his attempted suicide. Only the previous Saturday, he had taken his daughters out to see a film in the West End and later stopped by his local, the Hour Glass where he cracked jokes with the barman, Cecil Charrington. A chum of Dennis's reportedly said, 'He's nuts about those two kids, has kept himself poor, even on his salary, buying things for them. Often he has given up social engagements to take them out at weekends for walks.'

On that particular night in the pub, he had been having a serious discussion with a friend, a chap called Bobby, but the barman said he could not hear what they were saying as he was busy serving. He had also been seen talking with Vera Pearce, the Australian stage actress. She said, 'He came into the bar before leaving and said "Goodbye"—I took his goodbye to mean that he was going off somewhere on location for a new film.'

Dennis made a swift recovery and was transferred the same day to the Atkinson Morley Hospital in Wimbledon. By the following day, he was even said to be 'quite happy' and 'getting on nicely'. Matron Cecilia Fletcher, who was looking after him at Wimbledon said: 'All he needs now is rest after his nervous shock.'

One of the staff at Elstree Studios said, 'The film will do a lot to bolster his reputation.' He was scheduled to have finished the last shot on the Tuesday, but they said that the production was not held up because of his illness and it was hoped he would be able to re-join the film crew that Friday.

Dennis always appeared jovial and impeccably dressed in public and so no one suspected anything was wrong; he never allowed the 'other side of him' to be seen, though his struggle at having to deal with an ever-descending depression while maintaining this jovial facade finally took its toll. There was a debate about whether Dennis actually intended to go through with the suicide or whether it was a carefully contrived publicity stunt as a very desperate cry for help. Most people were reluctant to accept the worst and considered he had not actually wanted to die, knowing that his housekeeper would be calling at her usual time and would raise the alarm before the gas could claim his life. A friend of Dennis's, Jan Coombe-Dreyer, said that there was an additional character in this incident that was not reported at the time:

> Mrs Lamb had a pet dog and decided to bring it to the flat on that particular morning—something which she didn't do as a rule. It was her dog which ran down the basement steps ahead of her and on smelling gas, started to bark furiously and jump up at the door. Mrs Lamb realised from the dog's behaviour that something was very wrong so she summoned help. If Mrs Lamb hadn't had the dog with her that day, she'd simply have gone away again, thinking Dennis didn't want to be disturbed!
>
> I've no doubt in my mind that Dennis intended to kill himself that day. He came from a family who never accepted defeat and he felt totally humiliated by the embarrassment of his career slide and his divorce. His father's death had made him more relaxed about suicide since he had not lived to see these failings.

In the 1950s, admitting to having any form of mental illness, however sympathetically expressed, carried a terrible stigma. Dennis was lucky not to have been sent to a mental institution or even prison since taking one's own life was considered a criminal offence in those unenlightened times, and many people who attempted and failed were prosecuted. On top of all this, Dennis had an eating disorder sparked by his obsession to stay slim on screen and would regularly eat meals only to vomit them up later.

Jan Coombe-Dreyer elaborated on the reasons for his state of mind:

> He attempted to sustain old friendships, but people who'd respected him in the past as a prominent leading man when married to Joan now shunned him as if his misfortune would rub off on them. People were making excuses not to have him at parties, or thought he had nothing to offer in terms of putting in a good word for them with a film producer. He turned more to friends like myself who were less critical.

In the 1990s, many years after his eventual death, rumours sprang up that he tried to commit suicide because he was being blackmailed for being a 'secret homosexual'. This view was first aired in a Channel 4 documentary called *Those British Faces*, despite there being no evidence, just idle speculation. *Those British Faces* can best be described as a character assassination, written and produced by people who clearly disliked Dennis hugely. By showing clips from some of his best-known films, they suggested a biographical account of his private life was reflected by the worn-out old ham in *Charley Moon* (1956), the blackmailed gay actor in *Victim* (1961), and it was even suggested he was perhaps capable of murder, as illustrated by a scene from *Murder Without Crime* (1950). It certainly was not an affectionate look back across a fine career and actually stood out like a sore thumb among the rest of the series, which included profiles of James Robertson Justice and Jack Hawkins, who were regarded very favourably and complimentary by the filmmakers, with no details given about their private lives or any human failings they may have had.

Although, following his divorce, Dennis led the life of a bachelor once more, he liked to share his two-bedroom flat with fellow actors for the company they provided. One such flatmate was Patrick Macnee, who was heterosexual. In his autobiography, *Blind in One Ear*, Macnee recalls the time he spent with Dennis at Egerton Gardens, where Dennis let him stay 'at a peppercorn rent' and was 'much loved' as a human being. One day, Macnee sought his advice on a sensitive matter:

'Two of the most notorious old queens in the business invited me to join them in a sandwich and I asked Dennis if I should accept their invitation? It was the first time I had seen his unflappability leave him and he begged me not to do it.'

Surely, if Dennis had been homosexual, not only might he have made his own sexual advances towards Macnee (who was seven years younger and very handsome), but he would have encouraged him to join in the 'sandwich', which in this instance did not refer to food.

Macnee eventually left his company, not because of any improper behaviour, but because he was rather eccentric: 'Dennis used to keep a brood of chickens in the bathtub' and Macnee said he left the flat 'in a whirlwind of feathers'. Had Macnee endured the chickens and stayed around longer, it brings into question whether Dennis would have gone on to attempt suicide.

The week Dennis spent in hospital saw things began to pick up for him as his creditors agreed more time for him to pay off his debts and just a few days after admission, he was fit enough to leave hospital for the day so he could shoot his final scenes in *For Better, For Worse* on the Friday, where everyone Dennis came into contact with showed him nothing but kindness and concern.

Dennis spent a week in total in the quiet confines of the hospital, keeping his spirits up by ribbing Nurse Fitzmaurice, who had been caring for him. His weight had dropped though and his face was colourless, which was only to be expected of someone who had been through such a trauma, yet he was able to adopt a more positive approach thanks to the letters that poured in from well-wishers. 'Hundreds of them, mostly from total strangers scattered all over Britain. They lift me up, make me glow,' he said.

One devoted female admirer wrote, 'Thank God you are alive—I wish I could be beside you now, what an unhappy world it would be without you.' Another woman, from Nottingham, offered help, 'Anything we could do for you will give us the greatest pleasure. Could you come and stay with us? We have a little farm'. Many other letters contained offers along those lines too. 'Maybe there are still a few fans left', was his droll comment.

Expressing his feelings to journalist Donald Zec for the benefit of his fans, he said:

> When a person has been through a terrifying experience like this it is very, very pleasant to be alive and in some strange way I feel a hundred percent better. I was certainly depressed before it. Now in the last few days I've had a good look inside Dennis Price and unearthed some useful information. First, I'm going to stop playing these precious romantic juvenile parts. I think playing Novello in *The Dancing Years* was a major disaster for me. It drove Novello's fans into a frenzy and carved huge chunks out of my own supporters, who were entitled to expect much better from me. My plan is to try and get good robust costume films or solid acting roles similar to the part I had in *The Intruder*.... I don't intend to take life so seriously. I certainly caved in when the slump of 1947 killed my film contract—after that, things sort of slid downward. But they look much more hopeful now.

He was right as his agent sent him the following telegram: 'Firm offer for you—very good part in *That Lady* with Olivia de Havilland'.

Stars such as Robert Donat, Renee Asherson, and Valerie Hobson, to name but a few, sent letters of encouragement, which all helped to cheer him up further. The kindness that everyone had shown him, made Dennis regret his drastic actions: 'I wish I could tear last Monday out of my life. I am so sorry for the trouble I caused—particularly to my housekeeper,' he said. Yet he could not help laughing when he remembered the talk he had had with her earlier. 'I phoned her yesterday and she was so sorry. She said "I do hope I wasn't interfering, Mr. Price," I told her—I'll be grateful to you for the rest of my life.'

Joan sought permission from the authorities to care for Dennis on his discharge and on the Tuesday, a week after his admission, he left the hospital a changed man and upon the recommendation of his doctor, he and his ex-wife spent ten days on a farm by the coast in Dorset, taking in the sea breezes. They did not, however, rekindle their long-ago romance and after this break, they returned to their separate lives.

On his return from Dorset, refreshed and raring to go, Dennis began work on *That Lady*, which was an extravagant costume drama from Twentieth Century Fox; the 'lady' in the title role, Olivia de Havilland, was not one of the easiest people to work with, and she often displayed her temperamental behaviour on the set, much to Dennis's amusement.

The story was set in sixteenth-century Spain during the reign of an aged Philip II, played with great style by Paul Scofield, who was making his first screen appearance. His performance earned much acclaim, along with a BAFTA, establishing Mr Scofield as one of Britain's top actors. Dennis was given the role of the court schemer and for the first time in any of his films, he was provided with a false (Van Dyke) beard to echo his medieval Spanish costume; it really suited him. *That Lady* differed from other films of the genre by concentrating on a pair of ill-fated lovers and received a very warm reception. Shot in brilliant Technicolor, it was ostentatious in the extreme.

Costume drama *That Lady*, here with Dennis and Gilbert Roland pictured, reunited Dennis with director Terence Young who had helmed *Tall Headlines* two years earlier.

After another live guest spot on radio's *All-Star Bill*, Dennis found more offers coming his way, such as a starring part in his own radio series called *Happy Holiday*. The show was notable for being his first complete series for radio and was described as an all-star musical comedy, set in a fictional seaside resort. Dennis was a smooth-talking entertainments officer and ex-military man, Major Denzil. The series ran from mid-July for sixteen episodes. In September, he was back on television for a part in a thriller serial *Crime on Our Hands*, playing a mysterious poet.

In his private life, Dennis seemed happier and more content. Though he was often seen in the Hour Glass pub, he more frequently visited his favourite pub, The Star, where all the well-known celebrities hung out, including Robert Newton and Flora Robson. The proprietor Paddy Kennedy, a rough Irishman who was not afraid of speaking his mind, became friends with Dennis and spoke of Dennis being very fond of Flora Robson, with whom he made four films during his career; once, when she was very relaxed, having had a few drinks, she said to him, 'It's so unfair. Why am I so ugly when you are so handsome?'

Dennis remained on friendly terms with Joan, who phoned him often during the weeks after his discharge, and they often shared his latest joke. With money coming in, Dennis ensured his daughters and Joan were well provided for and was comfortably able to settle his debts too, but the temptations of drink and gambling were soon to raise their ugly heads again.

10

Bouncing Back (1955–1956)

In early 1955, Dennis returned to The Archers film company to take a starring role in Michael Powell's impressive musical *Oh, Rosalinda!!!* It was clear to the director that Dennis was in poor health, though Powell thought he was still 'excellent' in the part. 'We were all very fond of him,' said Powell, in his autobiography *A Life in Movies*, and having given Dennis his first film role in 1942, he reflected that the actor may have been pushed too far too soon by subsequent film-makers, hence his (then) depression. His rise to fame had been swift, and dealing with the inevitable comedown afterwards had been particularly tough, but they were pleased to be working together again.

Filmed in Technicolor at Elstree Studios, Powell set his story—ostensibly an updated version of *Die Fledermaus*—in Vienna during the spring of 1955, when the 'four powers' (America, Britain, France, and Russia) were in charge after the Second World War. Dennis represented the upper crust British, as Major Frank, Anthony Quayle played a Russian general, Mel Ferrer played USAF Captain Westerman, and Michael Redgrave was in the role of Colonel Eisenstein of the French Army. Dennis found the role very challenging since he was required to sing and dance as well as act, and had to take dancing lessons from a choreographer while his songs were dubbed. Quayle and Redgrave sang without assistance.

Powell's most celebrated films had been made during the 1940s and this new, and different, addition to his repertoire was not appreciated by the critics, who branded it a major calamity. Whenever seasons of Powell's films are screened on television, *Oh, Rosalinda!!!* is never on the bill, nor is it mentioned in documentaries, which suggests an attempt to disown it. Whatever Powell had in mind, the public were divided; some were perplexed while others either loved or hated it. Of the critics, Harold Conway at *The Daily Sketch* wrote: 'Strauss's score is chopped to pieces and the most startling voices dubbed on to the unlikeliest performers. A resonant bass booms from Dennis Price's embarrassed countenance ... but it is still the most emphatic failure of these brilliant film-makers' careers.'

After appearing in this, and the string of 'B' films that were still fresh in the memory, Dennis was acutely aware he had to choose his next part with immense care because it would undoubtedly determine the direction his future career would take. Unfortunately, Dennis did not show much insight when he accepted a part in *Charley Moon*. Never intended to be anything more than an amiable comedy film, *Charley Moon* concerned exposing the sleazy side of a life in show business as two aspiring actors struggle for recognition. The film was made primarily to showcase the talents of singer Max Bygraves, who was new on the scene. As the named star, Dennis found himself being shamelessly used to bring in the audiences while playing second fiddle to Bygraves, boosting someone else's career at the expense of his own.

Charley Moon is a naïve country boy who is enlisted into the army to do his national service. There, he is befriended by Harold Armytage (Dennis Price) who impresses Charley with reviews of his performances in obscure small-town productions. He persuades Charley to partner him in a double act after they are demobbed, and take to the stage with an awful song and dance routine that comes bottom of a variety bill.

Things go badly for the duo until Charley is spotted by a hard-nosed northern producer who wants Charley to star in the pantomime *Mother Goose*, but the offer does not extend to Harold. Being loyal, Charley insists there is a part for Harold. He is cast as the goose, completely hidden inside a ridiculous costume.

Then comes *Cinderella*, with Charley as Buttons. Harold gets to play one of the ugly sisters in full drag with heavy make-up. During the dress rehearsal, Harold interrupts the directions, suggesting how the scene could be played better, making the producer furious that Harold should dare to speak up, and roars at him to leave the stage, calling him a 'worn out, useless old ham' in front of the other actors.

Once off stage, Charley goes to see Harold in his dressing room, only to find he's departed leaving a goodbye note. The latter half of the film concentrates on Charley's rise to fame, only for him to leave the stage at the peak of his success, disillusioned by the artificiality and ruthless elements of the showbiz scene.

Dennis threw himself into the production wholeheartedly and did not mind how much he played the fool as this was a comedy so it was meant to be about raising laughs, but this was one joke that was destined to backfire and cause lasting damage to his reputation, as people laughed at him rather than with him.

Above: Another scene from *Charley Moon* in which the audience were laughing at Dennis, and not with him. Here he is with Newton Blick, Bill Fraser, and Max Bygraves.

Left: After a run of solid performances, Dennis's career wavered slightly when he starred in *Charley Moon*. Here, he is dressed as an ugly sister in the pantomime sequence.

It did not help that Dennis had upset Bygraves either, as his friend Jan Coombe-Dreyer recalled:

> Dennis was extremely insecure and so it was desperately important to him to know he was liked. This was especially true when he was acting with people he'd never previously met. He was therefore very anxious to be on friendly terms with Max Bygraves, since most of his scenes were to be with him. Dennis attempted to ingratiate himself with Bygraves from day one and approached him in a rosy glow of warm affection. He perceived Bygraves as being an amusing cockney fellow and reminiscent of the types he'd befriended in the army. Remembering how the other squaddies had mimicked his accent and he theirs, he approached Bygraves and spoke to him in his best imitation of an East Ender. Thinking he would be amused by his impersonation, he continued with a stream of gags on the theme of 'you're so common and I'm so posh!'

What he was trying to do was to make a joke out of the class system that sets people apart because in acting, everyone is united together irrespective of their social background. However, Max did not see the joke at all and thought that Dennis was trying to ridicule him. Max did not say much in protest, but it was clear that he had been offended.

> Poor Dennis was often misunderstood by people and made a lot of enemies that way. Those who really knew him loved him, but people who did not understand his humour and need to be liked, considered him to be a spiteful snob. Dennis often misinterpreted the way to befriend someone like Bygraves, because he'd been in the business so long that he'd forgotten what it was like to be starting out in films.

They were poles apart—Dennis's background was one of wealth and privilege, while Bygraves came from the humble dockside region of Rotherhithe in East London, and making a name for himself as a comedian and singer had been hard work. He did not want to be reminded—even as a joke—of his unglamorous beginnings. With a lot of working class people, it is not their own sense of value that matters but the view other people have of them. Bygraves was glad to move on from his association with Dennis, and many years later, when asked about working with Dennis, Bygraves was unwilling to discuss his memories. It was significant that when Bygraves was the subject of *This is Your Life* in the 1990s, there was much talk of his work as an actor but not a mention of his debut in *Charley Moon*. Instead, it was suggested his first film was *A Cry from the*

Streets, a black and white drama about a school teacher who deals with urchin children. This was made in 1961, some five years later.

Charley Moon may not be regarded as up among the best of British films but there are strong parallels between the character of Harold Armytage and that of Archie Rice in *The Entertainer*, John Osbourne's biting drama about a faded music hall performer. Dare it be said, the film version of *The Entertainer* appeared to borrow from the plot of Dennis's movie, though it was seen as being a much more important film, full of social comment. *Charley Moon* meanwhile was relegated to history as just another cheap British comedy.

Jan Coombe-Dreyer observed:

> The problem with Dennis acting the fool was that people expected him to be serious. For a decade, he'd played a romantic leading man idolised by scores of women. He was expected to maintain that image, perhaps appearing in classics such as Dickens, but *Charley Moon* was not good for his career at all. You never saw his contemporaries like Stewart Granger clowning around. He was only trying to prove how versatile he could be, but people weren't ready to accept that.

In July, there were reports of Dennis playing the Dame in a pantomime, obviously inspired by his part in *Charley Moon*. While it was a job in contrast to his usual line of theatre work, he was pleased to have the offer and suggested, in an attempt not to appear desperate, he was not the first straight actor to go 'illegitimate', though the press did suggest he was only doing it for the money. Dennis responded:

> I suppose that is true, but you know one becomes less snobbish about such things, one loses that star complex, one comes down to earth. It's a job of work and if it entertains people, it is worth doing.
>
> ... People jumped to the conclusion that I was unable to get work—that is not true. I was never broke. I was never really out of work. It is true the parts got smaller and the money got less, but I was working continually. It is true that I owed income tax, but then who didn't? Anyway, I decided to pay it off, rather than take the easier and more dishonest course of going bankrupt. I now have an arrangement whereby a fixed sum is deducted every week from my earnings to pay back tax and at the same time the current tax is also deducted. I don't want to get into a mess with the income tax again.

Dennis was indeed keen to economise and live within his means, and rarely dined out at expensive restaurants any more, reasoning 'For a young actor just starting out, I can see it is necessary to go to the smart places and be seen around,' he said, 'but I can talk to producers and agents at a pub round the corner or on the telephone.'

He had come to terms with his ranking in British films and did not hold a grudge towards the studios or up-and-coming actors. 'They cast me as Lord Byron,' he would say, 'but I haven't the profile to play such romantic heroes. I'm much happier now playing the wide range of parts I do.'

Dennis was undoubtedly putting on a brave face but financially, with *Oh, Rosalinda!!!*, *Charley Moon*, *Private's Progress*, and the pantomime, Dennis was doing reasonably well and was able to leave the basement flat in Egerton Gardens, which was just about as far removed from the type of home a successful film star would choose to live in as possible, to move into a flat at 90 Eaton Place, Belgravia, in one of a line of impressive lofty Victorian houses near to Sloane Square.

Once again, he could entertain his friends in style. However, he was still suffering from the occasional black mood and needed all the support he could get. Often, friends would spend long periods with him, chatting and playing cards to keep his mind off his worries.

The film *Private's Progress* marked the beginning of a happy working relationship and friendship with Ian Carmichael. Ian had not known Dennis in the years between seeing him backstage in 1948 and making this film, but he had heard on the grapevine that he was drinking heavily, and partly as a result, his career had not been going well. The Boulting brothers, John and Roy, were 'splendid men who believed in an actor's talent', said Carmichael. Whereas the majority of other producers had been put off by Dennis's rumoured drinking, using it as an excuse for not employing him, the Boultings were prepared to give him a chance on the strength of his talent and past record.

Carmichael remembered their first day on the set vividly because he had previously been the 'nobody' to Dennis's big star and now suddenly, just a few years on, Ian was top of the bill in his third starring role for the Boultings, and Dennis was supporting him. Ian had every sympathy for the man whose work he admired hugely, and found it 'a bit embarrassing'. While the camera crew were busily lining up for a shot on the first scene, John Boulting approached Ian Carmichael and suggested he had a chat with Dennis, because he appeared very nervous. John said, 'Go and make him feel comfortable—make him feel at ease.'

In the event, Dennis did very well and was professional as usual, though as a result of being humbled into going 'cap, or rather silk hat, in hand' for work (a quote from *Kind Hearts and Coronets*), it made Dennis very subservient to his directors and he did exactly as he was instructed; if that was what the director wanted, he was not going to suggest otherwise or object. By sticking to this approach, he was actually successful in getting many more parts and featured roles as word spread he was 'easy' to work with, so no longer did producers fear the seemingly alcoholic actor would cost them time and cause them headaches.

Roy Boulting and his twin brother John sensed quite accurately that audiences were getting tired of all the patriotic, flag-waving stories about the war and post-war years, which had been filling the cinemas for the past decade. Cinemagoers were ready for some incisive wit and that was exactly why they adapted Alan Hackney's novel exposé of wartime fiddling and crookery. John took on the task of writing the screenplay (with Frank Harvey) and also directed, while Roy produced. Dennis was an ideal selection for the role of Bertram Tracepurcel, one of the leading figures in Hackney's story—an ever confident, smooth talking rogue with a mind geared to working a nice cushy number for himself on the backs of others. The sharp Tracepurcel character was paired with that of his nephew, Stanley Windrush, a good natured young man who really does come up with the last draft when he joins the Army fresh out of college, and who better to play naïve Stanley, thought the Boultings, than Ian Carmichael? In bringing together Ian and Dennis, they discovered a duet of comedians perfectly in tune.

The Boultings shamelessly pulled out all the stops in lampooning what was formerly one of Britain's most respected institutions, and produced a great parody. It was not surprising that the War Office refused to lend them their facilities or any equipment to aid their production. Though undeterred, at the beginning of the picture, the producers stated they 'Gratefully acknowledge the kind and generous co-operation of absolutely nobody'.

Dennis was seen at his best, but for all his newly rediscovered suave self-assurance, it was Ian Carmichael who was destined to get the better of him in *Private's Progress*, an outstanding and very successful comedy.

During filming, Ian and Dennis were asked to present the awards at a local beauty competition being held in Reading. Dennis was to go up on the stage to present the winner with an orb, sceptre, and a sash. Ian was to crown her. Come the important moment, it went well—Dennis put the sash round her and gave her the orb and his job was finished. Then, Ian turned away to pick up the crown and when he looked round, the girl had disappeared. He discovered that Dennis had politely led her away up stage to give her his seat as he could not bear to see a lady standing while he was seated.

Following the release of the Boulting's film in the spring of 1956, Dennis wrote an article in the *Daily Express* to let everyone know how he had overcome his problems, which were still fresh in everyone's memory. It read:

> Two years ago this week, I nearly died. My landlady found me in a gas-filled room and saved my life. I spent the next two weeks in a hospital bed and my thoughts were far from pleasant. My career was at a low ebb. I had made a row of bad films in quick succession. My self-esteem was bankrupt, my private life too was in a mess. But it was in that hospital bed that I took my first steps on the hard road back. It wasn't easy. People I had known and worked with for years hardly knew how to approach a man who had almost died. There were awkward pauses, the wrong things said. I felt like a ghost who was haunting the wrong house.
>
> I decided the only thing to do was to behave as though nothing had happened. Not an easy assignment. I ate at the usual restaurants. I went to the usual clubs. I tried desperately to create the impression that I was living a thoroughly normal life. And my performance—the hardest I have ever had to give was a success. I went back to work and made five films—including one which I believe will be the success of the year—*Charley Moon*. Now I am playing in 'The Ball', a new play brought over from Madrid by the Spanish actress Conchita Montes. It opened on Easter Monday – an important date in my calendar. Work has put most things right in my life. My personal affairs have straightened themselves out. My friends—the ones who have helped me so greatly with their faith and kindness tell me—I am my old self. They are wrong, of course. No man can start life for the second time and stay the same person. It's two years since I took the turning for the long road back. I think it was well worth taking.

In April, Dennis made his first appearance on the newly formed television channel ITV, when he starred as Bob Herrick, ace reporter in an episode of the serial *Theatre Royal* called 'The Gloves'. Herrick is one of those people who has always been a non-believer in séances, but the gloves appear to have some spiritual connection with a man executed for murder and Herrick is assigned to discover what that connection is.

In the episode, Dennis was ably supported by Betty McDowall, a stalwart of TV plays and was directed by Don Chaffey, with whom he had previously collaborated on the film *Time Is My Enemy*. This TV production marked the start of a decade of outstanding performances Dennis was to give in classic and contemporary plays for the network.

The man whose job it was to decide which actor would get which part at the channel was Weston Drury, who was already well acquainted with Dennis as along with other casting directors, he had seen Dennis's potential in the early 1940s and put him forward for several film roles only to be frustrated by producers who had the final say, and it was 'no'. Ironically, after Dennis made his debut in *A Canterbury Tale*, those very

Among the better B-movies Dennis starred in was *Time Is My Enemy*; here, he is pictured with Alfie Bass.

same producers castigated Drury for not bringing this young star to their attention sooner. Drury kept his thoughts about them to himself, but did say: 'If ever a casting director could say "I told you so", I felt that I could over Dennis Price.' Thanks to Drury, Dennis had now launched himself into what would prove to be a successful TV career.

In one of the brief periods of spare time between engagements, Dennis took a trip to Ireland to visit his maternal ancestral home. He quipped it was quite nice to have a vacation as usually 'the nearest actors usually come to holidays is location filming—though with pay'. The home of his forebears, Dunboyne Castle, remained standing north east of Dublin with its 'seven guest rooms and every one of them draughty' said Dennis.

On returning to London, Dennis wasted no time in signing up for a run at the Fortune Theatre, in *To My Love* (originally entitled 'The Ball') from June 1956 onwards. He played Pedro, opposite the famous Spanish actress Conchita Montes, in a kind of tragi-comedy. During the run, Dennis appeared on the popular radio programme *Desert Island Discs*, in which he discussed his favourite records. Not surprising for someone of his generation, his taste reflected the fashions of his youth and that was the romantic period of the 1930s. The biggest influences in the British music and drama world then had been Noël Coward and Ivor Novello. When asked if he considered his taste in music to be high or low brow, he replied: 'I'd say I was in *The Dancing Years* department. Palm court selections, Strauss and so forth'. The nearest Dennis had got to being stranded on a desert island, he recounted, was three years previously when he had been out in Bermuda on location for a film and had whiled away his free hours sunning himself and lapping up the atmosphere on one of the small, uninhabited islands off Montego Bay. 'Quite perfect and quite peaceful,' he remembered. His choice of music on 'Desert Island Discs' was as follows:

Noël Coward—'Cavalcade'
Mary Ellis and Ivor Novello—'Waltz of my Heart' (from *The Dancing Years*)
Paul Whiteman and his orchestra—'Rhapsody in Blue' (recorded in 1924)
Frederic Chopin—'Etude in E major, opus 10/3' (soloist Tino Rossi)
Richard Tauber—'*Il mio tesorto*' by Mozart (as featured in *Kind Hearts and Coronets*)
Johann Strauss—'Oh, Rosalinda' (a.k.a. '*Die Fledermaus*', from the original soundtrack from the film)
Max Bygraves —'Out of Town'
Orchestra of Societe des concerts—'Iberia'
His choice of book was Giles cartoons by Carl Giles.
His choice of luxury item was painting materials.

Following a small part as a hotel manager in the comedy film *A Touch of the Sun*, which was actually a star vehicle for Frankie Howerd, Dennis next played the asthmatic husband of Arlene Dahl in the crime thriller *Fortune is a Woman*, his third film with Jack Hawkins. It seemed routine that Hawkins was set to woo Dennis's screen wife and win her from him, just as he had done in *The Adventurers*. The studios obviously considered Jack to be more attractive to women despite Dennis's outstanding looks, which did nothing to boost his confidence.

The most unlikely role (or roles) Dennis was ever cast in came next, when he portrayed Dr Jekyll and Mr Hyde in Philip Saville's production for ITV, which was screened in five half-hour instalments. In much finer detail than any of the old film versions, the episodes closely followed the book.

The debonair Dr Jekyll was a walkover for Dennis, but taking on Mr Hyde was a real challenge. Saville, who had previously worked with Dennis as an actor in the corny *Murder at 3am*, had high hopes for this series, which he also directed, and announced: 'I am going to scare the

A Touch of the Sun was written as a starring vehicle for Frankie Howerd, and featured Dennis in a cameo as the hotel manager. It was on this film Dennis perfected his impersonation of Howerd, much to the amusement of his regular dinner guests.

Jack Hawkins worked with Dennis several times; here they are again in *Fortune is A Woman*.

life out of every viewer! Everything that is bad is Hyde. But his evil, although complete, is utterly believable. One does not laugh at things one can understand'.

This version of Robert Louis Stephenson's most famous thriller was adapted by James Parish, who had every confidence with Dennis in the lead, that the series would be a winner. Dennis had to look more and more demented and sinister as Hyde's personality gradually took control—the physical side of the transformation taking place in front of the cameras.

Next, as part of the entertainment for Christmas Day, Dennis was heard on radio being evil again as The Bad Baron to Frankie Howerd's hero in an all-star production of the pantomime *Puss in Boots*. Also in the cast were Dickie Valentine as Idle Jack and Sabrina as the Good Fairy. On the last day of the year, Dennis was reunited with Tony Hancock in a radio version of *The Man Who Could Work Miracles* by H. G. Wells, along with several other actors and comedians making up an all-star cast.

Over the next few years, while Dennis re-established his film career and relationship with the studios, he concentrated on making a spate of plays for TV, especially ITV. It was a medium he was most successful in and though he never felt as comfortable (especially when appearing live) as on the floor of a film studio, Dennis proved the old spark was still there. The only drawback was that, now aged forty-one, many of the roles offered tended to be either worried fathers or ageing Jack-the-lads, but at least he had achieved his ambition of being established as a serious character actor at long last.

11

The TV Years (1957–1960)

In the new year of 1957, Dennis had numerous offers of work lined up and a nice fat contract with ITV, yet his past mistakes had taught him nothing about handling his financial affairs and he was still letting money drain away. He was drinking heavily again—his favourite tipple, Guinness, which he had come to rely on. It was also observed that he was not in very good physical shape for a man in his early forties.

After only a year living at Eaton Place, he was on the move once again, taking a flat at 29 Notting Hill, just along from the tube station. The sad and shabby Victorian buildings then provided cheap accommodation for the ever-shifting population and was a clear indication of Dennis's financial circumstances. Dennis continued to place bets with the local bookmakers whenever he felt like it, said he was a great believer in indulging in his pleasures, and furthermore believed he had nothing to save up for now that he lived alone. The tax man would not have agreed.

In February, he was seen in ITV's play *Myself When Young* by Dario Bellini. It was the story of how Paul/Constantine Chase changes from being a romantic and thoughtful young man—the kind you could really love—into a self-centred, scheming skinflint as he becomes more successful. For such a startling contrast in personality, two actors were required and the younger 'Paul' Chase was portrayed by Jeremy Brett, while the older Constantine was of course Dennis, whose character is involved in an adulterous affair. His younger self eventually confronts him, and the two halves of Chase compete to take over. This dramatic scene alone made the play compulsive viewing.

The girl in Chase's life is young and he is a successful playwright aged fifty who cannot help thinking that she is probably trying to secure a part in his next production rather than that she has any genuine feelings for him. Dennis described it as, 'A brilliant play and I love its setting and polished dialogue. It reminds me in many ways of a male *Blithe Spirit*. I took over a similar part in Coward's play after Cecil Parker had needed a holiday. In *Blithe Spirit*, a ghostly wife returns to haunt her husband. In this play, a young man is conjured up to bedevil me—as Constantine. He is myself when young. A youth full of romantic ideals and illusions which the adult me has destroyed.'

The same month, Dennis had been out in South Africa, making his first appearance on the stage there as Mr Malcolm in *Table by the Window* and also in Terence Rattigan's tense and moody play *Separate Tables*, in which he played Major Pollock.

He was next seen on British TV screens in 'The White Witch of Makala', an episode of the weekly series *Assignment Foreign Legion* in which the regular star of the show, Merle Oberon, played a female journalist who worked with the foreign legion during the Second World War. Each episode featured different guest stars and storylines, and Dennis was seen with Betty McDowall as an elegant French couple who brought a curse upon themselves when the Major ordered a native to be executed.

ITV's *Play of the Week*, J. M. Barrie's *Dear Brutus*, saw Dennis heading an all-star cast as Mr Dearth. The story took place on Midsummer's Eve, when eight people had the opportunity to live their lives again, and the consequences were quite surprising—a humorous story with a moral. The young Katie Boyle, later a famous agony aunt, was (then) a budding actress who could not believe her luck and said she was 'thrilled' to be cast alongside Dennis. The purpose of Barrie's play was to pose the question 'Do people have the ability to change, if given a second chance? Would they learn from past mistakes?' That was something Dennis should have asked himself.

Next, under Cyril Coke's direction, he starred in the TV play *The Age of Abandon* as another middle-aged Romeo called Peter Conway. Rumour has it that Conway, a handsome former movie star of advancing years, is set to embark on yet another romance, and his wife along with his ex-wife, tries to discover if he is having an affair. It was primarily a comedy about the way a lot of men and women (actors in particular) are coy about declaring their real ages.

At Walton Studios during the summer, Dennis took a break from television to make the film *The Naked Truth*, which has since become a classic. As in *Murder Without Crime*, he was cast as a blackmailer, only this time with the rather appropriate name of Mr Dennis. He is an unscrupulous magazine publisher who puts the squeeze on several well-known personalities with the threat of publishing their embarrassing secrets, his latest targets being Lord Henry Mayley (Terry-Thomas), television host Sonny MacGregor (Peter Sellers), writer Flora Ransom (Peggy Mount), and model Melissa Right (Shirley Eaton). Several of them decide independently that murder would be a better solution than paying. The four eventually join forces and try to do just that, but fail twice. Then, Mr Dennis is arrested for an earlier crime; when he threatens to reveal all at his trial, Mayley comes up with a scheme, with the help of hundreds of Dennis's other victims, to break him out of prison and send him to South America.

Although it was a film that solidified Peter Sellers as a box-office star, Dennis Price stepped into his role with obvious enthusiasm that breathed real life into the character along with sardonic wit and cool manners.

It was during this period that Dennis ran into trouble yet again with the Inland Revenue and was finding it difficult to raise the money owing. He reasoned he had already made cuts in his living expenses, while other careful actors were living it up. His co-star Peggy Mount observed:

> The rest of the team became extremely fond of him—both his fellow actors and behind the scenes people—which is very unusual in the profession. They were concerned about his welfare and couldn't help noticing he was going through a rough patch. The wardrobe department sent his shoes to be mended, had his clothes cleaned and repaired and sent him from the studio looking like a new man.

The truth, the whole truth and nothing but—*The Naked Truth*. Dennis was in terrific blackmailing form as Mr Dennis, here pictured with Terry-Thomas.

Terry-Thomas had always got on well with Dennis, and found his habit of toting Guinness bottles around very amusing.

The film was a smash hit, winning full houses at Leicester Square. One critic, among many equally enthusiastic, said: '*The Naked Truth* is ingenious and in places quite funny. For this we are mainly indebted to Dennis Price, effortlessly sardonic as the blackmailer.'

As the fictitious magazine in the film had been likened to America's famous scandal sheet, *Confidential*, their London-based European editor issued (unsuccessful) writs against the film-makers and scriptwriter, alleging they had broken the libel law by making a film about a scandal magazine. The writ stated it might prove detrimental to the sales of *Confidential*, which was planned to be sold in Britain—talk about life imitating art.

During October, Dennis was seen on television as Rupert Cadell in *Rope* by Patrick Hamilton; the two murderous students were portrayed by Alec McCowen and Ian Holm. It made a change for Dennis not to be the victim of the piece. He said of the play:

> I have played in numerous thrillers, but *Rope* is my favourite. I appeared in its first television production in 1939 at Alexandra Palace. Ernest Milton, for whom Patrick Hamilton wrote the play, appeared as Rupert Cadell, while I had the role of one of the undergraduates. Since then, I have twice appeared in *Rope* in repertory. This thriller is so good that actors clamour to appear in it.

Despite this enthusiasm, his co-star Alec Mc Cowen had another impression. 'He [Price] appeared depressed and uninterested in the production. He was always polite and courteous, but seemed to have already detached himself from life. I admired his work and was sorry not to have known him better.'

In 1958, Dennis guest-starred in a documentary feature entitled *Hello London*. It was a star vehicle for ice skater Sonja Henie and co-starred Michael Wilding. Eunice Gayson was another of the guest stars:

> The film was purely a story put together around Sonja Henie, set to music. I believe she and her husband financed the film in order to sell it purely as a skating fantasy. It was cast with other names in order to ensure its sale.
>
> When we were first sent scripts there was to be an item where Michael and I did a song and dance routine called 'We're a couple of swells'—that well known popular skit on a couple of down and out tramps. We worked hard on it and the shooting went very well. So you can imagine our surprise and disappointment when we saw the finished film, to find most of the number had been ruthlessly almost cut out, just leaving a few brief background 'bits' behind one of Sonja's scenes! We were furious

Michael Wilding and Eunice Gayson join Dennis in *Hello London*, also known as *London Calling*, supposedly the first in a series of location films for star Sonja Henie, though its poor distribution and her controlling personality meant it was the first and last.

> and so was the director, who told us he had been 'ordered' by Sonja to cut it out. When she saw it, she apparently told him 'Oh no they don't, they would steal the film with that—whose film is it anyway?'
>
> I can only say that as a lifelong fan of hers, it was so disappointing to find her such a cold, hard and jealous performer, quite the opposite to her screen persona. She never spoke to either Michael or I again—apart from writing us the obligatory 'Thank you' note at the end of the shooting. Not a nice lady! She was the artist the crew and everyone else disliked.
>
> I only met Dennis Price once for a photo shoot in *Hello London*. We never really 'met'. Michael Wilding I had worked with over the years though. I have never heard of anything derogatory about Dennis Price's reputation. Both Michael [Wilding] and I were known as 'Pussy cats' in the business, for which we were both proud.

The year 1958 brought more TV plays and when given the choice of doing it 'live' or pre-recorded, Dennis's answer was, 'I think a performance gets a fillip from knowing the director cannot say "Cut".'

With the war still being exploited as a subject in film, *Danger Within* presented a slightly different view by being set in an Italian prisoner of war

The concluding scene of *Danger Within* sees Dennis playing Hamlet as a diversion for the prisoner of war camp escape.

camp, which held a traitor among the inmates. It was a popular 'find the rat' story with a very distinguished cast, including Dennis's friend Bernard Lee. There were a few comic touches among the action and Dennis had a very good part as a frustrated thespian trying to offer up some culture to the others. His performance was reminiscent of his time as a gunner at Sevenoaks and it really was an excellent production, albeit strongly similar to America's *Stalag 17*. Among all the top names, it is interesting to spot an early appearance by Michael Caine, who has a tiny speaking part as one of the homesick squaddies; Caine was then a very inexperienced film actor and there were not many parts for Cockney wide boy types until the 1960s and *Alfie*. Dennis once wrote him an encouraging letter following one of his early TV appearances, and told the actor he could see that he was heading for greater things. They stayed in touch and reputedly became good friends.

Early in 1959, Dennis teamed up with Ian Carmichael again for the Boulting brothers' bitingly satirical slice of working life, *I'm Alright, Jack!* This was a sequel to their highly successful *Private's Progress*. It was especially penned by Alan Hackney, due to popular demand, and in bringing Bertram Tracepurcel back to the screen as (now) a director of a missiles factory, Dennis gave a marvellous variety of crafty looks and foxy smiles in perfect time with the jokes.

With an abundance of quality work, Dennis had every reason to be happy and content, yet he did not have the will to stop ignoring tax demands and paying them at the last possible minute.

During this period, he became a regular of the bar at the Cavendish Hotel and the Kismet Club, the latter being a popular haunt of the acting fraternity with its special licensing laws meaning it opened for drinking at 3 p.m. when most pubs closed. Dennis became a regular drinking friend of television director Nick Hague.

Hague remembers Dennis as having a very dry sense of humour, but also for being rather bitchy at times. He once asked Dennis if he liked to celebrate New Year's Eve. Dennis replied, 'Dear boy, New Year's Eve is for amateurs. It's full of office boys being sick in the gutter. I always stay at home.'

It was actually an actor named Tom Gill who first introduced Nick Hague to Dennis; they would often hang out at the club with fellow actors Ronald Fraser and Peter O'Toole, who together with Dennis, were bonded

Dennis excelled in the Boulting Brothers's comedy satire, *Private's Progress*, here with Jill Adams.

by their mutual love of drink. Dennis always enjoyed the company of 'off the wall characters' such as Ronald Fraser recalls Hague, and once having told Dennis he was going to a party, Dennis asked Hague, 'Do you think I could come, dear boy?' He said party was in St John's Wood and was full of lively people; Dennis was in his element. Hague describes himself as being 'a passing friend and drinking associate'. Indeed, despite being a generous host, Dennis lacked many close friends and confidents who may well have advised him on his priorities. Although that was about to change when he met a man who would have a profound and lasting influence on his life and career. While having a quiet drink in one of the several London pubs he frequented, Dennis met twenty-three-year-old Marcus Wootton, who was fresh from completing his national service. Wootton had the gift of the gab and soon had Dennis's undivided attention.

Having had a lengthy conversation, Wootton offered to sort out Dennis's financial problems by taking on the responsibility of becoming his manager, having had no previous experience of such a role. He soon took control of Dennis's diary and business affairs, and besides organising meetings and appearances for him, also had an instinctive knack for being able to précis and edit lengthy scripts. Wootton had a no-nonsense attitude, reportedly had no pretentiousness, and despised pretentious or foolish people. Anyone not on his wavelength was in line for one of Wootton's cutting and dismissive quips. Wootton liked to tell larger than life stories about his colourful past, including the claim that he had been held prisoner in a wartime concentration camp. Yet since he was born in 1936, that would have made him only nine when the war ended, so was highly unlikely to be true.

Something in Wootton's flamboyant nature really struck a chord with Dennis and their first meeting was the beginning of an enduring friendship. At twenty-one years his junior, Wootton represented the son Dennis never had, and although their personalities were poles apart, it was this striking contrast that Dennis liked—similar to the types he had befriended in the Army. Yet the main reason Dennis was 'attracted' to the stranger who had walked, quite literally, in off the street was to fill the void in his lonely life.

Many people wondered about the true nature of their friendship because after all, they were two unmarried men. Their relationship was never sexual, though it was complex. Wootton was primarily his bodyguard and shield, protecting Dennis from unwanted attention, but he was also a companion and confidant who was privileged to share the life of a very private man. Their friendship could best be compared to characters in the film *The Magic Christian* (which Dennis would appear in a decade later), where Sir Guy Grand (Peter Sellers) plays a very wealthy but eccentric businessman who is something of a loner. While strolling in the park, he comes across the epitome of a Swinging Sixties hippy (Ringo Starr) and they have a conversation. The hippy becomes known as 'Youngman Grand' and is adopted by Sir Guy as his son and heir. Dennis, like Sir Guy, was very eccentric and liked to play practical jokes on people, and with Wootton by his side, he had found a worthy 'play mate'.

Most of Dennis's colleagues and acquaintances took an instant dislike to Wootton because he acted as a barrier between them and Dennis. They did not realise it was Dennis's idea to have him around to ward off unwelcome approaches. Dennis and his new manager came to develop a coded language of their own, and Dennis would convey to Wootton when he wanted him to stay close and when he wanted him to vanish. Plus, they devised a series of phrases as a way of communicating privately in front of third parties. There were three different scenarios to suit every occasion:

Dennis would invariably be in the pub in the company of others, when he would turn to Wootton and say, 'Cyril phoned me earlier today. He was very impressed with the sample I'd given him and wants to discuss it with me.' This was the signal for Wootton to make himself scarce so that he could be alone with whoever took his interest.

Alternatively, Dennis would say, 'I've been trying to contact Cyril all week, but he never picks up the phone. He must be away on business.' This was Wootton's cue to stick to Dennis like glue and never leave his side.

Finally, in the last scenario, whenever Dennis found himself in the company of someone very obnoxious, he would invariably turn to Wootton and say, 'I managed to contact Cyril, but he said the sample isn't quite what he's looking for.' With those words, it was Wootton's cue to tell whoever it was that was bothering Dennis to 'fuck off!' The 'Cyril' dialogue never became obvious to others, so they used it for years.

Wootton's aggressive manner did not make him very popular among Dennis's chums, though knowing his fierce loyalty to Wootton, they thought better than to mention it. Essentially very modest and sorely lacking the confidence in his own abilities, Wootton provided all the push Dennis needed.

Accordingly, Dennis left the shabby surroundings of Notting Hill for the far better address of a flat at 16 Curzon Street, Mayfair, where he would reside comfortably for the next seven years. His flat was on the first floor above a hat shop, and Dennis invited his new manager to occupy the flat above him. Although Wootton managed his day-to-day affairs, Dennis still had an agent to bring in and filter offers of work; he had been on several agents' books over the years and was currently with the William Morris agency.

Wootton got to meet all of Dennis's family over time and observed they were 'very possessive of him, and disapproving of the fact he was an actor because they had to share him with the public'. The Prices moved among the right people and with restricted lifestyles, so never really understood

Dennis's desire to do anything otherwise. On one occasion, Dennis took his mother Dorothy and Wootton to have dinner in one of the restaurants in Shepherd's Market, just round the corner from Curzon Street. Wootton recalled, 'She was a delightful lady and the least pretentious of his relatives!'

Dennis took pleasure in seeing his teenage daughters whenever he could and often took them out for tea at The Ritz or other top places. 'He always liked the best', said Wootton, 'providing he could afford it—and wouldn't you?'

Dennis's two daughters' career interests did not turn towards acting and since he had parted with their mother, they had been brought up by their nanny, an Australian woman named Ross with a pleasant and kind nature. She got on very well with Dennis and he later invited her over to his house on Sark before she returned to her native country, which she had missed. Meanwhile, Joan was busy striving to make her break into big-time acting, though she was still unable to make a household name for herself and as time revealed, she never would. Wootton recalled that Joan was a very wealthy woman and 'lived in a six-storey house in Holland Park' at this time.

Dennis starred in another *ITV Play of the Week* called *Skyline for Two* and portrayed a successful playwright who became involved in a love triangle. He had lots of money, was top of his field, and had a snug lifestyle in a luxurious penthouse apartment in New York until a young girl entered his life. She was played by Lois Maxwell, an actress of twenty-six while he was fifty-three. He exudes charm on her, but when he asks if she finds him revolting because he is much older, she says 'You'll never be revolting', but adds 'after all, 53 isn't the age to make a girl's heart go pit a pat'. He later falls for his secretary (Wendy Craig), but finds he is rivalled by a young man. It is the men's battle over her that makes the play compelling.

When Dennis was asked his thoughts on the 'older man courts young girl situation', he said, 'A marriage between a couple who are about the same age stands the best chance of being happy', and added 'though this isn't the author's conclusion, I believe it is true—that there is something in a man's life which outlasts love, and the wise woman accepts it.' This statement is very telling and could account for the reason that Dennis (then aged forty-four and not as old as the character he played) seemed to have given up on pursuing a relationship. He went on to say, 'For me, the most discerning passage in this play lies in Stephen Gaye's description of audiences. Linda has just told him she hates audiences and he replies "You mustn't hate audiences—hate human beings if you want to, but not audiences".'

It was hard to imagine anyone as thoroughly British as Dennis playing a German officer, but that was exactly what he was asked to do as Captain von Krisling in the comedy film *Don't Panic, Chaps*, an amusing send up of military shenanigans during the war. Others who featured in it were George Cole, Harry Fowler, Thorley Walters, and Terence Alexander.

Terence Alexander worked twice with Dennis, and remembered him as, 'A sweet natured man who was very private.' Their first show together was a 1958 American TV film made in Paris. Alexander arrived on the plane from London, 'Dennis had flown from Germany and all his luggage was missing! He was sat at the airport and refused to move till the other actors arrived'. They filmed for a week, 'and of course, Dennis was always immaculate and totally professional,' he recalled. Terence Alexander used to go out to dinner on his own every night and have 'wonderful Parisian meals', but when he asked Dennis the following day what he had eaten, it was always 'just petit pois', which he thought to be very odd. They flew back together to London, 'the air steward was a friend of his, so he said "Just keep bringing Mr Alexander champagne and me Guinness throughout the flight", which the man did and it was quite the most pleasant flight'. Though Dennis liked to drink, a lot, he could not ever touch spirits as 'they sent him quite bonkers, so it was either water or Guinness,' Alexander recalled.

They also acted together in *Don't Panic, Chaps*, which was made on location at Runlestone, in Devon, where Dennis told many an amusing story between takes, but as Alexander remembered, 'It was always during or after dinner when we had partaken of the wine, that'd he'd often forget the punch line. Dennis once confided in me that he occasionally relied on his ex-wife for help, as with when he lost his car keys on Hampstead Heath in the middle of the night—he rang up Joan who came out to help him find them!'

Next came another comedy film, *School for Scoundrels*, which was based on *Lifemanship* by Stephen Potter. Dennis formed a comic duo with Peter Jones, as Dunstan and Dudley Dorchester, the 'Winsome Welshmen'. They are a couple of crooked car dealers into whose showroom walked naïve Ian Carmichael, hoping to pick up an impressive motor, but is naturally sold an old banger instead.

Dennis and Peter Jones's scenes were filmed in a genuine car salesroom in Harrow and their whole sequences were shot in one day. Travelling to the location, they shared a car and Jones observed Dennis was 'quiet and nervous, in such a way it seemed he might have been suffering a hangover, as he was reputed to be drinking heavily at the time. However, once in front of the cameras, he relaxed and the scenes were fun to do'.

Dennis lead the cast as Lt Price in the popular radio series *The Navy Lark*. His chief petty officer was Jon Pertwee, while Leslie Phillips played Sub-Lieutenant Philips; he and Dennis played great rivals for the affections of a Wren played by Heather Chasen. The series was an instant and lasting success and the team were on good terms. Dennis was well suited for his role, but his good looks and use of withering, sardonic expressions were wasted on radio. On tuning into episode three, Herbert Wilcox decided to produce *The Navy Lark* as a film, but Dennis was unable to take part and his role was

Dennis and Peter Jones play the scene-stealing dodgy car dealers, Dunstan and Dudley, with Ian Carmichael, in *School for Scoundrels*.

taken by Ronald Shiner. When the series returned for a second radio run, Dennis handed over his command to Stephen Murray. All Leslie Phillips can remember of working with him in the show was that 'he liked drinking a glass of milk stout or Guinness'. Sadly, it was a common memory of Dennis.

The Navy Lark radio show continued into the 1970s, though if Dennis had not left the series when he did, he would not have been able to take up the golden opportunity of starring as Hector Hushabye in an important production of *Heartbreak House*. It was with this play that Dennis made his debut in New York at The Billy Rose Theatre on Broadway; the show went on to tour during November. He remembered the opening night well as it was the day before Kruschev's visit to the city, and all around, security was tight with armed guards and flying squads operating; however, it was the arrival of Joan Crawford outside the theatre that took everyone's attention and kept the press photographers busy. Thus, 1959 ended on a high note.

After the tour, Dennis returned to his Curzon Street flat to find himself inundated with film offers, and all with good billing. He was also signed up by ITV to appear in their new series of works by Somerset Maugham; they turned out to be his favourite TV parts (prior to playing Jeeves) as they were the classics he had been longing to do since his college days. The first of these stories was 'The Lion's Skin', which was screened in March 1960, and in which Dennis played a captain in the Welsh Guards.

Then he was cast as Robbie Ross in the film *Oscar Wilde*, made at Walton Studios. Not only the same year, but just five days apart, a longer, colour film was released by a rival company, called *The Trials of Oscar Wilde*, starring Peter Finch; the latter version had all the advantages of budget, sets, and distribution. The character Dennis portrayed was a friend and sympathetic adviser to Wilde, who was played by Robert Morley, complete with his distinct and portly appearance. It is Ross who is with Wilde when he has his first encounter with Lord Alfred Douglas and is with him at the bitter end, when Wilde is in exile. Dennis presented an excellent portrait of a genuine friend; however, the critics argued that the unpleasing looks and performance of Morley as an over-aged Wilde pulled the film down and *The Trials of Oscar Wilde* was the bigger hit.

The film version of James Kennaway's punch-packing novel *Tunes of Glory* presented Dennis with his meatiest role in a long time as Major Charlie Scott. In complete contrast to his other films that year, it was a drama laden with acrimony, which tells of the battle between characters played by Alec Guinness and John Mills for leadership of a peacetime Scottish regiment. Major Scott was in the middle, provoking trouble while managing to dodge the sparks that fly. The story is set in the bleak surroundings of a Highland barracks, which the acting colonel (Guinness) runs like a leisure club. Charlie Scott is the second in command—the smooth-talking regimental Romeo who is the confidant of the Colonel, a whisky swigging slob he refers to as 'Old boy'. Even people who do not usually enjoy army films cannot fail to be engrossed in this finely made psychological drama, which is a credit to all concerned.

Dennis's co-star Gordon Jackson recalled:

> Dennis was a lovely man and a beautiful actor. I thought he was brilliant in it; he made the character he was playing so attractively sinister, a marvellous performance! Dear Dennis, if he did have a drink problem, I never saw it; he certainly never drank on the set; he was always on time, word perfect and completely professional. Sadly, every night he had to get a lift home from his stand-in, as the bankruptcy court wouldn't permit him to own or drive a car. Apart from the odd mutter of 'life is ridiculous!' and with a sigh when they turned the camera towards him, saying 'Oh no! You don't want a close up of me?' he was great fun to be with and had a wonderful sense of humour. I remember him once saying 'I've got to get back to town early tonight. They're running an Edie Martin season at the Baker Street Classic'. Edie Martin was a very small-part actress who popped in for odd moments in the Ealing comedies. I admired him tremendously as an actor.

Another of Dennis's screen highlights followed, when George Bernard Shaw's *The Millionairess* was made into a film by Twentieth Century Fox. He starred in his old Croydon repertory role of Dr Adrian Bland (shortened

Dennis relaxes on the set of *Tunes of Glory* with John Mills and Alec Guinness. He rated the film and his performance as one of his favourites.

from the original Blenderbland). The leading part of the Indian doctor was played by Peter Sellers and the millionairess herself by Sophia Loren. Though the plot was very time-honoured on stage, the film benefitted a great deal from snappy dialogue, big screen effects (including a judo wrestling sequence between Dennis and Miss Loren), and a memorable theme tune. Dennis enjoyed himself immensely as Dr Bland and was fast becoming one of the few regular actors Peter Sellers would work with.

Tony Hancock's colour film *The Rebel* was a wicked send-up of the modern art world, penned by his long-time writing collaborators Galton and Simpson. Dennis had an hilarious cameo as dotty eccentric Jim Smith, a wealthy art enthusiast and leader of a cult of existentialists who invites Hancock to one of his parties. This is after Hancock's childish daubs have been hailed as the work of a 'genius'. Dennis's part in the film ends when he retires for the night to the bottom of a fish tank. An all too brief appearance, it is still very memorable. The zany clothes he wore and half a moustache were an obvious parody of Salvador Dali, and a biting comment of art critics in general. The film was the sixth most popular at the box office on release, but it failed to make much of an impression in the US, probably due to its very English sense of humour. It also proved to be the final collaboration between Hancock and the writers who had served him so well. They failed to agree upon a script for a follow-up film and parted company.

It was a strange coincidence that brought Dennis, Tony Hancock, and George Sanders together in *The Rebel*, as all three men had tragedy in their lives, including broken marriages and drinking problems. Reading some years later about their suicides must have brought back poignant memories for Dennis, who had enjoyed much success since his own suicide attempt back in 1954. Yet despite the acclaim, all three actors were destined to die in lonely circumstances before reaching old age; they were all divorced at the time too.

Meanwhile during December 1960, Dennis appeared on TV twice; as a guest on *Alfred Marks Time*, a mixture of comedy sketches and song hosted by Alfred Marks and his wife, followed by 'The Letter' which was another classic from the Somerset Maugham season.

TV had put Dennis back on his feet and back in favour with the film studios, who were suddenly keen to sign him up. With his present income, he was able to keep the tax man at bay and that was half his problems solved—for the time being.

Tony Hancock's short-lived film career kicked off with *The Rebel*; Dennis played a Dali-esque cameo, which was as bizarre as it looks.

12

The Comedy Man (1961–1964)

Following the Boulting brothers' satires, Dennis was in demand for many 1960s British comedies, and there were plenty of them as studios were churning out a new farce every few weeks. He was one of the many popular actors who was thought to add a 'touch of class' to invariably frantic capers and whatever the part required he always made the most of it. When Dennis appeared in Hammer's *Watch It, Sailor!*, he chose to sport a large beard as Lt Commander Hardcastle, and his best scenes were with Irene Handl.

The allmovie.com website wrote:

> The two great scene-stealers in this comedy of errors are Irene Handl as the bride's eccentric aunt, whose ramblings have a surreal quality, and Dennis Price as the droll-witted officer who is forced by orders to interfere with the impending marriage, and then ordered to make it right. With the cock of an eye-brow or the slight curl of a lip, before he even utters a line, Price dominates every scene in which he appears, and even if the rest of the movie weren't as funny as it is, his performance would be worth the price of admission.

TV work continued apace too and in January 1961, ATV screened their *Armchair Theatre* adaptation of Oscar Wilde's *The Picture of Dorian Gray*, in which Dennis was given the plum part of Lord Henry Wootton, the character formerly played by George Sanders in the film version. Dennis was perfectly cast as the man responsible for corrupting an innocent young Dorian (played by Jeremy Brett) and came to the conclusion, 'Like so many key characters in Oscar Wilde's books and plays, Lord Henry must have been based on himself.'

Dennis worked a lot with Sid James that year and at one stage it looked as if they would form a long-term partnership, as along with appearing

Watch It Sailor gave Dennis a complete change of image, with a beard, which rather suited him.

with Sid in the films *What a Carve Up!* and *Double Bunk*, they also made a radio series called *It's a Deal*, which ran for twelve episodes; however, they each moved on to other projects and James became increasingly busy with the *Carry On* films, of which he made nineteen over fourteen years.

On the radio show *Movie Go Round*, Dennis was heard in excerpts from *The Rebel* one week, it being his latest film release, in which again he worked with Tony Hancock. Another week, he spoke from Pinewood where he had been making *Tunes of Glory*, giving the public a sample of the wide range of parts he could tackle. Yet perhaps the most challenging and controversial role of his career came when he was cast as a homosexual actor in the film *Victim* alongside Dirk Bogarde. Made six years before the law was changed regarding the legalisation of homosexual acts, there had been great pressure from the gay community for acceptance, and this film was made to highlight their plight, centring on everyday people whose careers were in jeopardy from blackmail. The supporting actors involved in the production did not really overanalyse their involvement in the controversial storyline; they regarded it as just another job. However, cinemagoers inevitably looked on some of the actors with a little suspicion, not least Dennis, a single man in a close friendship with his manager, with some even suggesting to the press that he may have been blackmailed in the past himself, hence his suicide attempt.

Sid James, Kenneth Connor, and Michael Gough were among the all-star British cast of *What a Carve Up!*

Noel Purcell, seen here with Dennis in the comedy *Double Bunk*, was probably his closest friend in the business. Starring Sid James and Liz Fraser, it was a film in the mould of the *Carry On* series.

Tackling the theme of homosexuality when it was still illegal in the UK, Anthony Nicholls, Dennis, and Dirk Bogarde starred in *Victim*.

The confusion between actors' own lives and their screen image was nothing new but these rumours were damaging and extremely hurtful to Dennis's family, especially his daughters; although totally unsubstantiated, it also did Dennis's professional reputation harm. In the 1990s, the leading actor in *Victim*, Dirk Bogarde, gave an interview for Channel 4 television about the film, and said: 'We were all straight—except, I think, for Dennis Price. I think he was homosexual'.

Of course, by suggesting Dennis was gay, Bogarde deflected attention from his own sexual preferences, and it was only after Bogarde's own death in 1999 that it was revealed not only was he homosexual, but had lived with his lover Tony Forwood for over forty years. Bogarde was quite desperate to hide his sexuality because he had a very large female following who adored him, even more so because he was a bachelor and, as they perceived, obtainable. He also went to great pains to maintain a heterosexual facade to please his parents, who had disapproved of his role in *Victim*.

Sadly, Bogarde was nothing like the heroic character he portrayed in *Victim*, lacking the courage to come clean about his sexuality, and continued to do so even after he played a gay man again in *Death in Venice*.

In his biography of Bogarde, the writer John Coldstream repeated the actor's unfounded thoughts about Dennis by stating, 'Dennis Price lived openly with another man'. The man he referred to is, of course, Marcus Wootton, but what Coldstream failed to mention was that Wootton occupied his own flat, with his girlfriend of the time, which was above Dennis's in the same building. In contrast to Dirk Bogarde, Dennis lived openly in the heart of London for most of his life whereas Bogarde lived in seclusion for many years in rural southern France—the ideal place for a gay man to avoid any exposure of his private life.

Victim was directed by Basil Dearden and still remains a most effective and compelling story. Dennis had previously played a gay man in a cameo in *No Love for Johnny*, but this time, the emphasis on his character was sympathetic, in one scene saying, 'I've never corrupted the norm. So why should I be persecuted for finding love in the only way I can?' The screenplay is extremely powerful and so is the acting, never allowing the audience to lose interest for a moment. Even in today's enlightened times, *Victim* is in a class of its own.

In May, Dennis considered the time had come to gather his memories and write his autobiography. Nearing his forty-sixth year and having lived through many different experiences—some not very pleasant—he wanted to put his thoughts on paper with the aim of helping others who had been in similar situations to him, with family expectations, and a struggle for recognition as an actor. He was so keen to do a book that he discussed it with a *Sunday Express* journalist. Subsequently, an article about his book appeared in the paper, and began positively by stating: 'This morning Dennis Price will be putting the finishing touches to his autobiography'.

In their discussion, Dennis told him 'I have no illusions about myself. I am a second-rate feature actor. I am not a star and never was—even in the old Rank days. I lack the essential spark, you see.'

Not quite a true statement, but a continuing example of how he constantly underestimated his own ability. He continued, 'but I have lived a fairly eventful life and met a lot of people both in and out of the profession, so I feel I have something to say ... something which may help those people who like me arrive at a stage in their lives when they feel they cannot go on. You'll remember I reached that stage seven years ago. I was unsuccessful. So my experiences may help others. I am quite frank about it in my book.'

Although he may have been fired with enthusiasm, the article was somewhat premature. 'The truth was', explained Marcus Wootton, 'He had only written the equivalent of a long letter, but had lost heart with his usual self-pitying attitude, "no one will be interested in me". He decided to scrap it and the few notes he'd assembled ended up in his waste paper basket.'

His recent films had shown he could still turn in a fine performance, even if in a small capacity, like his aforementioned cameo in *No Love for Johnny*.

'But there aren't many parts like that,' bemoaned Dennis, 'one takes what one can get. My eldest daughter Susan rang me up about some film in which I had only a small part and said "Daddy—what are you doing in a film like that?" "Earning money, darling", I said.'

News of his intended book soon got around the studio publicity departments, and they in turn announced that he intended the book to be a collection of reminiscences gathered over many years; the title was to be the rather twee, 'Looking Back with Pleasure'. He was also reported to be planning to move to Venice, which would have indeed been a wish come true, as he had been taken by the romantic atmosphere of the city while filming *The Bad Lord Byron*. Though he had a strong desire to change his surroundings, with his work base in Britain, moving to Venice remained a pipe dream.

Come summer, Dennis was back at Elstree Studios for the comedy *Go to Blazes*, in which he donned helmet and waterproofs as disgraced Fire Chief Withers, kicked out of the brigade for helping himself to goods. He then becomes involved with a trio of inept crooks, played by Norman Rossington, Daniel Massey, and Dave King, who ask him how to become 'pukka' firemen so they can use a stolen fire engine as a getaway vehicle when staging a robbery. All goes well with their plan and the comedy is funny up to a point, but that fun is spoilt by the unlikely and very moral ending, which has the rogues hearts melted by tearful children, whose burning tree house they extinguish instead of making good their escape.

Norman Rossington remembers, 'There were a lot of jokes cracked in relation to each other's parts. Dennis always had a twinkle in his eye and though never snobbish, would rib me over being "common" to his posh. He had an acid wit, but there was never any hurtful intention in his jokes.'

Following on similar lines to the antics of Brigadier Bertram Tracepurcel in *I'm Alright, Jack*, a new TV series was devised in which Dennis was the star. It was called *Colonel Trumper's Private War* and was screened on ITV. Described as a 'hitherto unknown' British undercover agent, Colonel Trumper was the man with the mind of a criminal and the morals of a Borgia. Dennis's co-star was Warren Mitchell, and joining the team throughout the series were William Gaunt, George Tovey, and the director Stuart Latham, a contemporary from The Embassy Theatre School, whose brief acting career had been quickly dropped in favour of working behind the camera. The series was not a success. Writer Barry Took explained:

> My original title was 'Colonel Futtock's Private War', but Granada made me change it and the idea was based on a story I'd read somewhere about a surreal group of army bods who got lost in the system and became

Disgraced fire chief Withers teaches three inept crooks how to become 'pukka' firemen. Dennis is seen here with Dave King, Daniel Massey, and Norman Rossington.

> a sort of private army. I wrote the pilot script and the producer Peter Eton cast the show. Actually, we wanted the actor Nigel Patrick but as he wasn't available we cast Dennis Price who was. That was the pilot. I have no memory of the series, except that it was a ghastly failure, written by a trio of authors none of whom were able to relate to the others. It was in a way a summer replacement for *Bootsie and Snudge*, but only six episodes were planned and made and no more were contemplated after their failure. Incidentally, in the series Moray Watson was replaced [much to my regret] by William Gaunt.

Dennis next played a high-class crook in *The Pot Carriers*, a film version of the play by Mike Watts about life behind bars and the 'pots' they had to slop out each morning. With the nickname 'Smooth Tongue Bertie', he had a memorable part with prominent billing and even sang little snatches of 'Oh, for the wings of a dove'. He also had to swallow raw eggs and say they were 'delicious'.

Michael Winner, a young director who was fast making a name for himself, cast Dennis in the musical *Play it Cool*, in the leading part of

Dennis excelled in his role as 'Smooth Tongue', a role which was made for him, in *The Pot Carriers*.

Sir Charles Bryant. It was a film especially contrived to feature a teenage pop idol of the day, Billy Fury. Dennis was the straight foil, a typically stiff upper-crust father, whose daughter (played by Anna Palk) became involved with a disreputable pop warbler played by Maurice Kaufmann. Many bands featured in the story, each performing in turn as the search for Anna's boyfriend takes her pals around different night clubs.

Dennis was well liked, as Anna Palk observed: 'He had a very dry sense of humour and was a pleasure to work with.' Anna was very excited to be given a starring role in her first film, aged just eighteen, and said she and Dennis met again several times over a period of three years while making films together. She found him, 'a completely dignified and charming gentleman of the old school who kept himself to himself. He was horrified when Michael Winner yelled at everyone through a loudhailer.'

While making *Play it Cool*, Dennis was asked by a film correspondent if he would give an interview. He agreed and chose one of the least likely places for their meeting—an East End pub. He reasoned, 'This is the best place for relaxing I know'. In one corner, a pianist was thumping out a pub tune, accompanied by a crowd of off duty dockers who were also playing darts. The journalist noted the pub was also full of lascars and

Above left: Michael Winner's first feature film was *Play It Cool*, though he had directed Dennis earlier in the year in a 'short' film.

Above right: With Anna Palk in *Play It Cool*.

sailors busily quenching their thirsts and that Dennis, with his suave and sophisticated air, stood out like a sore thumb.

> 'It seems an odd way of relaxing to me', said the reporter. 'Nonsense', Dennis replied, 'it's the best possible way; the only way; there's such an air of happiness here; people are content to be themselves here. It's not like those precious West End bars where everyone wants to talk louder than anyone else about their imaginary achievements. They're so depressing, dear boy.'
>
> 'Aren't you ever recognised here?' he asked Dennis.
>
> 'Sometimes, but I'm never bothered by it. Anyway, they all know me down here and I'm just another of the regulars to them. I was brought up in what would be called luxury today. My father was a General—he commanded the Welsh Guards. When I was a small boy, I used to meet all sorts of important people; I used to spend hours practicing bows in honour of Queen Mary; later on, when I left Oxford, I intended to enter the church.

> In the early 1930s, I used to spend a lot of time in East End slums. I was full of religious fervour in those days and tried to do what I could. I came to know and like the people around these parts; I have done ever since.'

In overhearing this statement, a small man in a brown cloth cap approached their table to tell Dennis, 'Saw you at the Odeon last night. Talk about laugh ... you were great; keep it up mate.' Dennis smiled and gestured to him with a wave of his hands.

Continuing, Dennis said:

> I changed my mind about becoming a clergyman and decided to become an actor. I appeared in *Richard II* in the West End. Not as the king, of course—I had a role as a minor servant. Then came the war and I served two years in the Royal Artillery. I didn't exactly follow in my father's footsteps, though. I went back to the West End stage, then Michael Powell gave me my first film part in *A Canterbury Tale*. Since then, I've made dozens of pictures.

The journalist asked what he looked for when making a film.

> I only accept a part if the producer or the director want me particularly to play it. When I started filming, I put myself completely in their hands. They know just how they see me in the film and it's up to me to do my best to act the part in the way they want; an actor's personal ideas, I'm sure, have nothing to do with the ultimate result. As far as I'm concerned, the director's word is law. A ship can only have one skipper. When I've done a scene and want an opinion on it, I always ask the boys on the set - the technicians, electricians, carpenters and painters; they are the potential audience ... and they make no bones about saying just what they thought of a certain scene.

They shook hands and departed the dockside pub for Dennis return to the West End and his small but cosy Curzon Street flat. As it was situated directly opposite the Curzon cinema, one of the most stylish in London, he was once asked if he often frequented the place after work. He surprised his interviewer by saying, 'Not very often; I prefer to see my films in suburban cinemas. The audiences there are less sophisticated; you can tell if they think a film is really good—or if they think it is a waste of their time; audience reaction is most important in my line of business.'

People's view of Dennis was changing; he was now becoming more and more associated with comedy instead of dark sarcasm and killer roles. Having previously thought that he must be pretty sardonic in real life or he could not have played a villain so well, it proved a great relief for Dennis to be accepted as a fun and comedic personality.

The film production of Anthony Kimmins's popular play *The Amorous Prawn* in the spring of 1962, saw Dennis working again with Joan Greenwood and (for the fifth time) with Ian Carmichael. He was superbly smooth as the eponymous Prawn and was equally amusing in his next comedy *Kill or Cure*, when he was teamed with other favourites Terry-Thomas, Eric Sykes, and Lionel Jeffries.

Among the successful comedies, there had to be the occasional flop—so came *The Cool Mikado*. It was billed as being a comedy based on Gilbert and Sullivan's *The Mikado*, though Michael Winner (who directed and wrote the screenplay) warned it had nothing to do with the original plot. When the critics heard, they did not even bother to see it, nor did the public it seems. Hoping his fleeting guest spot went unnoticed, Dennis returned to television to make a series of plays for ITV—*The Serpent Beneath* opposite Zena Marshall and *Some Other Love* with Virginia McKenna. The latter was a light comedy in which he played a successful businessman but neglectful husband whose wife attracts a new admirer, a Frenchman played by Eugene Deckers. It was a happy occasion for Dennis, as he and Eugene were old friends since the time they appeared together in the 1956 film *Port Afrique*.

'But I don't always agree with Eugene', he said of their friendship, 'certainly not in his theory of French women having greater individuality than ours! One has only to watch a big social function to see how marvellously English women dress for the occasion.'

Some excellently written and well-received comedies followed in swift succession—*Tamahine*, *Doctor in Distress*, and *The Cracksman*. In *Tamahine*, Dennis starred as a straight-laced public school head who has to look after his orphaned half-Polynesian niece, with the result that she causes a sensation among the masters and the boys alike. That was filmed during August and he enjoyed himself immensely, travelling to locations as diverse as Bora Bora, the boulevards of France, the River Thames at Marlow, and the famous public school Wellington College in Berkshire (where his elder brother was educated). Playing one of the housemasters was Michael Gough, who had known Dennis for years. As Dennis strolled out of his dressing room on the set (a classroom in Wellington College), he announced to the rest of the cast: 'Well, here I go, petal fresh and party pretty as my nanny used to say,' and Michael Gough took it up for his motto.

Derek Fowlds appeared in what was his first of two films with Dennis:

> As a young boy growing up I was an enormous fan of Dennis Price and all the wonderful films he made in the forties and fifties. Meeting him and working with him was a pleasure and a privilege. I didn't have many

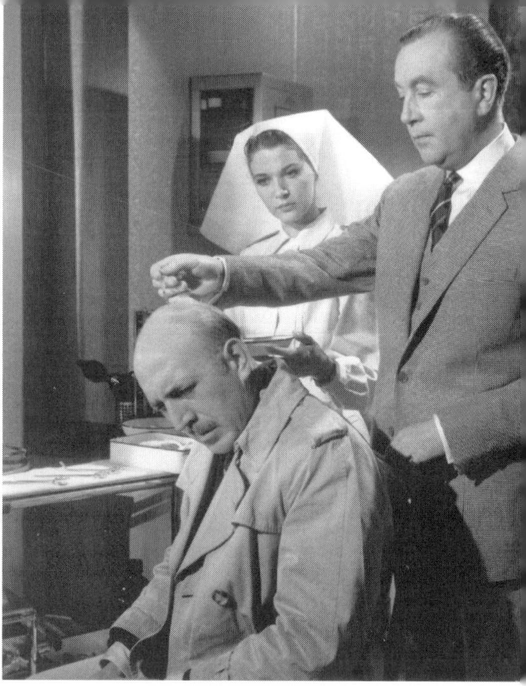

Above left: Initially a West End stage show, *The Amorous Prawn* was adapted for the screen by Anthony Kimmins and reunited Dennis with Ian Carmichael.

Above right: Terry-Thomas, Eric Sykes, Ronnie Barker, Lionel Jeffries (pictured), and Derren Nesbitt star alongside Dennis in a health club-set comedy.

Below: Dennis back to playing a more dramatic role in *Port Afrique*, with Rachel Gurney, in 1956.

scenes with him in [the second film together] *Tower of Evil* but we did socialize when we were filming *Tamahine*. He was charming and very helpful to all of us younger actors, he did have a very self-deprecating sense of humour. I often felt he was quite lonely and kept himself very much to himself and I'm not sure what he felt of the two films I made with him. I don't think either of them were hugely successful. It was a huge honour to meet Dennis and I will always remember him being brilliant in *Kind Hearts and Coronets*—one of my favourite films.

In *The Cracksman*, Dennis played a sophisticated crook and confidence trickster. Charlie Drake was the lead character of a Cockney master locksmith whose innocence is the answer to a thief's prayers. He and Charlie have a series of sketches together, then Dennis bows out halfway through and George Sanders's character steps in. Sanders was one of his biggest screen rivals, yet although they were in films together such as *The Rebel* and *Five Golden Hours*, they never shared a scene. In fact, the two men may not have even met up on the film sets.

Of making *The Cracksman*, Charlie Drake said, 'Dennis was a charming man—but very private and he took his work very seriously; his sense of

Charlie Drake had a bit of a reputation for throwing his (diminutive) weight around and when Dennis worked with him on *The Cracksman* he found himself replaced mid-way by George Sanders. A touch of the green-eyed monster perhaps?

comedy timing was immaculate and it was a great pleasure to work with him. I shall always remember the man with affection and admiration.'

There was a rumour (most likely true, given the circumstantial evidence) that Charlie Drake was a very jealous man and had Dennis removed from the film halfway through simply because Dennis was getting too big a share of the laughs.

Dennis's next part was in the large screen version of Terence Rattigan's *The V.I.P.s*. It was one of his shortest roles in which he was absolutely wasted, though it could be said his brief appearance as the rich man's butler could well have inspired his later casting as Jeeves. The main characters of a rich man and his spoilt wife were played by Richard Burton and Elizabeth Taylor who virtually dominated the whole film, although many other big names featured. On the set, Dennis was asked if he preferred films to the stage and answered, 'I suppose I was born bone lazy. I couldn't bear to give all my energies to the same play night after night and two matinees a week' and went on to hand all the credit to the director as usual. This was a very odd statement coming from a former repertory actor.

The V.I.P.s had been filmed in one of the bleakest winters for eighty years and Dennis bore the brunt of it, being outside near the airport runway to meet a helicopter.

Five days before Christmas, he appeared on TV in the first episode of a series of stories by Sapper (author of *Bulldog Drummond*). In 'A Two to One Chance', Dennis portrays a wealthy hypochondriac whose curious hobby is collecting rare spiders. He is self-centred, eccentric, and becomes suspicious of his wife when she pays attention to a young doctor. What begins as an informal triangle between them changes dramatically when the curious husband goes down with a rare illness and gambles with his life, but the odds are against him.

Ralph Michael, who played Sapper in the introduction, described Dennis as, 'An enigma to his colleagues; though a thoughtful man of great charm and intelligence.' They amused one another because their sense of humour was the same—'quiet and astringent'. He thought Dennis was, 'Very witty and a wonderful actor in parts that called for urbanity and sophistication. Not good when called upon for heroics'. Incidentally, Dennis had gone to school with Sapper's son before joining Radley.

The Comedy Man, which far from being an amusing story as its title might suggest, was a rather depressing film about a group of actors struggling to make a name for themselves. Dennis was cast as a ruthless theatrical agent who makes the actors' lives even more depressing. He gave a marvellous observation of a cold businessman as he had done in *The Intruder* a decade earlier; yet if the story was true to life, it was a miserable account of unpleasant people scrabbling for fame.

TV viewers saw Dennis reunited with Tony Hancock again in 'The Girl', as part of Hancock's new series for ATV after he had dissolved his partnership with Sid James. Dennis and Tony got on well and their attitudes towards comedy were in tune; when he was confronted by Hancock's often asinine remarks, Dennis would adopt his marble-cold look of distain and everything about his aloof manner suggested he was praying for someone to relieve him of this fool. In 'The Girl', Hancock was at odds with everyone from the medical profession to the stereotype cafe waitress.

Next, appearing alongside Margaret Rutherford, Dennis took a supporting role in the MGM Agatha Christie thriller *Murder Most Foul*, and was seen again in early 1964 when he was given a part in a new science fiction film called *The Earth Dies Screaming* in which robots from outer space tried to take over the earth by touching everyone, which in turn killed them with an electrical shock. They then revived the bodies as mindless and sightless slaves. Only a few people escaped and they formed a group of survivors. The scriptwriter clearly thought that with a story as packed full of action as this, they did not need to bother too much with dialogue; as a result, the characters sounded like zombies long before the robots got to them. An American actor, Willard Parker, was picked for the leading role of the devil-may-care hero. Dennis was landed with the part of a bumptious old windbag with the strange name of Quinn Taggett; another American, Virginia Field (a one-time glamour starlet), played his on-screen wife.

When the BBC adapted the Edwardian tragedy *The Lady of the Camellias* for television, based on Alexandre Dumas's tear-jerking story of two French sweethearts, Marguerite (Billie Whitelaw) and Armand (John Fraser), Dennis was offered a good supporting role in the tale of social differences. Also in the cast were Alexander Knox, John Le Mesurier, and Bruce Montague. Montague recalls:

> The only time I worked with Dennis was on this production, directed by Rudolph Cartier and broadcast on 12th February 1964. We rehearsed in some territorial army club which had a little bar for their evening meetings. Needless to say it wasn't open at ten in the morning when rehearsals started, however, Dennis Price and his co-star John Le Mesurier were thirsty thespians and in no time discovered a way of getting the bar to open each morning soon after ten a.m. I too liked a drink but was never in their league; I joined them to talk at a little table outside the drill hall and there were always pints of Guinness with generous chasers on the table. Dennis had the capacity to drink Guinness without any apparent effect. I noticed the same ability later when I worked with Dirk Bogarde.

Left: With Mervyn Johns in *A Jolly Bad Fellow.*

Below left: Dennis plays Quinn Taggett, a zombie with grey blobs for eyes, in sci-fi film *The Earth Dies Screaming*—as did most of the people who saw it.

Below right: Murder Most Foul was Margaret Rutherford's third appearance as Agatha Christie's Miss Marple, and Dennis took a cameo as theatrical agent, Harris Tumbrill.

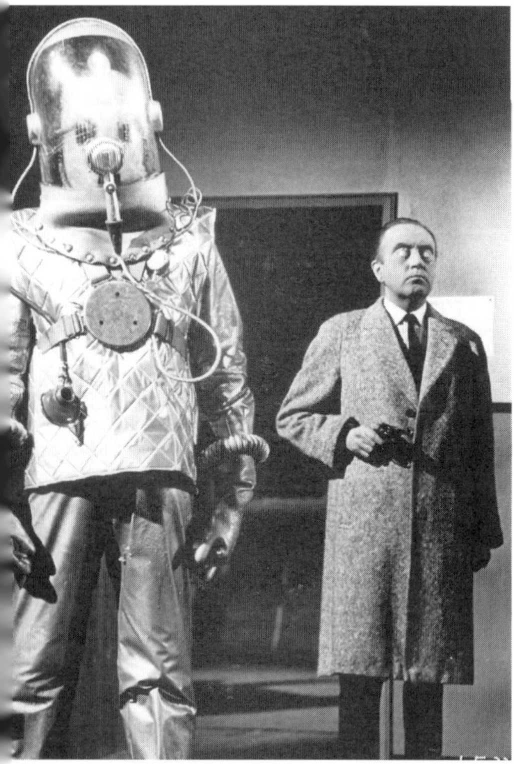

It has always amazed me how heavy drinkers remember their lines. I'm thinking now of John Le Mesurier, Wilfred Lawson, Mark McManus, John Hurt, Burton and so on. Anyway, I found Dennis affable, urbane, amusing, anecdotal and impeccable in performance. I don't know how he did it, it seemed effortless. We all chain smoked in those days - and again this seemed to have no ill effects. Dennis and John Le Mesurier were good buddies. 'Outside guests' sometimes wandered in to join them for morning cocktails. Wilfred Lawson, who I knew from the Old Vic, I remember came to watch rehearsals.

My part in *The Lady of the Camellias* was there to demonstrate a happy love life (as opposed to Marguerite's). My amour was Suzan Farmer. Marguerite was called Lady of the Camellias, because she wore a white camellia when she was 'available' and a red camellia when she had her period and was not available.

I don't remember Marcus Wootton, so don't think he could have been around much at that time. Rudolph Cartier was a no-nonsense director and wouldn't have allowed friends and agents on the set—at least, not for any length of time.

I listened to Dennis's reminiscences with eager amusement. He and John Le Mesurier shared memories of the British film industry that to my ears sounded as if it made movies on a shoestring budget. The huge salaries that seemed to be paid in Hollywood were not reflected on this side of the pond. Twenty or twenty-five pounds a day seemed to be the general rate for an actor in a picture and the stars didn't make a great deal more. Of course, £25 per day in those days seemed reasonable. In the early 1960s jobbing stage actors in the theatre were lucky to make £25–£30 per week.

At the bottom of the cast list was a forty-eight-year-old actress named Mary Barclay. Miss Barclay found making a name for herself very tough going and had to accept work whenever it was offered, though often felt upset at being treated as just a 'bit' player, rather than one of the team. Her memories of Dennis are vivid because of his kindness towards her. She recalled:

The director, Rudolph Cartier, was very grand, and during rehearsals, ordered all the actors with small parts to sit at the back and all the stars together in the front ... When Dennis saw me get up, he said "You can come and sit next to me," which I did and got on well with him. He was a conservative man who had no starry attitude or side to him whatsoever.

He was often kind to struggling actors, which was not something Miss Barclay encountered very often.

When director Sidney J. Furie and Cliff Richard got together to make the singer's third musical, *Wonderful Life* in June, Dennis was cast as Douglas Leslie. From his point of view, the film presented very little opportunity to do much acting as it was mainly given over to musical numbers. Yet disaster struck when the team were halfway through location shots in the Canary Isles as Dennis became ill with stomach trouble and was taken to hospital in Las Palmas, where it was discovered he had contracted dysentery. A spokesman for the film company was reported as saying, 'He is not expected out of hospital for at least eight weeks.'

After treatment, Dennis was flown home again and actor Derek Bond went out to the Canaries to take his place. The film was certainly cursed, as Furie went on to say, 'We had eighteen days looking at clouds and rain—at a cost of £100 per minute. It was like pouring gold down the drain.'

Another cameo part not worthy of Dennis's talent, here he is in *A High Wind in Jamaica* with Deborah Baxter.

Once recovered, Dennis found other offers, including a TV play called *Spare the Tears for Happiness*, were forthcoming. In it, he played a famous Hollywood screen lover whose real-life lack of stamina in the bedroom was threatened to be exposed by a spurned ex-girlfriend.

In a short space of time, Dennis completed a spate of films and plays calling for everything from an ageing or out to pasture actor to a comedy foil. He had greatly enjoyed making his recent comedy movies, but now they were beginning to thin out a bit; also, at forty-nine, Dennis could not think about reverting to romantic leads, so it looked as though his immediate future would be in small 'guest appearances' in film, such as *A High Wind in Jamaica*. He popped up in the concluding courtroom scene as a barrister, questioning a group of children who were mistakenly held by pirates when capturing the ship they were on. Dennis had his hair permed into curls, as he had worn during his romantic period, but his face was showing signs of middle age and he was beginning to move around more slowly.

He rounded off the year by appearing in the joint American/British horror film *The Curse of Simba*, which was a classic example of the low budget, fill-in picture destined to be confined to the B-movie shelves forever more.

Yet whether the quality of Dennis's films was good or bad, and the roles small or significant, his income was still a King's ransom to most people.

13

Jeeves (1965–1966)

The year 1965 proved to be an eventful year for Dennis. On 16 January, his presence was required at the Brompton Oratory in London, where his daughter Tessa was married to a chartered accountant, Hugh Burnett. To give her away in style, Dennis went dressed in traditional top hat and tails, accompanied by his manager Marcus Wootton in similar attire.

Afterwards, Dennis left London for location work on the film *Ten Little Indians*, another adaptation of the popular Agatha Christie thriller in which everyone ends up as a corpse (bar two in the screen version). Shot in black and white and supposedly set in the Alps, it was actually all shot in Ireland. Dennis gave a very convincing performance as Doctor Armstrong, with Wilfrid Hyde-White as the murderous and resourceful Judge Cannon. The other six destined for 'the chop' were Israeli actress Daliah Lavi, Stanley Holloway as a private detective, Leo Genn as a general, Fabian playing a pop singer, and Germans Mario Adorf and Marianne Hoppe as the servants who cater for them. Shirley Eaton and Hugh O'Brian played the statutory love interest. Critic Ann Pacey said:

> By far the best scenes are reserved for Wilfrid Hyde-White and Dennis Price, who play snooker together between murders and still worry about where the breakfast coffee is coming from, even when death has reduced the party by half.

Then a great opportunity came Dennis's way—the chance to play the impeccable butler Jeeves from P. G. Wodehouse's famous stories, which were being planned for a television series. It had already been decided that his friend Ian Carmichael was to play Bertie Wooster, but before considering Dennis for Jeeves, other actors were auditioned and, understandably, it did not please him too much when he discovered he was not first choice.

Dennis as Doctor Armstrong in his second Agatha Christie story of the year, *Ten Little Indians*.

Being the refined, sardonic, and sharply intelligent Jeeves came as second nature to Dennis. It was a role that suited him extremely well and after seeing his performance, it was impossible to think of anyone better. Ian Carmichael was a perfectionist and so it all made for a happy and enjoyable show that lingers on in the memory of those lucky enough to see them.

Reading through the script in the week before filming an episode had Dennis and Marcus Wootton curled up with laughter at some of the lines, so it took Dennis a while to compose himself enough to keep a straight face while recording. One of the minor problems of playing the character was finding the right hat for Jeeves to wear as butlers have a slightly flatter crown to a bowler. Yet as the studio had not provided him with this necessary prop, he was left to find his own, and had great fun searching around London till he found one suitable.

Beginning transmission on 30 May 1965, *The World of Wooster* (as the series was called) became a favourite nationwide. The combination of Dennis Price and Ian Carmichael as Jeeves and Wooster proved a wonderfully successful one. The dialogue was always very comical and the stories adhered to the original Wodehouse books closely. Dennis's portrayal of Jeeves, with the disapproving sniff, the upraised eyebrows, expressing annoyance of Bertie's choice of tie, or very often a long suffering 'Oh Lord, he's done it again!', brought the character to life. A must for viewers, it ran for three years. Dennis's only recorded comment on the show was 'I enjoyed it so much.'

With the popularity of the Wodehouse series came a lot of good publicity, and there was also talk of Dennis being 'rediscovered' as a star, as if he had spent the past decade hibernating. Soon after the first show had been transmitted, journalist Peter Dacre went to interview Dennis at the Irish Dance Hall in Tottenham Court Road where the rehearsals took place. He wanted to find out how he felt about playing the butler.

Dacre's first impression was of a tall, well-built man in an elegant check suit who spoke, as he described, like a 'real life Bertie Wooster'. Dennis suggested, 'Let's toddle round to a pub I know—handy place; landlord's a friend of mine, gives me the odd tips on the horses.'

At the pub, Dennis sat down to answer his questions over a pie and salad with a glass of his favourite stout. 'This role of Jeeves', he said 'is the best opportunity I've had for a number of years. I know damn well they tried to get other people before they turned to me, but when I was offered it, I took it with open hands. I know what competition is like in this business, but that's part of the fun of the game.'

When asked if he ever regretted choosing acting for his career, Dennis said quite firmly, 'No, never. I always wanted to act ever since I took part in amateur theatricals in the hols from prep school.' Did he wistfully remember the years of big stardom?

> They are behind, dear chap. The truth was, I was inflated too high for my worth. I had some damned good parts and a very reasonable income, but I don't think I could have kept going as a juvenile lead. I wasn't born with the kind of looks that last. And let's face it, there's no use in being an overaged juvenile lead. You must always look to the future in this business.

Thinking back to not so happy days, he continued:

> That film about Lord Byron was the turning point, I suppose; the critics slated me. I still have the notices papering the walls of my bathroom. The critics really pulled the plug on me that time, but it was probably just as well. You know, when you are reasonably young, you have a revolting conceit of yourself?—and then suddenly you find that what you have set out to do isn't going to work. After that film, I realised that I would have to get down and be a character actor playing bishops and butlers.

> I had a rather tatty period in my life, but that's all behind me; I don't think about it.

Asked what life had taught him, he contemplated for a while, then said:

> I've learned that in this business there is no possible chance of wavering; you have to fight like the blazes. You must be grateful when an opportunity comes along and must never retreat. I come from a soldiering family and so I've never retreated. In this game, you don't need vast ambition—just tenacity of purpose. As Harry Lauder said in his song, you just keep right on till the end of the road, even if you slip a bit on the hills.... there was a time when people jumped to the conclusion that I was not able to get work. That was not true; the parts got smaller and the money got less, but I was working continually. One of the things I've learned is that as the years pass and you go along the road, you must be kind to people. I've always practiced that—and it is surprising how many people are kind to you in return. I take life as it comes, day by day. You must enjoy yourself in this business.

The World of Wooster was such a success that its writer Richard Waring planned to make a musical version and present it in the West End, something along the lines of *My Fair Lady*. Waring wrote the words and Sandy Wilson composed a complimentary music score. Waring was keen that Dennis should repeat his portrayal on the stage and asked if he would care to do so, but knowing his own limitations, Dennis told him, 'I can't sing!'

Waring replied, 'Well Rex Harrison does'. However, they were piped at the post when Andrew Lloyd-Webber brought out his musical version in London, called simply *Jeeves*, and cast David Hemmings as the gentleman's gentleman. It was a fitting irony that his musical was a complete flop and sunk without trace; it was one of the few Lloyd-Webber compositions that was not raved about.

The BBC series was meanwhile voted 'Best Comedy of The Year' in 1967.

The make-up artist on one of the *The World of Wooster* episodes was Julie Crattenden, who had also worked with such celebrities as Peter Sellers, Vanessa Redgrave, and The Beatles during her years with the BBC. On meeting Dennis, Julie described him as being 'just delightful'. He came in dressed as the butler, sat down in the make-up chair and she asked 'Is there anything particular you'd like?'

He replied, 'You know your job—I'm quite happy for you to do whatever is necessary'. With those words, he put his head back in the chair and closed his eyes as if going to sleep, though she sensed he was actually going over his lines. With significant experience behind her, one of the things Julie had learned was that you did not always need to chat, as although some artists liked to gossip, others liked to just rest and concentrate in silence; Dennis was in the latter category. Her overriding impression of Dennis was 'a warm, nice person', though she added you couldn't tell that from his 'inscrutable face'. He was 'amazingly polite' and had a good skin which did not require a lot of makeup—his was a strong face with a lot of character and she didn't want to lose any of that, but rather just emphasise his features. When she had finished, she enquired 'is there anything else?', but he just thanked her and got up to start filming.

Dennis received encouraging words from Wodehouse who, on seeing recordings of the first series in New York where he lived, had sent a telegram to the BBC: 'Thank you all for your perfectly wonderful performance. I'm simply delighted with it. Bertie and Jeeves are just as I've always imagined them and every part was played just right. Bless you, P. G. Wodehouse.' Dennis, in the fashion of the butler he portrayed, commented 'Most gratifying, you know'.

It was little wonder he got into the part so well; 'I was brought up in it,' he explained. 'I've been in very many places where there were butlers, magnificent people. They scared me when I was a youngster, because I never had enough money to tip them in the manner to which they were accustomed, but I think they terrified everyone ... they absolutely ran everything in the household.'

Jeeves was by no means the first time he had played a butler either, for back in his repertory days, he had often put on his tailcoat and bowler to bring a tea trolley on stage before rushing away and studying a long part for a show the following week. As for walking in the correct fashion, it was hard for him to define, as he explained:

> Wodehouse always describes Jeeves as 'Flickering' into a room or 'Shimmering' out of it or 'Gliding' somewhere. Flickering and shimmering are difficult to say the least, so I've settled for a sort of semi-glide, unlike some real-life butlers, who on leaving the dining room, ran like mad for their first glass of port.

It was never easy to bring popular fictional characters to life, and many people had their own idea of how Jeeves should look and behave, as Dennis recounted:

> One lawyer was absolutely horrified when he heard I was going to play the part. He said 'You can't put someone like that on the screen, he's

immortal, everyone knows what he looks like'. In the face of this minor argument, *The Times* printed that, 'Dennis Price, suavely dignified and episcopal in diction, is uncontroversially near the universal picture of Jeeves'.

Dennis particularly approved of their 'episcopal' description.

Ian Carmichael, while working on the series, noted a change in Dennis's attitude to work and life. He had been given a hard time by the industry, having fallen from grace and now said, 'I'm not going to argue or question a decision, I'll just do exactly what the director or producer tells me'. Yet by sticking to this idea, Carmichael observed 'Dennis became quiet and reserved on the set', whereas in his heyday in the 1940s, he would have put across quite a few of his own ideas, or objected to something he disliked in the script. At rehearsals, Michael Mills, the director, who was a friend of both Dennis and Ian, invited the team to discuss the shows, the script, and ideas as to how they could improve on things. Ian always liked to voice any worries he had and suggest possible alterations to the text, and because they all worked together as a team, new ideas were always welcome, but Dennis sat quietly in a corner during these proceedings without ever adding to the discussion in any way. Whenever he was drawn into the conversation, he would just break off, saying he was quite happy to go along with the decisions. This new 'hermit crab' approach of his worried Ian Carmichael, who would love to have heard him put forward his own views for a change.

On the set, Ian would exercise his need for perfection, asking Dennis to go over a particular scene again and again. Although Dennis never objected to doing it, Ian observed that it was anathema to him. In fact, Dennis referred to the tediously long passages of dialogue as being his 'Gethsemanes'. He adopted a lordly and slow manner of delivery, which Ian suspected gave him more time to remember the next line; he appeared to have trouble remembering dialogue, as indeed they both did, because it was so lengthy.

Marcus Wootton remained close to Dennis and was described by Ian Carmichael as his 'Eminence Grise'. As Wootton was such a contrast to Dennis's quiet, pleasant nature, he was not a popular man, so much so that it seemed people did their utmost to discredit him; for example, having completed the last *The World of* Wooster series, Richard Waring next wanted Dennis to star in another series he had written (especially for him) called *The Gold Watch Club*, about a man who had just retired and how he faced up to his first day. They made the pilot show and Waring declared, 'It went beautifully. Dennis was excellent in the role,' fulfilling all that the writer hoped it would be, but the BBC decided for some reason that they did not want to commission a full series. It was to be the last occasion Waring worked with Dennis and although despite not being

Dennis with Marcus Wootton, his manager and bodyguard, taken during the late 1960s.

a close friend, Waring claimed in a 1990 interview that Dennis and his manager Marcus Wootton, together with Wootton's girlfriend of the time (a snake charmer named Zarita), had engaged in regular 'three in a bed sex sessions'. He claimed Dennis himself (who had long since died) revealed the information to him, which rather goes against Dennis's reputation of being extremely private about his personal life. It was in fact a further attempt to discredit the still (then) very much alive Marcus Wootton.

Soon after celebrating his fiftieth birthday, Dennis enjoyed a triumph when he appeared on the stage in London, after an absence of eight years, in Muriel Resnik's witty farce *Any Wednesday*. The play ran for a week at The Hippodrome, Golders Green, and, having been well received by the audience, transferred on 4 August to the Apollo Theatre for a West End season. Dennis starred together with Moira Lister as his wife, Amanda Barrie as his mistress, and John Fraser as a younger love rival.

Dennis did not forge any close friendships with his co-stars; this was again blamed on his manager acting as a barrier between them. In years to come, in their various autobiographies, his co-stars made some pretty negative and extraordinary statements about Wootton.

John Fraser took an 'instant dislike' to Wootton and described him as having 'a high pitched voice'. Fraser wanted to get to know Dennis better, and as they had previously worked together on *Tunes of Glory* and *Tamahine*, he invited Dennis to dinner at his house; however, when he realised that Dennis would be coming with his manager, the invitation was called off. Dennis was aware of the reasons, though did not choose to ask Wootton not to accompany him. Fraser was intrigued by Dennis's unusual relationship with Wootton and claimed to have discovered the 'secret'—that Wootton was actually a lesbian in men's clothing. Amanda Barrie makes similar claims in her autobiography.

In his book *A Kentish Lad*, the comedy writer Frank Muir made equally bizarre observations, claiming Dennis was living with a man who had undergone a sex change operation. These suggestions were quite a contrast to the rumours of Dennis and his manager being in a homosexual relationship. Yet none of it was true—Wootton certainly was not a woman in men's clothing, nor had he undergone a sex change. He was entirely masculine, and subsequently fathered three children with his wife.

Colleagues and journalists could only guess at what went on behind the door of Dennis's Curzon Street flat; their assumptions only went to show they knew absolutely nothing about Dennis's sex life, or that of his manager. It was to protect him from such intrusions into his privacy that Dennis engaged Wootton as his shield and defender and it greatly aggravated all those who aimed to get close to Dennis, whether they were predatory women or homosexual men (like John Fraser). Dennis was a master at hiding his private life as evidenced by his affair with Margaret Lockwood, which was never known about during his lifetime. The more people did not know about him, the more they seemed to invent.

On 23 August, Dennis's Curzon Street flat was broken into and the thieves made off with scrapbooks, clothes, tape recorders, records, and liquor. It seemed rather sinister as all these items, though holding sentimental value, had no real monetary value. It clearly was not the work of regular criminals and the police assumed they were taken for souvenirs by a crazy devotee.

Rounding out the year was yet another cameo role in a film, *Just Like A Woman*, a very contemporary sixties British comedy written and directed by Robert Fuest. The most remarkable thing about the movie is that it has virtually no plot. It could be summed up best as 'bored and zany housewife leaves home to build her own house.' Stretching it out into a full-length feature film made it very boring and tedious to watch, not helped by insipid characters that are not well defined or given anything to do. Even Dennis's part as a bath salesman lasted just one minute, which must have been his shortest performance ever, though it likely fitted in nicely with his stage commitments at night. It was screened once at the Edinburgh Festival in 1966 and rather bizarrely gained a diploma of merit for its 'wit and originality'.

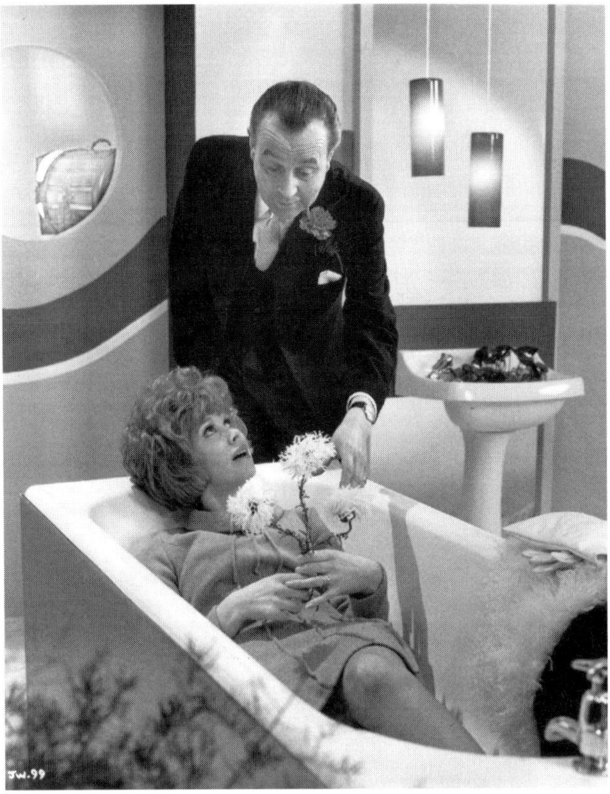

Another cameo—the zany comedy *Just Like A Woman* saw Dennis help Wendy Craig out of the bath.

By now, Dennis's face had begun to show the wear and tear of heavy years of drinking and appeared more rounded and fattened compared to his former neat oval look; his changing look began to affect the roles he was offered.

14

Guernsey (1966–1967)

The year 1966 kicked off with Dennis still starring in *Any Wednesday*, which had switched to the Wyndhams Theatre for the conclusion of what was to be a six-month run.

A memorable event occurred a month later with Dennis becoming a grandfather for the first time at the age of fifty, when Tessa gave birth to a daughter, Lucy Eleanor. Yet before he could spend much time with his new granddaughter, Dennis found himself moving overseas. Due to a sudden demand from the Inland Revenue ordering the payment of his back taxes within the space of a week, Dennis who was both unable and unwilling to meet their terms, was forced to quit the flat in which he had lived for the past seven years and make speedy alternative arrangements. The bill should not have surprised him as he had 'thrown several demands in the waste bin as soon as they arrived', according to Marcus Wootton.

On the advice of Wootton, Dennis decided to settle on Sark, one of the Channel Isles and a known tax haven. Wootton rented a bungalow on the island and gave Dennis the keys to it. It was called 'Les Rocquettes'. With his possessions packed, Dennis left on 6 March, leaving his manager in London to face the music.

As always, Dennis had been too preoccupied enjoying himself to notice he was heading for financial disaster. He did not like being interviewed over personal matters, so made no comment to the eager press reporters waiting for a scoop. Appropriately, there was no phone at 'Les Rocquettes'.

Wootton, who promptly moved into Dennis's old (and bigger) flat downstairs, thus inheriting Dennis's phone line, was plagued by calls from inquisitive journalists, all wanting to know the ins and outs of the story. He told the national newspapers, 'Dennis has been forced into retirement and driven out of England for good by the tax man.' Growing tired of their continued inane questions as to what Dennis was doing on Sark and what he was thinking, Wootton told them drily, 'Mr Price is decorating a friend's cottage and enjoying himself growing daffodils,' never dreaming they would actually quote him word for word the following day. Wootton later explained further:

> Dennis simply cannot afford to live in England any longer. The income tax man has driven him out. He was paying £50 a week in tax and suddenly the income tax man said it wasn't enough. They wanted his entire back taxes paid within seven days. It amounted to quite a few thousand pounds. He loves acting, he loves the stage, he loves television, but can't afford to live here anymore. I am afraid that the English public will be deprived of the face of Dennis Price in the future.

Many people would have been thrown into depression by such a sudden uprooting and move, but Dennis had an ability to adapt to any situation and soon felt at home in his new surroundings. The islanders took to him immediately with his friendly outgoing nature; he, in turn, liked them. They were at pains to point out to anyone who asked that they regarded him as 'just another of the residents' and not in any way special because he was famous.

All his trouble with the tax man had a familiar ring—it had only been twelve years since a similar chain of events had made him suicidal—but he had now taken an easier way out. By leaving the shores of mainland Britain, he annoyed a lot of people; he was accused of running away from his responsibilities and that he was a tax evader. In an interview years later, Dennis said:

> Those ridiculous reports written in the newspapers about my going to live on Sark. They suggested I was trying to avoid tax. Quite ridiculous, my dear and untrue. I am subject to tax as is any other British subject. I'd have gone to Switzerland like many others if I'd had other intentions.

It is common knowledge in the islands that when the Dame of Sark, Sybil Hathaway, heard of the substantial debts Dennis had amassed, she took a very dim view of the wayward actor's plans to live there; in fact, she ordered him to leave Sark unless he raised the money owing and paid the tax man. The prospect of being sent back to London worried Dennis, and he agreed to prioritise his debts as soon as possible. Though he was allowed to live on Sark, the Dame never warmed to him.

Dennis was taken ill on 18 April with suspected abdominal issues and was transported across to Guernsey for treatment at the Princess Elizabeth Hospital. It was thought he might be suffering from a common complaint known as 'Sark tummy', caused by the primitive water supply on the island, but it was in fact found to be his beloved Guinness—or rather too much of it—which had upset his system, and he needed to 'dry out' for a while. He was moved from the Princess Elizabeth to another hospital on Guernsey and by 1 May, he was transferred yet again to a nursing home in London, of all places, to continue his recovery there. His condition, Wootton reported, was 'very satisfactory' and he returned to the islands later in the month.

Dennis's arrival in the Channel Islands had aroused the interest of Edward Willis, the director of the Guernsey Repertory Company, a small group based at the Little Theatre made up of lesser-known actors and local talent. He had been planning their summer season and was keen to ask Dennis about starring in one of the productions, to bring in the crowds. The first move was to contact his lodgings and ask him, or rather his manager who was by then on Sark too, if he would be willing to take the leading part in their opening play, which was called *Not in the Book*.

Getting down to business, Wootton wanted to know how much he was going to pay Dennis; this was an embarrassing query as Mr Willis had not given the matter any thought. The usual fee he offered his leading actors was £20, but rarely having dealt with such a well-known star, he did not

One of the rare images of Dennis on stage in Guernsey, with Gerald Tarrant in the production *Not in the Book* (1966).

have an idea what to offer. 'Shall we start at £25?' he asked tentatively. Dennis agreed to his suggested terms and so began his association with the Guernsey rep.

Mary Mitchell, the company's leading actress for that season, was one of the first people to be told that Dennis was coming to join them. She announced the news enthusiastically from the stage to the audience the following week, but in her excitement, she got his name wrong. Dennis, however, who was sitting in the audience at the time, forgave her slip-up straight away.

Subsequently, for a week from 26 May, he appeared at the theatre in the leading role of Andrew Bennett in the rather obscure comedy by Arthur Watkyn, which was not quite to Dennis's liking—that is until he got into the part and gave it his professional touch; the house was packed for the whole run. Unfortunately, when word got around, the theatre was mobbed by national press reporters (William Hickey in particular), hounding Dennis for the low-down on his tax arrears. He absolutely refused to give an interview and asked they should be kept away from his dressing room. 'I'm here to do a play; if you wish to discuss the production or the company that's fine—but otherwise I'm not interested' was his brusque statement. To ensure the coast was clear at night, his fellow actors would take a look around, then let Dennis know when it was safe to leave the theatre.

Dennis's star status had made Willis hesitant to give him any direction while rehearsing for the play, but Dennis was quite the exception and had the same approach to his work as the others so was mildly annoyed when he realised this; he gave the director a ticking off. Dennis said, 'I'm an actor. Now look, if you're not going to direct me, then why are you here?'

The *Guernsey Evening Press* were particularly enthusiastic about the play and, in particular, Dennis: 'He brought to his part all the professionalism and polish which have earned him a deservedly high reputation. His every movement, his timing and the apparent ease with which he played the part were a rare pleasure.'

Dennis had no trace of 'star' behaviour and soon became one of the company. He was all too aware there was not a lot of room for 'side' in weekly repertory and just knuckled down to work with the others.

Following the success of *Not in the Book*, Willis asked Dennis if he would like to do another play, and suggested *Any Wednesday*, something he felt was bound to be a hit after its West End run. Dennis was pleased to accept, and they discussed the cast, along with a more realistic fee for Dennis, and settled on the third week in June for the run. The last performance actually fell on the eve of Dennis's fifty-first birthday and, as usual after the show, he went up to Willis's office for a Guinness. He

Dennis with Edward Willis, director of several plays at The Little Theatre, Guernsey, in which Dennis starred. 1966. (*Courtesy Edward Willis*)

was surprised they were the only two people present, as generally on last nights, the cast and crew would all assemble for a drink.

'It's my birthday tomorrow', Dennis said, thinking Willis did not know. At this point, a loud chorus of 'Happy Birthday' broke out and the rest of the cast appeared, to present him with an iced cake, with 'Happy Birthday, Dennis' on. Overwhelmed, Dennis fought back tears and was genuinely touched by their gesture and display of affection for him as a person, rather than a star. His warmth of character had certainly made him very popular with the company and more was to come when Willis led them all into the theatre, where a party had been arranged on stage. Dennis was 'weepy-eyed' when they gave him an engraved pewter tankard for his Guinness. A bottle of champagne was cracked and after he had sipped one glass, Dennis opted to drink his favourite brew from his new tankard. It was fairly late before they eventually made their way home.

The show had been widely praised, and the *Guernsey Evening Press* had much praise for Dennis:

> Dennis Price, in the role of John Cleeves, is, of course perfectly at home in a part he has played hundreds of times. It is good to watch him move,

> to hear him speak, and generally to see at work an actor of his calibre. Yet he does not overshadow the other performers ... all four play as a team and the result is very satisfying.

Dennis used to pop into the theatre quite often to see his friends and watch their other productions, and throughout July and August, he often treated members of the company to a social evening at his hotel, always insisting on paying for their drinks. He was often with them until the early hours and certainly enjoyed the companionship of people on his wavelength; they were not a bitchy group and one of the actresses actually said, 'If we heard any nasty gossip or spiteful talk about the other actors, we ignored it.'

Not long after the run of *Any Wednesday*, Dennis breezed into Edward Willis's office with a new one-act play, which had been written by Marcus Wootton. He asked Willis to read it. On taking a closer look, Willis realised it was a poor script with an unpleasing storyline and he was not at all keen on it. Titled *Why Don't You Bring Her Home?*, it is the story of a possessive father and the way he tries to keep a hold over his grown up son, becoming jealous when girlfriends threaten to take the boy away from home. When Willis had finished reading, Dennis asked for his opinion, but realising Dennis was very enthusiastic, Willis found it difficult to be honest and say he thought it was rubbish. At the same time as being diplomatic, he tried his utmost to persuade Dennis not to pursue it, and instead suggested a part that would be perfect was the school master in *The Browning Version*. Dennis declined and persisted with the Wootton play, saying he really wanted to do it. Realising a golden opportunity might slip away, Willis offered a compromise; he (grudgingly) agreed that he would put on *Why Don't You Bring Her Home?* as a curtain raiser, on condition that Dennis starred in *The Browning Version*. Dennis agreed and subsequently starred in both plays.

So pleased was Dennis that after the first rehearsal, when the cast and crew went out for lunch together, they found to their great surprise that Dennis had paid the bill discreetly without saying a word. It was his way of showing his appreciation for their support.

The company was divided into two to perform the plays, with a different set of actors in each but Dennis taking the lead in both. Wootton personally supervised the production of his 'little gem'. On the first night, the curtain lifted on Leon Shepherdson's son to Dennis's possessive father and the audience seemed to like it, but the undoubted highlight of the evening was Dennis's portrayal of the pompous school master in *The Browning Version*, opposite Mary Mitchell. Willis had fully expected him to be excellent in the part and was not disappointed when during that week (1–7 September), he gave, 'A most wonderful performance' in what the director considered—and he had directed quite a few in his time—the best production he had had the privilege of helming.

There was one scene in particular that made an impact on the audience; it was the point in the play when the boy Taplow (John Berryman) had just called his master 'Himmler of the lower 5th'; Dennis repeated those words in indignation, and had everyone in fits of laughter—not at all the desired effect—simply by the way he had delivered the line. He did not move a muscle and carried on. By the second time he had said it, there were a few giggles and by the third time he calmly said the words, there was absolute silence.

The *Guernsey Evening Press* was diplomatic in its review of Wootton's play, saying: 'Dennis Price had his part well under control ... and all four [cast] gave a very good interpretation of a rather unusual theme'. However, when it came to *The Browning Version*, the same reviewer was a little more enthused: 'All the hardness and bitterness of this [headmaster] character and the moment of emotion too, are very finely portrayed by Dennis Price in the role.' It was clear which was the favourite and in which Dennis gave the better performance.

Part of Dennis's calm and collected air was due to a strange ritual he performed, without fail, before going on stage each evening; he deliberately made himself sick through sheer nerves. He preferred to do so in his dressing room than risk any possible embarrassment in front of his public. He never drank alcohol on the day of a performance, but had a glass of glucose and lemon before each show, then every evening, he had a crate of Guinness delivered and relaxed with a Rothman's cigarette. To boost his confidence, Dennis kept three mascots in his dressing room—a pink elephant, an old pig and a white furry dog. Another 'lucky charm' was the gold signet ring on the small finger of his left hand, which he had worn on and off stage for the past thirty years or so. Latterly, he had acquired a second ring, which he wore on the third finger of his right hand. He was one of the few actors who did not wear any stage make-up and only used hair cologne.

Away from the theatre, he continued to be a very shy man who did not like to be recognised or praised for his work, being increasingly more modest about his achievements. That did not mean he was stand-offish to his public, far from it; he would talk about any subject with anyone and took pleasure in buying numerous rounds of drinks for his conversational companions to keep the chat flowing. When someone once told Dennis that he had 'neat hands', he replied, 'good for holding a glass'.

A member of the repertory company was Dee Macdonald, a professional actress who had been appearing in a show on Guernsey with Richard Murdoch, who often covered stints in the ticket office. It was there she encountered Marcus Wootton at close quarters. He went over to her one evening and said 'Order a minicab for me immediately'. Thinking he was rather sharp, she asked why he did not order it himself, whereupon he announced 'because I am Dennis Price's manager. I'm twenty-nine, a writer and I have been in a circus and I now manage Mr Price. I'm bored with Sark and want to go shooting, but I can't get a license in this Goddamn place', a statement that she found extraordinary, not to say perturbing. The taxi was duly ordered.

Another active member of the Little Theatre company was Joyce Cook MBE. She sat with Dennis on a panel to choose the winners of a talent competition, which after several weeks had reached the final stages. Dennis kept insisting they 'had trod the boards together', but she was equally sure they had not. Her uncanny resemblance to Dame Peggy Ashcroft (with whom he had appeared in *Richard II* many years before) was said to blame.

Being comprised of people much younger than Dennis, the theatre company always thought he looked very old for a man of fifty-one. He certainly was old beyond his years, moved very slowly, and occasionally

Dee MacDonald-Harris, actress and friend of Dennis.

stooped over, cutting a sad and lonely figure walking the streets of Guernsey on his own. Happily though, the five months they spent in each other's company was a joyous period for all concerned and they were like one big family.

During the same summer theatre season, Dennis also gave a recital in Guernsey's smallest private theatre (a converted barn) of poems written by the ever-versatile Marcus Wootton. It was in aid of the Flying Christine boat fund, a worthwhile cause as the people of Sark badly needed a special boat to take their sick and injured to the Princess Elizabeth, Guernsey's chief hospital. It was ironic to think that in just a few years, it would be carrying Dennis on what was to be his final journey. The poetry event was attended with great interest by his friends from the theatre, who sat through forty minutes of verse before dutifully applauding. Later, Dennis went to Jersey, Alderney, and Sark to give similar poetry recitals, always in aid of charitable causes. At the end of the recital, many attendees were lost for words when asked 'What did you think of that?'

'Well, Dennis read it very nicely' was the best reply offered.

The promoter of the first event, in the converted barn, was the author of the book *Parkinson's Law*. Afterwards, he and his wife held a little reception at their home where Mrs Parkinson, intrigued by Wootton's appearance, asked him 'Why do you wear your hair so long?'

Wootton snapped, 'You don't like me, do you?' They joined the ranks of many of Dennis's other friends who disliked Wootton and his work, but in large bit their tongues, preferring to talk behind his back. Wootton always appeared surly and wasn't a person you could get close to; he kept his distance from everyone.

Anytime Dennis happened to be visiting Guernsey, he would always stay at The Mayfair Hotel in Hauteville, St Peter Port. He liked it so much that he stayed there from May right through to September while appearing at the Little Theatre. The proprietors, Mr and Mrs Jack Drabble, became friends and described how on many occasions, Dennis enjoyed an evening there with a group of friends from the theatre company, and had them all highly amused by doing imitations of Frankie Howerd and telling stories about his time with Noël Coward. All his stories were usually jolly ones apart from when he recalled the film *That Lady* as he reserved particular scorn for Olivia de Havilland, describing her as 'the lady with the tantrums' and 'hard to work with'. He reserved most scorn and bitter feelings towards the Germans; when he was asked to explain why he disliked Germans so much, he looked at the nails on his fingers and quipped, 'Yes, they've grown again'.

Mr Drabble recalled the type of friendly exchange he enjoyed with Dennis:

'Oi,' Drabble would say.

'Oi,' Dennis called back.

'Come for a coffee, Mr. Price?'

'Call me Dennis, that's the name on my passport.'

'Ok, Dennis,' said Drabble, 'coffee?'

'I loathe the stuff! It's time for my cot, so goodnight' and with that Dennis went upstairs.

When dining out, The Absolute End seafood restaurant at Longstore, St Peter Port, was a must for Dennis. He had a friendly relationship with the owners, Clive and Gwen Wales. Although he was a regular visitor, he did not eat a great deal, instead picking at bits and pieces. He always drank stout while ordering champagne for his friends. Once, he took some actors from the company out for a meal at the fish restaurant and the waiters treated them like royalty; despite Dennis ordering all sorts of food for himself, he did not touch a morsel.

Clive and Gwen Wales frequently went over to Sark with Dennis, taking him across in their boat, which had an irritating knack of cutting out. When they arrived, he would entertain them at his lodgings and they were usually very merry by the end of the evening. He was fond of taking snapshots of his guests, though he was admittedly hopeless at photography, with his favourite camera, an old fashioned 'box brownie', as he refused to use what he called a 'newfangled job'. His consideration and kindness certainly made him popular with people on Guernsey and Sark alike.

On the last night of *The Browning Version*, the company gave a farewell party for Dennis, and sadly, this particular production was to mark the end of his stage career. He continued to occasionally perform in Wootton's plays at private parties for charity, but was not cast again in a professional production.

Dennis made just one film that year, *Jules Verne's Rocket to the Moon* from a story by Peter Welbeck (the writing pseudonym of producer Harry Alan Towers). It was said to be inspired by Verne's books and was a comical send-up of the pioneers of long ago. Dennis had a starring role as The Duke of Barset, described as 'a patron of the arts, a peer of the realm and a trifle dim', but among the other eccentrics, it was hard to tell the difference. Several unlikely actors were originally considered for the leads in this comedy and William Mervyn was all set to play Barset until he fell out with the producer. Had Dennis known, he would have been quite upset as he thought he was first choice, though sadly at this latter stage in his career, he was often viewed as a good standby when prominent actors turned down a film or wanted too much money. Knowing he could not afford to be too choosy, producers often had Dennis at an advantage. The

With old friend Terry-Thomas in *Rocket to the Moon*, filmed in the land of the 'Liffey water'.

film was actually very comical and provided a happy occasion for Dennis to team up with Burl Ives, Gert Fröbe, Terry-Thomas, and Lionel Jeffries. Shooting began on 21 September and finished five weeks later on location in County Wicklow, Ireland, where Dennis made the local press when a photograph of him welcoming his daughter Susan on set appeared.

Within a month, Dennis had pretty much frittered away the money he had earned from the film on fancy drinks parties and gambling, mostly at cards. Six months later, on 5 May 1967, his partying and gambling lifestyle caught up with him when the Inland Revenue petitioned for a receiving order against him in chambers at the London bankruptcy court.

Dennis was not present for the creditors meeting on 25 May, but during the discussion, his earnings were disclosed by the assistant official receiver; the full amount he owed in tax was revealed and also how he had spent his cash over the past decade. Dennis had confessed that for years, he had let his substantial income as a movie star slip through his fingers. On 4 July, he had the wearisome task of travelling to London for public examination at the bankruptcy court where he admitted that he owed the Inland Revenue the staggering sum of £10,452, plus £250 to his accountant; 'this disgraceful debt I have incurred' he said. His only assets, shown in a statement of affairs, were given as £500 held by his agents, which were

After a string of cameo roles, it was good to see Dennis playing a leading part in *Rocket to the Moon*.

fees for his old films, recently shown on television. Far from suggesting the money should go to the tax man, Dennis said he was hopeful that some of the money could be given to him for personal expenses.

When questioned by the official receiver, Dennis tried to explain his long history of struggling with tax demands and how the money was spent. Since his film career began in 1943 up to 1955, he had been earning around £5,000 a year, and during that time had lost up to £100 a week on gambling, but in the years following 1954, he had released £17,200 tax arrears together with paying his current tax debt.

Then from 1955 to 1966, his average income increased to £10,000 a year, and he admitted about a third of which was spent on gambling at race courses, casinos, and card games; as a result, he had not put by sufficient money to pay off his tax. Added to the money he had lost to the betting shops, he had spent a vast sum entertaining his friends (and hangers on). He told the court his annual wines and spirits bill was about £1,000. Since January 1965, he had received £17,000 in annual income, the bulk going on 'very, very extravagant living and most inadequate gambling.' That statement undoubtedly won him little sympathy with the tax authorities. They asked how he would pay his debt.

Dennis told the official receiver that he would start to make good the money he owed his creditors as soon as he received fees for playing Jeeves in a new TV series. Mr Registrar Parbury ordered Dennis to prepare an account to show how he had spent his earnings between April 1965 and 1967, to be ready for his examination, and adjourned until 24 October.

No sooner had Dennis returned to Sark than he was flying back to London again in August to start working on his third and last series of *The World of Wooster*. On arriving at Heathrow, he was immediately pestered by reporters asking him to give a statement on his tax trouble. Dennis replied politely, 'I don't wish to be rude, but I have absolutely nothing to say'. When they went on to ask if he planned to go back to Sark in the near future, he said, 'Not in the slightest.' The baggage handlers were complimentary about his portrayal of Jeeves, and for transporting his two suitcases to a waiting car, Dennis gave one of them a generous £1 tip.

Dennis was reportedly rather subdued on the set, but he kept his problems quiet. In truth, Dennis found the whole tax situation very embarrassing and after already trying to reason with journalists his sudden move had nothing to do with tax evasion but a desire for a change of scene, they were after him again, never giving him a moment's rest. It was a trying, sensitive time for him and he appreciated those who did not discuss the subject of tax with him.

While making the series during September, his eldest daughter Susan married Thomas H. Mapp, a divorcé, in a London registry office. The first Dennis heard of it was when he was sitting in the bar of the Whitehouse Hotel near Regent's Park. Susan swept in and proudly announced, 'Daddy, I've just married Tom' and he almost choked on his Guinness. The name Tom had haunted Dennis since childhood, with his grandfather, father, nephew, cousin, and one son-in-law (Hugh Thomas Burnett) all bearing it, so he was not overjoyed to hear another one was going to join the fold.

Dennis always stayed at the Whitehouse Hotel while doing *The World of Wooster* and kept his trusted manager Marcus Wootton with him at all times, in case the press got too inquisitive.

In October, Dennis returned to court for his adjourned public examination when he agreed that, in the two years, from April 1965 to May 1967, he had spent £18,588. Yet he also pointed out he had recently paid the Inland Revenue more than £3,000. The official receiver demanded to know the names and addresses of people to whom he had lost £8,200 within the past couple of years, gambling, but Dennis replied, several times, that he could not give this information.

'Do you understand it is a criminal offence not to make a full disclosure of your assets?' asked the receiver.

Dennis replied softly, 'Yes, I know that'.

'Cannot you produce any confirmation at all?'

'I don't know exactly at which betting shop, which racecourse or which card table I lost it,' said Dennis.

'You have no friends who will come along and tell the official receiver in confidence that they have seen you lose these large sums of money?'

'I don't think so,' he replied, and went on to say the cause of his failing to pay his taxes was 'I'm afraid, extravagance.' On this note, the hearing was wrapped up.

It was going to take Dennis years to pay all the money he owed, and with Jeeves behind him, he needed to find a new source of income in a hurry, but where was his next work coming from? Would he continue to get good parts or would he have to look further afield? He returned to Sark and waited for the offers to come in while downing his favourite Guinness. Despite his debts, his 'extravagance' continued unabated and amid an island population renowned for its drinkers, it was unlikely he would be encouraged to stop.

15

Life on Sark (1966–1973)

Sark held and still holds a great attraction for many people, not least Dennis Price, because of its tranquillity and picturesque scenery, and apart from cycling, the only other method of travel is by horse-drawn carriage, as cars are banned. Yet walkers have to look out for the farm tractors that regularly pass, raising clouds of dust, and though farming is the main industry, their chief source of income is now tourism. Numerous hotels and guest houses around Sark provide very comfortable lodgings for visitors from March to October though, unlike the other Channel Islands, it is devoid of any night life apart from bars.

In the years that Dennis lived on the island, the 493-strong community were ruled over by the Lady of the Manor, Dame Sybil Hathaway (a direct descendant of a successful pirate), famous for her autocratic manner. Then in her eighties, the Dame had the first vote in Sark's parliament and Chief Pleas on any local decisions, one being there should be no unemployment benefit or pension allowance, though that was offset by very low taxes, meaning anyone living there kept virtually all their income for themselves.

Docking on Sark is at the foot of Harbour Hill, a steep incline between the harbours of Creux and Maseline and the shopping village, which is the hub of the island. Ferry passengers and their luggage are transported by open-sided, ramshackle buses pulled by tractors up the hill, which itself is half a mile long with an incline of 300 feet at the top. This journey over the rough track is bumpy, though the natural wooded slopes either side of it are a mass of bluebells in springtime, making it a very picturesque landing point, and certainly help give the first impression of the island as being an old-fashioned, unspoilt community, with clean, fresh air and lovely views—as England used to be.

For Dennis, the peaceful atmosphere and friendly attitudes made a refreshing change from his life in London, which seemed to be under increasing scrutiny of late. It was seldom he was ever troubled by inquiring minds or reporters on Sark. His favourite pastimes included sampling much of what the local bars had to offer and strolling down the long, winding lanes to the sea, or sometimes taking a short cut over the fields from one pub to another. Having lived for most of his life in and around London, Sark must have been a startling contrast, yet from the moment he arrived, he became very much attached to the place. Of course, some people suggested the island proved an attraction to Dennis solely because it was free from the tax laws of the mainland, and while that undoubtedly contributed to his swift relocation, he again explained if tax had been his only motivation, he could have chosen more exciting countries in Europe such as snow-capped tax haven of Switzerland, the shady Monaco, or lovely Lichtenstein, all of which had much more happening than sleepy Sark.

Dennis was a friendly, outgoing person who liked to mingle in a crowd and join in the conversation when invited; that continued apace in Sark, and when the occasional visitor would ask for his autograph, he was always pleased to oblige, often adding a lengthy and amusing message while chatting away like an old friend. Anyone who chatted with him would say he rarely ever mentioned acting or talked about himself, much preferring to tell jokes or discuss news in general instead.

The pubs on Sark opened at 8 a.m. and stayed open all day, so it was not unknown for some of the regulars to become a little animated and argumentative, but Dennis was a gentle and good-natured man who did not approve of brawls, so he avoided getting involved in any heated debates that flared up by moving on to the next hostelry.

Whatever the day or time, locals always said Dennis's dress was immaculate. He wore a blazer in the summer and in the winter months, he chose a Guernsey sweater with casual slacks, always with a tie or silk scarf tucked into his shirt. Never was he seen to be bare chested, unlike Marcus Wootton who often went without a shirt in the long hot days of summer. In fact, Dennis continued to dress elegantly until the last couple of years of his life, when his year-round look became more of a casual one. However, whenever he was needed for work—he did a lot of advertisements across the water in neighbouring Guernsey—he would transform himself instantly into the perfectly attired gentleman again. Marcus Wootton said of Dennis's latter years' change in dress code, 'His family couldn't be bothered to come over to Sark and visit him, so he wore an old pullover, but if he dressed up and took them to dinner at the Ritz, the daughters were all for it.'

Dennis was not new to Sark as he had spent several holidays on the island and stayed at different hotels (notably Stocks and Dixcart), though this time, Dennis moved into the bungalow Marcus Wootton had rented, but as soon as Wootton followed him over a short time afterwards, Dennis moved into the hotel Aval du Creux at the top of Harbour Hill, which was noted for its excellent cuisine and in particular its dressed lobster. Dennis loved seafood, even more so when it was freshly caught by the local fishermen.

In those days, the hotel was run by Peter and Nita Hauler, who got to know Dennis quite well during his time there, as did most of the staff; there was certainly no scope for much privacy in tiny Sark and Dennis's daily habits soon became noted. For instance, he invariably slept in room five as he liked a double bed; he was very fond of cheesecake, but no ordinary brand would do; whenever he went to the mainland, he would take the opportunity to bring back a supply from Fortnum and Mason's—'the only place for a gentleman to shop'. Each morning, before breakfast, he would have a crate of Guinness sent up to his room and referred to it as 'Liffey water', after the river in Ireland, an expression he'd picked up while making *Jules Verne's Rocket to the Moon*. He liked to mix his Guinness with champagne to produce 'Black Velvet'—his absolute favourite drink—or else he would have a 'gin and it' in the hotel bar. Whenever Dennis received a script and wanted to know how he might appear in the part, he liked to test it out on the locals in the hotel. He only needed to read a script once to memorise it, and would then walk around performing the part to his gathered audience.

At times, he was known to be wistful over his days as a Rank star, perhaps frustrated by the type of roles he was being offered versus the ones he relished playing. One thing was made quite clear—Dennis did not like the new trend for films with either sex or shocking scenes and he was never happier than when playing in a good family comedy.

When the Sark hotel closed for the winter months, Dennis rented one of the five self-catering chalets owned by the Bel Air Tavern, his, being the only one with a veranda, was called 'Petit Friponnerie'. It was there he was suddenly taken ill with liver problems and spent the best part of six weeks resting in bed, helped to recovery by Mrs Edie Hamon, a member of the family who ran the Bel Air, who had taken a shine to Dennis after first becoming acquainted with him at the pub; having grown used to his sense of fun, she did not mind him pulling her leg when she dropped by to cook him a meal. She soon discovered that making a pie or large meal for him was a waste of time as although he always appreciated good food, he only ate the smallest of portions and often only managed a bowl of soup. Dennis affectionately called Edie 'The Arch Duchess' for reasons unknown, and later thought up different nicknames to suit all his local pals. Conversely, a woman fan from the mainland once referred to him as

'Lord Byron' and the nickname stuck, so he signed himself as the poet on his Christmas cards.

Everything about Dennis was well-mannered, which endeared him greatly to islanders. This included the elegant way he held his cigarette, giving the occasional flick of the wrist to dispel the ash, to his cheery nature and his witty exchanges, such as with the manager of the local branch of Midland Bank Mike Terry to whom, whenever Dennis saw him in the street, he would call out 'Morning, Michael—are you going to open your little shop today?'

Moving between the various watering holes, islanders often saw Dennis toting an airline bag with his personal supply of bottled Guinness chinking away inside. There were always half a dozen bottles; 'That's as much as I can carry' he used to say. It was known as his 'blue bag'. He certainly never went thirsty.

Marcus Wootton remained the complete opposite of Dennis and caused quite a sensation with the locals when he first arrived, walking around in the summer months with just a pair of shorts; in a belt around his waist, he kept a 12-inch bowie knife, which he was fond of throwing like a dart. Once, in The Mermaid Tavern, he pulled this knife on the lighthouse keeper who, presuming he was going to cut him, landed Wootton a blow that sent him across the room. Wootton said he carried the knife because he had worked as a knife thrower in a circus before becoming Dennis's manager, and that he and Dennis would put tin cans up on a ledge to throw knives at. Though Wootton was also fond of guns and told the islanders larger than life stories about supposed escapades involving him as a sharpshooter, his knife-wielding bravado and colourful bragging only served to rub people up the wrong way. He had a strange, very quirky nature and was extremely touchy, so much so that holding a conversation with him was like walking a tightrope—one false move and you'd fall from grace. If anyone asked him a direct question about himself, he would glare and snap 'That's none of your damned business!' or words to that effect, though Dennis did not tolerate language in front of ladies. The few who got on with him usually only did so because 'he was Dennis's friend'. Without even trying, Wootton soon made himself *persona non grata* on both sides of the Channel.

Wootton had long nursed his own interests as an aspiring playwright and poet and would have surely excelled in fantasy writing. By this point, he was married to a girl named Judith, nicknamed 'Kitten' because of her love of cats, and with her, Wootton produced three children; however, tragedy befell them when one of their sons, Andrew, died as a baby. Dennis was very fond of Wootton's two surviving children and being around them was a small compensation for his own grandchildren being far away on the mainland. By 1973, Dennis in fact had six grandchildren, balanced neatly between three boys and three girls. Tessa, the first to marry, produced Lucy, Emily, and Rupert while Susan had Stephen, Peter, and Kat. He saw little of his daughters and even less of his grandchildren.

When Wootton's marriage to Judith later turned sour and followed in divorce, he married the local school teacher Jenny who he had met during her time doing Dennis's typing. It did not surprise anyone when 'Kitten' Wootton left her husband and he found little sympathy among the islanders; he had gained nothing by riling the locals and once, when Wootton was totally inebriated, he wandered into a field near the Bel Air and shouted for someone to come and 'help'; nobody did.

Journalists continued to probe as to why on earth Dennis chose to live on Sark. What did a man with a taste for the finer things do all day for amusement? In reply, he said in an interview for Hammer Films:

> People always get the impression that life is so very different. I do what anyone else does when at home. The family [his daughter Susan was the only one to visit Sark] come over to stay, I play some golf, go to the pub and watch television. It doesn't seem strange that we have no cars on the island. You just get the buggy to the wharf to handle your baggage, otherwise you walk. Very pleasant, but not so different from life in any other part of the country.

Dennis became an unofficial ambassador for Sark, telling everyone how much he enjoyed the place. He was also the island's biggest attraction, with holidaymakers and visitors returning time and time again as the prospect of seeing him and hearing his showbiz stories was just too good to miss. He was funnier than a lot of stand-up comedians, and there seemed to be no end to his resources; when he was not joking, he was doing impersonations. Dennis was one of the few big names to land on Sark and the locals made the best of it; he was always good fun at a party and was the 'must invite' person to ensure a gathering went off with a swing. Other celebrities visited Sark from time to time, including Molly Weir and Alec Guinness, but Dennis was the only actor to ever reside there. The poet Marcus Conig was a regular visitor, being a close mate of Dennis's, and whenever Conig went over with his girlfriend, the radio actress Mary Wimbush, they always had a ball, drinking champagne and Guinness, and playing snooker.

Over seven years, the locals built up quite a picture of Dennis's life through their conversations, yet never knew him intimately. Charles Falle, a member of an old Sark family who owned the tractor buses that went up Harbour Hill, knew Dennis since the day he first arrived for a holiday and took rooms at Stocks Hotel. At the hotel, Dennis stayed with Charlie's family (his mother-in-law ran it then) and became a friend. Dennis was also a friend of Charlie's cousin, Regina, who some of the locals unkindly referred to as 'vagina', and the three often spent a leisurely afternoon together. It was while Dennis was staying at Stocks that his daughter Susan came over for a few days. She was then a student at Oxford and a cub reporter for *The Oxford Mill.*

Far away from his family and without any firm guidance, Dennis often drank far more than was good for him, so he made frequent use of Charlie's carriages—the next best thing to a taxi service. One night, Dennis and Wootton were drinking in the bar of Stock's Hotel and ordered a carriage to come and collect him and take him back to his home as his legs were not very strong. As it grew later and later, and the carriage had not arrived, Dennis phoned the office to ask what had happened only to discover that they were still out in the fields trying to catch the horse.

Dennis was also a friend of James Le Feuvre, who worked down at the harbour. They, and some others, often got together to have a drink and rib one another. The young chambermaid who had just been tidying Dennis's hotel room, asked James indignantly: 'Do you know this man Price?'

'Do you mean Dennis Price, film star?'

She said, 'Yes, and do you know what I found under his bed? I was hoovering underneath and hit this chest—I thought it was a dead body! It turned out to be a case of Guinness, about twenty-four bottles, with empties decorating the room.'

Following Dennis's bankruptcy hearing, when his life was returning to order again, he moved into his own house, Le Clos du Vivier (French for the enclosed fishpond) near the old mill. With six bedrooms, it was really too big for a man on his own, so Dennis invited Wootton and his new wife Jenny to come and live upstairs while he occupied the ground floor rooms and was catered for by his housekeeper. Sometimes, when Dennis was not feeling 100 per cent, Mrs Wootton popped down to look after him, but other than that, Dennis and Marcus Wootton lived fairly separately to one another.

When James Le Feuvre and his friends were in a field adjacent to Le Clos du Vivier digging potatoes, Dennis called out 'Come and have a drink, boys'. They drank whiskey all night long and through into the next day and got so merry that the boys all fell down on the veranda. Just behind the left side of the house was a well, which Dennis happened to look down one day and complained 'Bloody thing is full of cans and bottles!' After their all-night get-together, they all ended up in the Bel Air, where a couple from the mainland cornered Dennis and asked him which number bus would take them to Little Sark. He told them 'The number thirteen', later saying to James 'Good God! I hope those idiots don't come in here again!'

He did not suffer fools gladly and often had a good rejoinder. Failing that, he would just walk away as was the case when another tourist, a woman visitor to the pub, had such a high opinion of herself as an entertainer that she was quite immune to Dennis's suggestions she was boring. He carefully chose the right moment in which to slip away quietly.

Having spoken to numerous people and regular visitors to Sark who knew Dennis, there is no evidence to suggest he ever had any romantic ties during his years there. His excessive drinking probably was not conducive to establishing a relationship, though Dennis enjoyed some close (platonic) friendships with the opposite sex and, despite his aged appearance, was still considered to be a very attractive and desirable man. He would have had no shortage of takers if he had wanted to take a wife, but his bitter experiences with Joan had forever put him off marriage. As Wootton phrased it, 'He was a case of once bitten, twice shy'.

Dennis only spent part of the year on Sark; the other time, he was usually away working, particularly in Spain and Istanbul when he was under contract to do a series of films for Jesus Franco, the Spanish director of sex-horror pictures. When he was not filming, to avoid boredom, he often spent a lot of time writing to all the friends and fans he had met, like London train driver Peter Green:

> I had the pleasure of being a friend of Dennis Price during the last five years of his life and was one of the few people to see him alive the Saturday prior to his death. My friendship stemmed from the time I decided to stay on Sark and booked into the hotel Petit Champ. It was a very posh place indeed and not the sort of hotel I was used to. It was situated just down the lane from Dennis's house, Le Clos du Vivier.
>
> Then I found out the hotel to stay was Stock's, where anything goes and where I'd be in good drinking company; and that included Dennis. One afternoon, Dennis invited my friend Les and me to his house. Stills from all his films covered the walls and photographs of his actor friends were all over the place. It was a beautiful house with a view of the sea from the bottom of his back garden. Dennis drank Guinness and smoked menthol cigarettes and the only alternative drink he could offer us was Scotch. We were all gradually getting drunk, then Les knocked his Guinness over Dennis's script for *The Horror of Frankenstein*; he was hugely embarrassed and full of apologies, but Dennis just said 'Don't worry, dear boy, have another Guinness. I know the script off by heart and it's a rubbishy part anyway, but it will help pay the bills.'
>
> When we finally left his house to go back to the hotel where we were staying, we were both so drunk, we nearly fell into the fish pond in the front garden.

> I wrote to the Guinness brewery at Park Royal and told them of Dennis's love of their drink and that he never drank anything else. Back to me came a large packet with all sorts of Guinness items and a letter from the secretary who was also an admirer of his. I parcelled them up and sent them to Dennis who was thrilled.
>
> When I last visited the island in September 1973, Dennis was in hospital on Guernsey, so naturally we missed him on the island and the place wasn't the same without him. On the Saturday I left for Guernsey to get my plane home, I had about four hours to kill and fortunately a Guernsey couple drove me to The Princess Elizabeth Hospital where I visited Dennis in the ward and told him how much we had missed him on Sark. He certainly looked very ill though. When we left, we turned and waved to him and he called, 'Don't worry, dear boys, I'll soon be back in action.' That was the last I ever saw of him, the end of a really wonderful friendship. He truly was a gentleman.

Dennis spent much of the winter months at home in his bedroom, where he stored his Guinness, and used it like a living room. On entering the room, his visitors were at first surprised to find he had a large collection of cuddly, soft toys of all types and sizes adorning the mantelpiece and the shelves. They were mascots from his many fans, wishing him good luck. He always treasured his gifts and would not have dreamed of discarding any; to him, they represented the affection his admirers had shown for him over the years. Among the toys, photos, and beer bottles, a notable feature of Dennis's bedroom was a rope that ran from the door to his bed. At first, its purpose escaped the visitors, until Dennis explained he used it to guide himself into bed at night, in case he stumbled on the bottles and did himself an injury. As the island was without street lamps, nights were particularly dark and when the moon was obscured by clouds, you could not even see your feet. When Dennis was between the pub and his front door, he was particularly vulnerable and almost helpless in an intoxicated state, and in time, it became a nightly ritual for someone to assist him, as Heather Laughton recalls:

> In 1971, I spent a holiday on Sark. Walking into a pub one evening, I found Dennis Price flowing bonelessly over a chair, with a permanently benign smile sliding down his chin. There are many pubs on Sark and the locals told me that on the dot in the mornings he would be waiting for one to open and would then gently progress through most of them until closing time, when in turn someone would help him home. It fell to me to be the helper that evening and under a beautiful starry night, he clasped my hand, and, elbow to elbow and leaning only a little, managed

> the journey to his front door. He was very courtly—just like his screen image so often—and his 'Thank you, my dear' was delivered with great dignity.

His whole home smacked of cosiness and comfort though the house was very cluttered. Dennis never was tidy, and the empties stayed where they rested until his housekeeper came in to clear them; tidying up had never concerned him. Marcus Wootton on the other hand was quite the opposite and had no such place for mementos or photographs; he said he had a Peter Pan approach to life and liked to look only to the future so did not keep any photos, not even of Dennis. In the years to come, he found even the memories irritating, so he pushed them to the back of his mind. In truth, the past only reminded him of his advancing years.

People seeing Dennis staggering around and walking in an odd, awkward fashion naturally assumed he was drunk. They were not always correct in their assumptions as for a number of years, he had been suffering from a painful bone disease (*pyelonethritis osteomalacia*), which makes bones brittle and joints stiff; it is caused by a lack of nutrients, resulting from a poor diet, so getting around by foot was not always easy nor well-coordinated.

However, illness aside, Dennis's drinking habit was no frivolous matter, as the older he became, the more he succumbed to the effects of alcohol. With his steadily ailing health, it was quite amazing how he managed to stay articulate and on his legs all day. His drinking also often gave people the impression that he was a tragic man, attempting to drown out some great sorrow in his past life. The fact he was on his own and in the declining years of his career encouraged the theory.

It is hard to believe that Sark in the Swinging Sixties was still a very primitive place, which had advanced very little since the Victorian era in more ways than just the architecture. Most buildings, outside of the hotels and La Seigneurie (the Dame's home), were wooden or corrugated shacks. At one time, they had thatched roofs, but the locals seemed more inclined to replace them with tin rather than pay a thatcher to come over. The majority of islanders did not have a bathroom or any proper washing facilities, and made do with old-fashioned washtubs and pitchers; though if other islanders were content to go without the basic luxuries, Dennis was not. One of the first things he did when he moved into Le Clos du Vivier was to have his own bath installed, and the 'event' was talked about for years to come, as everyone went around to his house to see the new wonder of Sark. On one occasion, Dennis, while drinking in the Barn Bar, learned that some friends of his who were staying there had not had a proper bath, so he let them use his whenever they needed, as he did with some of the locals. Sark has since caught up with the times but even so, some people have never forgotten Dennis's gesture; few can say they used a famous actor's bath.

Dennis's favourite walk on Sark was along the path leading to the Pilcher Monument, on the cliffs above the fishermen's harbour, Havre Gosselin—the stone memorial commemorating those lost at sea. Across a cascade of wild flowers and a clear blue sea can be seen marvellous views of four other Channel Islands, the furthest being Guernsey and the area of coast around St Peter Port, to the left is Herm and Jethou (both once privately owned by the writer, Compton Mackenzie) and the nearest island is the privately owned isle of Brecqhou. One rocky end of Brecqhou juts out into the sea like a crocodile's head, with bulging eyes and snout. In the summertime, Dennis occasionally enjoyed taking a swim in the safe waters of Dixcart Bay, a nice secluded spot separated from the rest of the coastline by a natural arch of rock where he could go to unwind. Places like this appealed to his need for privacy; when exposing himself to the elements, he needed all the self-confidence he could get. He became keen on amateur photography, having previously decried new-fangled cameras, and had piles of snaps he had taken around the island. Since developing bone trouble in his legs, walking had taken the place of more vigorous activities, like horse riding. As a rule, first thing in the morning, he would take a leisurely walk around the island with his camera, pausing occasionally to take snaps of the countryside and people. One of the features of Sark was an incredibly long washing line of up to 100 yards, which belonged to the DeCarteret family, who helped in the running of the Beau Regard Hotel. Dennis was out walking early one morning, taking photos, when he came across Sybil DeCarteret hanging out clothes—some thirty-four pairs of knickers, to be precise. She found his sudden presence off-putting as she was busy and waved him on, but he would not go and followed her all along the line, exclaiming, 'My God, you wear some knickers!'

At home, Dennis relaxed by reading a book in bed, his favourite subject being biographies, and playing cards with a group of friends, but he never played for money with them; only Marcus Wootton was the exception and they regularly had a wager together. Being a poor gambler, Dennis lost a lot of money and his manager eventually refused to play with him because Dennis had put him in such an awkward position—if he went on taking Dennis's money, he would be accused of sponging off him and if he let him win, Dennis would leave Wootton without any wages.

There were times when living on an island made for problems when it came to travel, as Sark has no airport, and the only means of getting to the nearest airport (which is on Guernsey) is by boat though the unpredictable currents in the channel; an engine breakdown sometimes prevented

Dennis on Sark, awaiting the boat to Guernsey. (*Courtesy Lynn Bragg*)

crossings at the scheduled times. Once, Dennis needed to catch the ferry for a flight when he agreed to make a television commercial with actor Peter Jones for an Italian company.They had been asked to repeat their highly amusing double act as the crooked car salesmen from *School for Scoundrels*, but it was never filmed as Dennis missed the ferry and arrived too late for the shoot. The opportunity was lost.

A very pleasant moment for Dennis was meeting up with his old friend and Radley master, Charles Wrinch, who was living in retirement on Guernsey by that time. Since finding fame in the 1940s, Dennis had been so busy that he had lost touch with the Wrinches, so they had a lot to catch up on when they chatted over a drink together at the Barn Bar. Dennis was subsequently invited back to their Guernsey home when he next visited the island, but when Wrinch produced some bottles of stout as a treat, Dennis declined and produced his 'Blue bag', to the amusement of his host.

Of course, when he performed at The Little Theatre on Guernsey, his tutor and wife were there to enjoy the plays. It was an especially memorable and nostalgic evening for Barbara Wrinch since she had acted herself with Dennis some thirty years earlier during their college days, playing Nerissa to his Gratiano in *The Merchant of Venice*. The physical contrast between the young and older Dennis may not have seemed very remarkable to people who had watched his films year by year, but friends such as the Wrinches who had not seen him in ages could not help thinking how old and tired he looked. It was a marvel he kept going so long since he lived mainly on Complan, which led to a marked loss in weight at one stage. 'If he turned sideways, he'd disappear' said Wootton. Dennis had a long-held suspicion that his health was getting worse and often talked to Wootton as if he was going to die the next day.

On two occasions during his Sark years, Dennis was asked to be a guest on *The Golden Shot*, the quiz and archery game show hosted by Bob Monkhouse. Dennis reckoned 'it was a real fiddle' but was nevertheless grateful for the fee. Wootton next arranged for Dennis to appear on a TV chat show, but he had to really talk him into it, and even then, he did it very reluctantly. Dennis objected to being interviewed because of the probing questions interviewers asked about sensitive subjects like his divorce, bankruptcy, and attempted suicide—they were definitely taboo. Live TV also worried Dennis as the camera work was so intense and the many close-ups were unforgiving; it became harder for him to conceal his emotions. Dennis believed a person's eyes were the window to their soul, which can be a disadvantage to an actor. He said it was the reason he admired actress Sylvia Syms a great deal; 'her eyes never gave her away'.

Dennis remains an institution on Sark, an integral part of their history; he certainly did all he could to enliven the place. A lot of the friends he made among the visitors admitted that without his presence, they would not have visited the island; people who knew him realised just how much he had added when they returned in later years to try and recreate that fun atmosphere they experienced, but it was not there. Dennis has left a gap that has never been filled. Consequently, without him, Sark life returned to being pretty dull.

16

The Horror of It All (1968–1973)

To everyone's surprise—not least his own—Dennis embarked on a series of horror films in which he suffered all manner of nasty ends. He gained two contracts, the first with Hammer Films, the second with Spanish director and writer Jesus Franco and his producer Harry Alan Towers.

In a way, he was pleased to be in so much demand, and his grateful employers used his name to beef up their humble productions. Despite making thirteen horror features between 1965 and 1973, Dennis was never regarded as a 'horror star' like Vincent Price or Christopher Lee; nevertheless, it was the genre that made Dennis his living towards the end of his life.

In 1968, Dennis filmed *The Haunted House of Horror*, a blood-curdling thriller involving a group of trendy youngsters who explore an old house only to have a madman hack one of them to death. The film contained some exciting scenes, but Dennis had the very flat and uninteresting role of a police inspector called in to investigate the victim's disappearance. Anyone could have played the part, but he was the crowd-puller, the biggest name on the bill, which comprised rising actors and two pop stars—Frankie Avalon and Mark Wynter. Wynter recalls:

> Sorry to say I never met Dennis or heard anything about him. As filming goes, one often never meets fellow actors; shooting out of sequence often precludes this. I was not enamoured of the finished product—and said so, rather politely, but I gather it has a cult status of sorts. I remember a critic said 'Mark Wynter died wonderfully'.

It has not been as enduring as other thrillers of the time because it involved characters that were quickly dated as fashions changed.

Soon though, Dennis was given one of the lead roles in the low budget brainchild of producer Harry Alan Towers, well known for his cheaply

Left: The Horror of it All was one of Dennis's first forays into the horror genre; he is pictured here with Pat Boone.

Below: Dennis was heavily disguised for part of his role.

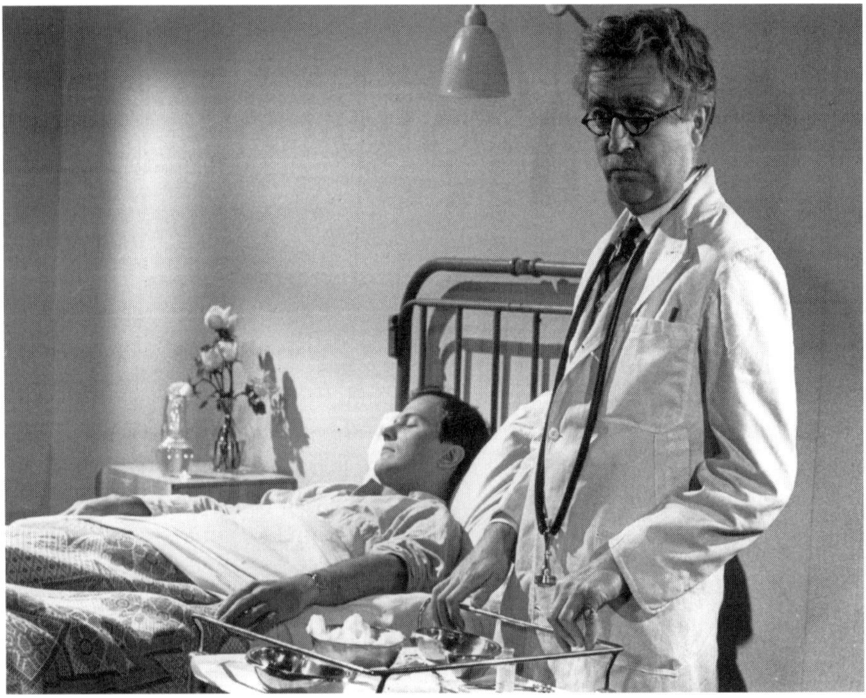

and hurriedly made films, with frequent sexual content. The title of his latest work was to be *Venus in Furs*, and was an idea very loosely based on the famous novel by Leopold von Sacher-Masoch, who had made a study of men deriving their sexual pleasure through enduring cruelty, usually at the end of a whip.

As usual with Towers, the picture was a product of co-productions with several countries, which accounted for the cast being a mixture of all nationalities, requiring the film to be dubbed into English. For the more liberal European market, there would be a second cut of the film featuring extra nudity scenes, though not, it should be pointed out, featuring Dennis Price. Harry Alan Towers certainly knew his market, though as he insisted on writing a lot of the scripts himself without any story editors, and with his Spanish director throwing every character and angle he could think of into his plots, the storylines were often hard to follow.

In *Venus in Furs*, Dennis was cast as Kapp, a homosexual deviant and degenerate who joins forces with a lesbian, played by Margaret Lee, and a sado-masochist as portrayed by Klaus Kinski. Together, the characters plumb new depths of depravity when they violate, mutilate, and kill a young woman before dumping her corpse on a beach. Yet they had not banked on the woman returning from the dead to exact revenge on her killers. The story is told by a young jazz trumpeter (James Darren) who is haunted by the dead woman wherever he goes. Yet for all its titillation and exploration of sex acts, the film was criticised for being 'old fashioned' in its approach to perversions. Sadly, it only showed how hard-pressed Dennis was to find work. *Venus in Furs* was released in the UK in 1969 but had only a limited showing in adult cinemas. People took a dim view of Dennis for ever being involved, and to make matters worse, two of his co-stars, Margaret Lee and Klaus Kinski, narrowly escaped being arrested when the film, with the title *Paroxismus* (meaning orgasm), was released in Italy and subsequently banned. The judges who watched it in private said: 'Too much explicit sadism, abandonment, unusual confidences and disfiguring acts of pathological sex proves *Paroxismus* has neither artistic nor entertainment merit.'

Miss Lee, Kinski, and the Italian co-producer Inigo Bianchi were each sentenced to three months in prison, but the terms were conditional unless further complaints were made against them. They were also fined £30 each. Separately, Margaret Lee also faced the possibility of a six-year jail sentence for allegedly smuggling 4 pounds of marijuana into Spain when she returned from location filming in Tangier. Customs officers claimed to have found it in her suitcase and she was released on a £600 bail.

Meanwhile, the English producer Harry Alan Towers was expelled from America after being charged with 'bringing girls into the USA for the purpose of illegal prostitution'. Towers had suggested, in meetings with potential financiers, that his female companions would stay behind after he left for other meetings to help said financiers make up his mind about backing a future project. He remained banned from entering the US again for decades.

Over a period of five years, until he was too ill to travel, Dennis appeared in at least five of Towers and Franco's pictures, but *Venus in Furs* was perhaps the most controversial, though far from the worst, with a strong and uncomplicated storyline. There is also a musical score by the sixties band Manfred Mann. In later years, Dennis came in for a lot criticism for working with Towers and Franco, yet he was far from the only star to appear in his films; Christopher Lee was a regular, and his work included the *Fu Manchu* films and *The Bloody Judge*, which told the story of hanging Judge Jeffries. Christopher Lee was never berated for being one of Franco's actors and in fact considered *The Bloody Judge* to be up among his best films. Lee, unlike Dennis, was however not desperate, so his work with Franco was a personal choice after, no doubt, a bit of arm twisting by Towers about how their next film together would be bigger and better.

To stay in the public eye and for the benefit of those who assumed he had retired, Dennis accepted guest and cameo roles—anything as long as it helped pay his debts. One such part was in *The Magic Christian*. The script was written by Terry Southern from his novel, with additional material from Peter Sellers, John Cleese, and Graham Chapman; it was basically a laboured attempt to prove the point that anyone, despite their position, can be bought for the right price. It was rather ironic in Dennis's case. Once again, he worked with his friend Peter Sellers, who was starring and being his usual zany self as an eccentric millionaire, Sir Guy Grand, who squanders his vast reserves, playing practical jokes, with the help of his 'adopted son', Youngman (Ringo Starr). As in the case of *The Magic Box*, the filmmakers tried to cram in as many celebrities in small parts as time would allow, with the result that some sketches were amusing but ultimately did not add up to a strong film. This was a passion project for Peter Sellers, and was a film idea he had nurtured since first reading Terry Southern's book; the far-fetched antics appealed to him immensely and he was determined to bring it to the screen. Sadly, it bombed at the box office and Sellers was left with egg on his face, while Dennis looked decidedly uncomfortable and out of place with Sellers's Goon-style brand of humour; he was sadly wasted, although no more so than forty other guest stars.

Dennis happily found himself playing a butler again when he appeared in the film *Some Will, Some Won't*, a very amusing comedy that the reviewers damned when they compared it to the 1940 original version,

Laughter in Paradise, with some saying they preferred the original to the colour remake.

On 11 November 1969, Dennis's mother Dorothy died at the grand age of eighty-eight, having survived her husband by twenty years. Her funeral was a private affair with only family and close friends present, but Dennis did not attend. Of all his relations, she had been closest to him. His absence was never explained.

His next film was for Hammer and under the direction of long time studio screenwriter Jimmy Sangster. Entitled *The Horror of Frankenstein*, it was a parody of their earlier hit, *The Curse of Frankenstein*, with Ralph Bates in the lead.

Dennis was delicious in the part of a gin-swigging grave robber who revels in his grisly work and is employed by Frankenstein to provide the raw material for his monster. His cameo brings great amusement to the film, not least in the way he delivers such lines as, 'Anything I bring you will be so fresh—it will get past the government meat inspector'. The grave robber's admiring wife and helper was played by former Rank starlet Joan Rice, and marked her last big screen appearance; in one of their best scenes together, they take a delivery of corpses to the castle, 'Read me that bit again, lovey' says Dennis as his lips curl into a wicked leer, and she reads an account of bodies being washed ashore after a shipwreck. He says enthusiastically, 'I love that phrase—more and more with each passing hour!'

To lend a gothic feel, part of the picture was filmed in a church crypt, though the floor kept flooding with water, so by the end of the various takes, everyone had pretty much gone down with flu. For most of the time, Dennis kept his spirits up by drinking in the studio bar between takes, which did not help his billing, both on screen and in the studio. In fact, during production, which was at EMI Elstree Studios, it was common knowledge that Dennis needed the work and was no longer regarded as a big star, so he was given a shabby old dressing room with only an upright chair for furnishings. The excuse for not offering their guest star anything better was, 'He'd turned to drink.' Marcus Wootton, incidentally, was ever present on the set and claimed to be getting on with his work as a script editor in one of the studio caravans.

Another witty part came Dennis's way in *The Rise and Rise of Michael Rimmer*, with a screenplay by the zany trio of Peter Cook, John Cleese, and Graham Chapman and director Kevin Billington. Although two of the writers were responsible for the misfiring *The Magic Christian*, this actually turned out to be much funnier and made good use of Dennis. One of his scenes was filmed on the Mappin Terrace at London Zoo and sees him eating kedgeree while he eyes the penguins; it was Peter Cook's quirky sense of humour to have Dennis dressed in pinstripes with a black tail coat resembling the birds.

Above: Leslie Phillips and Barbara Murray starred, with a little support from Dennis, in comedy *Some Will, Some Won't.*

Left: Supplying the good doctor with body parts—Dennis played the graverobber, in Hammer's *The Horror of Frankenstein*, with Ralph Bates in the title role.

After making *The Rise and Rise of Michael Rimmer*, Dennis wrote to actor Derek Nimmo who had recently been singing his praises:

> While filming in London, a friend of mine told me you had spoken most generously on your programme about self and Ian [Carmichael]. I wish I'd heard it. Very many thanks anyway. So glad you are up to the gills in good work and all well. If you ever penetrate this outpost of the empire, I'll be livid if you don't look me up! I've just been filming at the zoo—the animals won.
>
> All the best, Dennis

Later in 1970, Dennis returned to Spain to appear in Towers and Franco's *Vampyros Lesbos* (The Lesbian Vampire), which was another strange blend of the erotic and supernatural, albeit it with even more sexual than artistic content. It was happily followed by *Twins of Evil*, the third in Hammer's saga of the Karnstein vampires. Dennis was second on the bill to Peter Cushing in a plot that had everything from witchcraft to sex; Dennis's character manages to make it halfway through the film before he gets killed by a vampire's bite. *Twins of Evil* had a strong cast and impressive production design, which all helped gain good box office takings throughout Europe, especially Italy and France.

When on a driving holiday around England in a hire car, Dennis suddenly felt the urge to pay a visit to Copthorne Preparatory School, to have a good chin wag about his boyhood. Dennis spent most of the day chatting with the headmaster, David Sayle, and was introduced to the staff and matron, Florence Lever. His rather puffy appearance, pallor, and lined skin shocked everyone who had watched him in the *The World of Wooster* and they could tell he was ill. The headmaster's wife said, 'He was not at all the larger than life character I'd expected to meet, and seemed *passé*'. Yet they were pleased that he had taken the time and trouble to see them, though the tutors and headmaster Dennis had known as a boy of nine had long since retired.

Perhaps Dennis looked pale because he knew his next film, and quite possibly the worst film he ever made, was coming up. The ghastly *Dracula, Prisoner of Frankenstein*, was his third picture for director Jesus Franco, in which he starred as the notorious Doctor Frankenstein opposite French actor Howard Vernon as the Count. Franco wrote his own storyline, which was a crazy jumble of both Dracula and Frankenstein tales. As there were so many foreign actors on the bill, finding a common language they could all use on the set was a problem and even those who spoke English did so with very thick accents. Franco solved the language barrier by keeping the dialogue down to a bare minimum and as a result, the actors moved about like clockwork dummies and had to resort to facial expressions as in the

'Look, he's calling up the devil', but Count Karnstein (Damien Thomas) is unimpressed in this scene from *Twins of Evil.*

silent days. The sets were (forgive the pun) wooden, the direction jerky, the story unfathomable, the camera work wobbly, the make-up crude, and what dialogue there was comes across as banal. For some reason only known to Franco, Dennis was not allowed to record his own voice and was later dubbed by an American actor who sounded nothing like him. When ITV bought up *Dracula, Prisoner of Frankenstein* for late-night showing in the 1990s, they cut out all the sex scenes; seeing what's left of a Franco film without them is like buying a pie without the filling.

One more Franco film later, and on his return from Spain, fed up with horror yarns, Dennis was very pleased to be included in Columbia Pictures' *The Adventures of Barry McKenzie.* With a plot taken from the *Private Eye* strip cartoon character created by Barry Humphries, the film starred Aussie singer Barry Crocker in the title role, with Barry Humphries in support as Aunt Edna Everage. Together, they cause havoc among British society. Now seemingly viewed as an ageing eccentric by casting directors, Dennis was given the juicy part of a superficially respectable family man with a penchant for having his bottom thrashed. He pushed all embarrassment to one side and entered into the spirit, making this one of

Perverted Mr Gort asks Barry McKenzie to thrash him as he dresses up as a naughty schoolboy. Outrageous is the word when it comes to describing *The Adventures of Barry McKenzie.*

his most entertaining latter comedy roles, and with it delighted the critics. His ability to laugh at himself and let others laugh at him on screen was a most endearing quality and a great contrast to his early days with Stewart Granger. His co-stars Peter Cook and Barry Humphries were on good terms with him though observed he had 'fallen on hard times', but Dennis never burdened them with his personal problems.

In early December, Dennis left the cold, windblown island of Sark and flew out to sunny Malta for a cameo part in *Pulp*. It was advertised as being a comedy-thriller and turned out to be an outrageous parody of all those stereotype characters who fill the adventures of Philip Marlow books and the like. Following their working association on the film *Get Carter*, producer Michael Klinger, director Mike Hodges, and star Michael Caine found they had an affinity and decided to form their own production company, The Three M's, with Klinger producing, Hodges directing and writing the satirical script, and Caine starring. This was their first project. Dennis enjoyed the sunshine and was rewarded the following summer with glowing reviews about his hilarious performance as an eccentric Englishman, using his acid wit to put fools in their place. Although he is

Can you spot Barry Humphries?

mostly seen sitting or in the distance, there is a glimpse of his bandaged wrist, which was the result of a nasty injury he had endured when falling at the harbour on Sark. His brittle bone condition caused him to fracture easily, and he had to walk with great care.

His part in *Pulp*, though irritatingly small, came as a result of his friendship with Michael Caine. Twelve years earlier, it had been Caine who had a tiny part in *Danger Within* and he had since come far, thanks to films like *Alfie*. It was the big star Dennis Price who was now reduced to accepting a cameo in his film, yet in giving him that part, he detracted from his own performance for Dennis stole the show. It was the mark of a real artist to earn critical acclaim for just a few lines.

After the awful low-budget *Tower of Evil* and Jesus Franco's *The Erotic Experience of Frankenstein* (a sequel to *Dracula, Prisoner of Frankenstein*), Dennis was cast as the King of Hearts in a musical version of *Alice's Adventures in Wonderland*.

His fearsome dragon of a Queen was Flora Robson, and likely lad Rodney Bewes was cast as the naughty Knave of Hearts. It promised to be a triumph, with an endless parade of celebrities hidden under the fur and fabric. The film follows Lewis Carroll's story meticulously from the moment

Right: Dennis won critical acclaim as 'The Mysterious Englishman' in the offbeat comedy *Pulp*—at last a worthy cameo.

Below: With Flora Robson in the musical, *Alice's Adventures in Wonderland*; sadly, the music let the film down, which was unfortunate with it being a musical.

Fiona Fullerton as Alice drops down the rabbit hole, to when she wakes on the river bank. The incidents, set designs, and clever costumes brought the book vividly to life, but the songs were rather unmemorable. Shooting commenced at Shepperton Studios in the early summer, so it was no wonder Dennis remarked it was 'very warm work in that costume'. The heat was not the only discomfort he suffered as his costume, comprising beard, wig, crown, and heavy red robes, not to mention under garments, took more than half an hour to remove. Dennis's poor diet often resulted in urgent visits to the lavatory, and fearing half an hour in the make-up chair towards the end of the working day, he sent a messenger to fetch some diarrhoea curative medicine from the studio nurse post-haste. He had always suffered from acute nervous tension, and it seemed to be just as problematic then as if he was giving his debut performance on the West End stage.

The first time he had encountered the story, he recalled, was at Copthorne Preparatory School when as a boy of nine, he had selected Carroll's novel for reading over the holiday, in preference to one of Kipling's works. Later, while studying at Oxford, he had canoed along the Danube representing his college and *Alice* was his evenings' literature, together with the amusing and exclusively adult novel *The Diary of a Nobody*.

He had a favourable leaning towards the book and thought it was a laugh throughout, and not frightening in any way. 'I don't think Alice is even terrified of the Queen of Hearts. They have good old ding-dongs, great verbal battles for a girl versus an old lady. She's not a smug thing that's going to grow up into a horrible modern teenager—I think she'll grow up very happily married,' he said. The idea that the girl's safeguard relied on a subconscious awareness of her social status, he dismissed. 'Oh, I don't think so. Carroll takes the mickey, as they say nowadays, out of everyone and everything. The King and Queen are made to look complete poops more or less, the animals get away with murder and they, I imagine, are supposed to be the common people.'

In contrast, Dennis went straight from this jolly children's story into a starring part in Hammer's black comedy feature of the TV series *That's Your Funeral*. Bill Fraser, as a fat and wheezy funeral director with a very irreverent outlook, made light of the undertaking business. Dennis was employed as Mr Soul, an outrageous caricature of a funeral parlour beautician.

Dennis had always kept his teeth beautifully clean and in good condition, but following a routine check-up, tobacco stains from his constant smoking were mistaken by a dentist as tooth decay and two of his front teeth were removed, ruining his smile. As Mr Soul, he shows his teeth, and that was when the bad dentistry was fully revealed.

One of the blackest jokes in the film happened for real. In one scene, David Battley said he had to push 'a dear old extra about in a wheelchair':

They kept getting worse—*That's Your Funeral* with Sue Lloyd and John Ronane was really quite dreadful, but Dennis needed the money.

> He was playing the part of a dead body. When they'd done a few shots with him, the extra wasn't needed again for three or four days and come time for him to be recalled the Assistant Director telephoned, only to be told by his wife 'He can't come'.
>
> 'Why?'
>
> 'He's dead!' she replied.

Dennis was asked on the set whether he preferred the old days of film making, when a couple of minutes of screen time in a day was considered to be good compared to the somewhat rushed proceedings on the modern-day sets. His feelings were stirred and he replied, 'It's a matter of keeping this great industry alive, not regret what has gone. We all have to work to that end.'

Though only eighty minutes long, the storyline of *That's Your Funeral* was neither funny nor believable and the film fared badly with cinemagoers. Tellingly, the TV series was also axed after just one series.

The best of Dennis's horror films was unquestionably *Theatre of Blood*, which he started filming after *That's Your Funeral*. It had the advantage of an excellent screenplay and sharp direction by Douglas Hickox, who never allowed the pace to sag for a moment. Unlike some of Dennis's other horror pictures, which had been laughably bad, this film set out to be tongue-in-cheek from the off and the end product is an extremely gruesome but very funny black comedy. Dennis's namesake Vincent Price played the main character, an eccentric Shakespearian actor whose refusal to change with the times results in his performances being slated; Dennis played the aptly named Hector Snipe, one of the eight theatre critics murdered.

As the story unfolds, we are made to feel the pathetic actor's anger and frustration, his absurd vanity, and the mad devotion of his daughter (Diana Rigg) who aids him in the murders. The critics are shown to be a rotten bunch, thus eroding any sympathy that might have been shown for them as they get slaughtered. The Snipe character is out for what he can get and is completely self-centred, and when told of a fellow critic's brutal murder, he quips: 'At last a headline, instead of a byline'.

Despite a few noises of disapproval, primarily in objection to the bloodletting and violence, the main critics declared *Theatre of Blood* a success. Film Facts called the film, 'A triumph of stylish, witty Grand Guignol'. David Bartholomew noted that it 'Combines comedy and horror

Hector Snipe makes a flippant remark about the death of his fellow critic. At last, a horror film worthy of Dennis's talents, in *Theatre of Blood*. With Madeline Smith, Robert Coote, and Ian Hendry.

with a deft and stunning effectiveness'. Director Douglas Hickox described it as 'A modern version of *Kind Hearts and Coronets*, and who better to feature in the film, than the man who made *Kind Hearts* so famous in the first place!'

Although the casting was excellent, Dennis would have certainly been happier playing Vincent Price's part, for he would have gained much satisfaction from killing the critics, remembering how they had slated *The Bad Lord Byron*.

His co-star in *Theatre of Blood*, Madeline Smith, recalled:

> Dennis Price was a bit of a misery with very little personality, and seeming much older than his years. I had zero conversation with him. The others were much quirkier and more fun—mostly anyway. Maybe Dennis was more exciting in his younger days, but seemed to my young self to be very much 'a spent force'.

It seemed odd that Dennis should have been so unhappy and not at all his usual jolly self, considering he was among friends such as Jack Hawkins and Robert Morley. It could have been he was suffering pain because of his bone condition, or perhaps the dark spectre of depression had raised its head again. We perhaps will never know, and it is a great pity his usual wit and charm was not in evidence. There was a jovial, relaxed group photograph taken during a break, with all the 'critics' assembled on the steps of a cemetery chapel, joined by Vincent Price as the killer cum grave digger; however, Dennis was missing from the group—he had gone off to have 'all that ghastly red muck' (the fake blood) cleaned off as he could not bear to have it on his face another minute.

There was an element of personal nostalgia for Dennis, as the Putney Hippodrome in Fesham Street, South West London provided the setting for Hector Snipe's demise. It brought back memories of when he had appeared on the stage there in the early days of his career and he said he could 'sense the presence of unseen ghosts from the past'. The old theatre had once been a Vaudeville variety playhouse before it was converted into a cinema during the late 1930s, but it had closed its doors permanently in 1958. To temporarily restore the building for use in the film, a team of cleaners was given a weekend to clear out pigeons' droppings and generally tidy up the mess of the intervening years before new theatre fittings were installed.

Very clever stunts made it look as though Dennis was going through a really tough time, though he was actually aided around the sets and given all the time he needed to complete his scenes; he found people were extremely kind and considerate, though sadly it was obvious to them his days were numbered.

His next project was another comedy, with a slight horror twist. *Go for a Take* was written for the screen by Alan Hackney and Harry Booth (who also directed) from their original story. With Hackney responsible for creating the hilarious characters in *Private's Progress*, this film should have been a winner, but it ended up a low-budget caper devoid of any sparkle. It is a tale of two crooks on the run (Reg Varney and Norman Rossington) who take refuge in a film studio. A stream of well-known faces ranging from Anouska Hempel to David Lodge, Bob Todd, John Clive, Bill Fraser, and Sue Lloyd pop up in cameo parts, plus, of course, Dennis. In the film within the film, 'Mr Price' was on the set of a Dracula movie, playing the title part, but before casting Dennis in the cameo role, the film company had actually approached Vincent Price, who had said he would never demean himself by accepting such a small part. The paper-thin storyline became just an excuse for bringing together actors in comic 'turns' that were puerile. The film was chewed up and spat out by the critics.

The paring down of many scenes to fit a time slot meant they shortened Dennis's (already small) part and killed the punchline of a very funny joke. As 'Dracula', Dennis is supposed to hate his leading lady, as played by Julie Ege. In his second scene, Hackney has him on the point of biting Julie Ege who is reclining on a four-poster, when Reg Varney and Norman Rossington crash through the canopy, landing on either side of her. So, Dennis bites Reg Varney instead, with the cue for Dennis to say 'Blast, missed her again!', but in the final cut, Varney just pulls the fangs from his neck, hands them back, and departs.

In *Go for a Take*, and despite only being in his fifties, Dennis's health was visibly deteriorating. Despite having put on weight, the effects of cirrhosis and heart disease were taking their toll. The scene in which he mounts some stairs, supported on the arm of his co-star Aubrey Morris, was particularly daunting for him, as he had developed a dread of heights in case he fell. He was sad at having to forgo many of his past pleasures like riding, rowing, dancing, and anything else that was vaguely energetic. In fact, Dennis continued to become more fragile and unsteady on his feet, but had no intention of retiring and made a concerted effort to take on all new offers. It took great determination for him to carry on and a degree of physical pain.

He next appeared in the British-made equivalent of a hotchpotch horror movie, the Apple Films' production of *Son of Dracula*, which was Ringo Starr's debut as a producer, aided by director Freddie Francis. When casting for lead role in the film, Starr chose rock singer Harry Nilsson, who was a total newcomer to acting, for the reason 'he was tall'. Having any previous experience was deemed unnecessary, as Starr admitted he had not had lessons either, and it showed. Set in modern England, it was billed as 'The first rock and roll Dracula movie'. Has there ever been a second? Starr was meanwhile heavily disguised under a white beard as Merlin and, together with a host of rock musicians, set about telling the story of Dracula's offspring.

It might have just worked as a black comedy, but it lacked the necessary wit to place it anywhere near that category. Instead, it was a confusing mish-mash with an assortment of characters that were very reminiscent of Jesus Franco's *Dracula, Prisoner of Frankenstein*. Even talented actors like Dennis and his co-star Freddie Jones could not elevate the film from being fifth-rate.

Dennis's part as Van Helsing in this instance was supposed to be Dracula's saviour, and saw him sitting in a wheelchair throughout for no explained reason. Following his broken wrist, as seen when he made the earlier films *Pulp* and *Barry McKenzie*, one cannot help but wonder if the wheelchair was required for his own ailing health reasons. Dennis was also seen to be sporting a wispy goatee beard that appeared to be his own facial hair, and as he had never grown a natural beard before, it seemed as though, at this late stage in his life, he was keen to try something new in his characterisations.

Son of Dracula did not receive a UK release. Freddie Jones remembers:

> On the set Dennis looked tired and rather dissipated. I suspect he drank quite a lot of Dubonnet and although he was pleasant with me, I believe he had tantrums with his 'aide'—a sort of general assistant. He invited me into his caravan for a Dubonnet and seemed profoundly depressed. I reminded him of the great pleasure he had given to millions—a fact he flatly denied! The film belongs to Ringo Starr—he made it when he had pretensions of being an actor. The film never came out!

In the autumn of 1972, Dennis spent a few weeks working in and around London on what was sadly to be his last film, yet another tale of blood and gore as produced by Richard Gordon (who was also responsible for the ghastly *Tower of Evil*) called *Horror Hospital*—a rather unfortunate choice of title as Dennis was soon to end his life in one.

The supposed black comedy had a simple plot—that of a mad brain surgeon (Michael Gough) turning any youngsters staying at his remote health hotel into mindless zombies to do his evil bidding. Dennis played a travel agent who is paid to send people there. Although described as a 'guest role', it provided a lovely opportunity for Price connoisseurs to savour one last performance, in this case as an outrageously flamboyant homosexual who gets killed in the first thirty minutes.

With Anna Palk, Derek Fowlds, Bryant Halliday, and Jill Haworth in *Tower of Evil*, which, despite Dennis's one scene, was promoted as 'a Dennis Price film'.

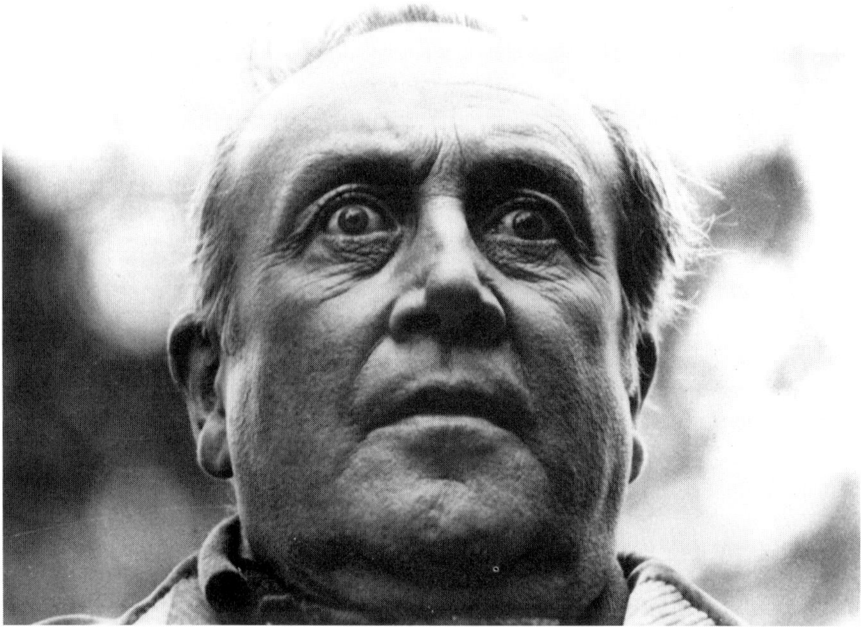

Mr Pollack is mortified as he realises he is about to have his head chopped off in *Horror Hospital*. That may have actually have been more fun than having to watch this dire film.

Dennis used to arrive on the set by car from his accommodation, already made-up, while his co-star Ellen Pollock had to share a cramped little dressing room with Michael Gough. When she saw the finished film played back, she warned her friends not to watch it. Miss Pollock comes to a sticky end in the film when she is smothered by a thing that looks like a walking heap of porridge. It was filmed inside Battersea Town Hall in South West London, which was the perfect location for a horror movie with its gothic architecture and unkempt grounds. Dennis was thankful to have an easy role that did not require a lot of strenuous activity, as even walking (such as from the manor doors to the gates) he had to do slowly, and stiffly. The twinkle in his eye was not because of the lines he was given, as co-star Robin Askwith recalled:

> Dennis Price used to arrive on the set every morning with a very impressive old fashioned doctor's bag which he said was full of scripts. However, he would slip behind curtains or whatever cover was available to study these scripts and all that could be heard was the clanking of Guinness bottles and much gulping. He would appear half an hour later, looking refreshed!

Horror Hospital was first shown at the New Victoria in April 1973, together with a complimentary film *The Corpse Grinders*, to a mixed response. The awful storyline was the major grumble. It may not have been the best of swansongs for an illustrious film career, but it was certainly an unforgettable one.

Dennis continued to work in TV alongside films, and with the huge popularity of Lew Grade's many one-hour adventure-style series, he accepted reoccurring roles in both *Jason King* with Peter Wyngarde in 1971 and *The Adventurer* with Gene Barry in 1972. He completed just three episodes of the latter show before ill health prevented him working further.

17

The Final Curtain (1973)

It was in April 1973 that Dennis made his last appearance at The Barn Bar and Bel Air taverns on Sark. The locals thought nothing of his subsequent absence as they were used to him being away filming for weeks, but his health was really breaking down and he was barely able to walk.

A few months later, July seemed like any other summer on Sark. For the inhabitants, it meant the island was swamped with tourists from Guernsey and the mainland, bringing in the revenue that would last them through the dreary winter months. It was a time of prosperity, liveliness, and activity on an island that had little industry outside of the tourist trade. Yet for Sark's most famous resident, this particular summer was very different, because it was to be his last.

Drinking had become Dennis's main interest while confined to his home, and it soon spiralled into a vicious circle. While he waited anxiously for his next offer of work, he needed alcohol to banish his depression, thus his intake increased exponentially. By drinking more, he was not only destroying his appearance and health, but it had reached the point where studios were reluctant to employ him in case he fell over and got seriously hurt as just taking a few steps on screen was problematic for him.

After one of his all-day drinking binges, Dennis slept off the effects and dreamed blissfully about the days of his stardom. He had covered the walls of his bedroom with photos of himself when young, to protect him against the dark forces that surrounded him—his own personal demons. As he fell into a drink-induced sleep, he took great comfort from seeing the images again.

When his housekeeper Edie let herself in to make his breakfast the following morning, she found him thrashing about wildly in his bed and babbling incoherently. He was having a bad attack of delirium tremens and Edie knew exactly what to do, having experienced this situation many times before. She immediately called for Sark's ambulance boat, *The Flying Christine*, and alerted his manager Wootton.

Edie and Wootton attempted to comfort Dennis, staying with him and ensuring he was safe until the ambulance crew arrived. Sark had no adequate facilities for people suffering from any serious complaints, so it seemed inevitable he would soon be bound for Guernsey.

The medics who attended were treated to a vision of the great Dennis Price completely inebriated. They gently pulled him out of his bed as he struggled to hold a conversation with a stream of slurred noises. Edie and Wootton were used to dealing with him in this state, so were able to get him from his house down to the harbour and on to the boat without much trouble and any unwelcome onlookers. Once again, they saw that his dignity was protected. Dennis was taken in the boat across to Guernsey and was then transported by road to the island's main hospital, The Princess Elizabeth.

Word soon got around that he was hospitalised and his friends flocked to see him. Primarily, they were just ordinary people who were used to seeing and chatting with him on their holidays. At first, it appeared that this was to be yet another 'drying out' period and everyone took for granted that he would soon be back propping up the bars of Sark, keeping all amused and entertained. Sark without him was boring indeed and his visitors were secretly quite unhappy to find that their carefully planned excursion had coincided with one of his bad turns.

Where other famous actors would have been open only to visits from close family and showbiz friends, Dennis welcomed all, for he was a man of the people. He was in the newest wing of the hospital and quite surprisingly for someone of his standing, he did not have a private room, but was placed in a public ward, among a row of beds.

Dennis was thrilled to receive a visit from his Radley master, Charles Wrinch, and made a joke about one of the other patient's loud and incessant snoring. 'Last night, there was a wonderful performance of The Warsaw Concerto'. Wrinch was dismayed to find Dennis in this situation and could not believe that the handsome, thin, young man he had tutored as a teenager, with such a promising future ahead of him, had disintegrated into the bloated apparition in front of him. He looked far older than his years and was a physical wreck. Worse was to come. Dennis continued to have attacks of the DTs (delirium tremens), so the hospital staff thinned his blood daily. As the summer advanced, Dennis needed help with moving around, and had he been able to pay for the luxury private treatment befitting his star status, he would have got it, but within the confines of a busy general ward, he was often neglected.

One day in August, he attempted to get out of bed, only to find his legs gave way under him and he fell badly. He let out the most agonising scream, which resonated loudly in the echoing rooms of the hospital, as he had fractured his hip on the polished floor. It was a terrible injury to sustain and would mean he would be spending many months more there with treatment, recuperation, and aftercare. This, on top of his alcoholism, was to prove all too much for him. His hopes of getting back to work seemed more remote than ever and he fell into deep depression, contemplating only a bleak future. Friends rallied round, knowing that they needed to lift his spirits with jokes and encouragement, including Wootton and Edie Hamon, who brought his cigarettes; even though he was not supposed to have them, they always found ways in which he could indulge in a smoke.

His sense of humour never left him and, if anything, helped him endure his ordeal. However, as his health deteriorated, there was a strong feeling he was not going to recover. At first, he believed that with sheer 'tenacity of purpose', he would make a good recovery, but behind the scenes, tests were revealing his body was breaking down from years of alcohol abuse, and in order to regain his health, he would need to have multiple organ transplants. The hope of finding the donor organs required was slim to zero and surgeons were reluctant to waste their skills on seasoned alcoholics. It seemed he was doomed. It greatly saddened his closest friends who saw him, though they were not totally surprised that his long battle with drink had finally got the better of him.

By September, Dennis's broken hip was not mending properly due to the brittle nature of his bones, leaving him completely miserable. Having fewer visitors and being bedridden for most of the time, the cold reality of his situation began to kick in as he accepted he would most likely never leave the hospital alive.

During one of Wootton's visits, he gave him instructions for his funeral. His plans were to be passed onto his daughters who, as next of kin, would be making the arrangements. He stated that he wanted a very simple service with no fuss. He was to be cremated and his ashes then placed in a casket and buried on Sark, a place he had a great affection for. He wanted no wreaths from any of the mourners, just bunches of cut flowers, and these were not to be placed on his grave, but following the service, they were to be given to the other patients on the hospital ward.

He further added that he did not want to have the customary memorial service that follows the death of a big actor such as he; that again, he considered, was making a fuss and he felt he did not deserve it. His instructions did not include a request for what was to be put on his gravestone or who was to attend his funeral; he left it open to Wootton and the Price family to issue the invitations.

The funeral service that Dennis had proposed was entirely at odds with the traditions of his family, who were all buried in the family vault at Trengwainton Manor in Cornwall. As the most famous member this family was ever likely to have, it seemed unthinkable he would not be buried where he belonged, but exiled on a tiny island in the Channel; yet there is a strong connection between Dennis's request and a scene from his most memorable film *Kind Hearts and Coronets*. There is a scene halfway through that could have had a bearing on his decision; it is where he accompanies Edith (Valerie Hobson) to her husband's funeral and meets the odious head of the family, Uncle Ethelred, the present duke (Alec Guinness). On leaving the church together, Edith, deeply upset, pauses to bid Ethelred farewell whereupon devoid of tact, he announced: 'Wonderful thing, a family vault, great reminder of one's heritage. Take this new cremation nonsense—who wants to see one's nearest and dearest put in an incinerator?' Alec Guinness, doing a great job of bringing out this character, delivers the line with such pomposity that it may well have prompted Dennis to act for himself against his own family's customs. After all, he had never done what they had expected of him in life, so why not defy them in death? It certainly could be taken as a rejection of them.

Right to the very end of his life, Dennis remained the perfect gentleman. Only two days before his eventual death at the hospital, Charles Wrinch and his wife came to see him and tried to make things seem less grim. As they rose to leave, he was so apologetic for not being able to get out of bed and see them to the door.

He had endured a long and painful ordeal, but was able to face the prospect of death with great calm and good humour, accepting the situation completely.

After spending nearly three months confined to hospital, the end came for Dennis in the early hours of Saturday morning. He succumbed to heart failure and died at 1.10 a.m. on 6 October 1973.

The medical examiner, Dr T. W. Parsons, attributed his death to no less than three separate causes. These were *pyelonethritis osteomalacia* (a disease of the bones), cirrhosis of the liver from acute alcoholism, and pulmonary oedema (when the heart chambers fill with fluid). In such a poor state of health, he had stood no chance of survival.

It was tragic that a man who had brought so much pleasure to generations should come to such a miserable end, before even reaching sixty. He was a dedicated and extremely professional actor who had spent all his life in the industry he loved, and perhaps his life is best summed up in words he had said the previous year: 'When people are paying you a great deal of money, it is unthinkable that one is not ready to work when required, or that one queries the boss, the director, or that one doesn't bother to learn one's lines. Frankly, I've always felt grateful to be allowed to work.'

In his last decade, Dennis Price may not have been the beautiful young man of the Rank days, but he always retained the characteristics that were his trademark, those fine aristocratic manners that made him perfect in the role of 'Jeeves' and a sensitive nature which always came through, even when he portrayed the nastiest people. After gaining experience in *Kind Hearts and Coronets*, he was even funnier (when allowed to be) in subsequent comedies, though despite his huge talent and star quality his compulsion to drink and gamble just went to show he was as human and vulnerable as the rest of us.

The following day, a very true and touching statement appeared in *The Times* obituary column:

> He will be remembered with pleasure by a younger generation who never witnessed his style on the stage or in films, for his television appearance as the Wooster manservant Jeeves, eyeing the peccadilloes of the young master with urbane omniscience, for Price was always at his best when displaying emotion tempered with refinement.

Dennis's passing left many people feeling a great sense of loss and sadness. There was a feeling that if he had been given proper guidance, he may have taken better care of his health and diet, but it must also be observed he was a proud and stubborn man, so it would have taken great persuasion to change any aspect of his life.

For some reason, the nature of his death being drink related caused derision from some quarters. yet he was in good company among the acting fraternity. So many legends of the stage were hard drinkers, including Oliver Reed, Richard Burton, Richard Harris, Tony Hancock, Sid Field, and Trevor Howard to name but a few; the list is endless. It never did their post-mortem reputation any great harm—in fact, it brought them admiration in many quarters for being 'real men'—yet somehow, Dennis was excluded from the honour of being a 'hell raiser', perhaps because during his life time, his drinking had been kept a private matter for which he sought no publicity. Maybe if he had become well known for his drinking, it would have elevated his status much further.

As Dennis passed into theatrical history, it was left to his family to organise his final curtain call. His relatives were acutely aware that the eyes of the media were upon them, therefore what they said to reporters had to be carefully prepared and scripted.

Dennis's conduct over the course of his life had caused the family considerable embarrassment, shame, and humiliation from what they considered to be one disgrace after another. If he had come from an ordinary background, it would not have impacted so much, but the Rose-

Price clan felt they had an obligation above all else, to uphold the honour of a lineage belonging in the pages of Debrett's Peerage.

Whatever his motives were, Dennis had always been the 'black sheep' of the family, going in for acting against his father's wishes, failing his exams, avoiding fighting during the war, divorcing his wife over his adultery, his attempted suicide, going bankrupt, lived in exile, and finally dying from alcoholism. In their eyes, these were deeds that placed him as a social outcast and quite beyond redemption. Yet these attitudes, if aired publicly, did not seem charitable or understanding, so his family realised the importance of closing ranks and presenting a united front.

The funeral was to be a public occasion open to scrutiny from reporters, so the family arranged a conference to decide what they should do. Dennis's daughters Susan and Tessa, as next of kin, legally owned his body and could do with it whatever they wished, but as Robin was head of the family, he would be in charge of organising the event.

Susan decided that Dennis should be given the funeral he had requested and did not consider for one moment putting him in the family vault, alongside his mother who had only died four years previously. Among the chief mourners should be the people closest to Dennis, those who shared his life and knew him best. They included his ex-wife Joan and his manager, Marcus Wootton. On contacting Joan, she declined to be present, too upset by his untimely death and too afraid to face the painful memories that would come flooding back. She also feared the possible interest from reporters tackling her about their marriage breakdown.

Inviting Wootton was another matter. The family were fired up with bitter resentment at the manner of Dennis's passing. It was the culmination of a life they considered had gone badly wrong and they needed someone to blame; that blame fell on Wootton. They chose to ignore the fact that Dennis's problems arose long before Wootton appeared on the scene, but on making enquiries, they discovered Wootton was very ill and confined to his bed. He was unlikely to attend the funeral, but in case he was thinking about it, they left word that he was not welcome.

Susan carried out her father's wishes to the letter. Dennis's funeral went ahead on Wednesday 10 October and the service was held at 2 p.m. at the parish church of St Marie in Castel, in a quiet part of Guernsey rather than in the central town of St Peter Port. Leading the mourners were his daughters, Susan, then aged thirty-three, and Tessa, who was approaching her thirtieth birthday. His brother Robin addressed the small congregation, which included Charles and Barbara Wrinch, Graham Jenkins (brother of actor Richard Burton and a Guernsey resident), and Clive and Gwen Wales of The Absolute End seafood restaurant. Also, one of the actors who had appeared with him at the Little Theatre attended, though the others had all returned to the mainland by then. There were no famous stars of the stage and screen.

However, support came for Dennis from a surprising quarter. Despite his request there were to be no wreaths, a huge one arrived from Elizabeth Taylor who, together with her husband Richard Burton, had worked with him on the film *The V.I.P's* ten years previously. Taylor and Burton were very much the stars of the production as a rich jet-setting couple, while Dennis had a tiny cameo appearance as their manservant and his scenes were over within the first fifteen minutes. With such a brief association, it was ironic that Taylor thought enough of him to send a tribute where others had not. The wreath was very large and caused concern among the family, who did not know what to do with it.

When the church service was over, his coffin was carried out along the aisle and as the bearers passed Gwen Wales, who was sitting in an end seat of the pew, said quietly under her breath 'Goodbye, Dennis'. In that same instant, one of the huge chrysanthemums on top of his coffin suddenly burst open and the petals landed in a shower on the floor, as if in answer; this was a very unusual occurrence that she did not forget, almost as though Dennis was trying to let her know he had heard her.

The funeral cortege travelled on Foulon Cemetery in St Peter Port for the cremation, which was arranged for 3 p.m. It was just as well that few fans were present as they were left to imagine a grand affair, but this was no movie star's funeral. To make it even more unglamorous, the crematorium in Guernsey must be one of the most depressing in the UK, being dreadfully small and standing forebodingly on the summit of a steep hill to the rear of the cemetery, surrounded by unkempt graves and waving grass. The island's governing authority had been too mean to build a proper crematorium set within its own grounds, so in 1929, they converted a tiny Victorian chapel. It was wholly inadequate for holding funerals; there was no waiting room, toilets, or hall of remembrance to put flowers in. Inside the chapel, it was even worse; the furnishings were a few rows of cramped together pine chairs of the kind used in old state schools, set around the catafalque on which the coffin was placed. The mourners were seated only a few inches from the coffin, which was practically in their faces, and was only hidden from view when some shabby net curtains closed around it. The interior was bleak stonework with no comforting floral displays; it was truly awful.

It is extremely sad to think of Dennis spending his last moments in human form inside this place. The committal service was over within fifteen minutes after some final words from the priest and melancholy recorded music played as the curtains closed around his coffin.

It was on this day that a bitter dispute arose as to what had become of his estate. Old dislikes, hidden while Dennis was alive, suddenly came out. What sadness there was at his passing became buried under deep resentment and anger—anger because he had died what the family considered to be a shameful death; anger that he had apparently left no money to share around; and resentment over his friendship with this Marcus Wootton, a man they hardly knew, yet regarded as an 'outsider'.

The family had been on tenterhooks the whole time, constantly vigilant for the presence of Wootton, who they expected to appear at any moment. The air was electric with simmering grievances and if Wootton had really made a dramatic last-minute appearance, the fat really would have been in the fire.

Talking to Charles Wrinch, Susan announced bitterly 'Wootton exploited my father'. Wrinch, remembering Wootton's 'atrocious poetry', was inclined to agree with her. He too had never understood why Dennis needed to have Wootton around when he had cultured friends like himself.

With the funeral itself over, the mourners went their separate ways, but the family stayed on in Guernsey for the next stage of the ceremony and to discuss what to do about the mess of affairs he had left behind.

The following day, Thursday the 11th, Dennis's ashes were collected from the undertakers. They had been sealed inside a bevelled wooden casket, approximately 12 inches × 10 inches × 6 inches deep, bearing his name on a plaque. The family caught the ferry across to Sark for the service at St Peter's church, arranged for 12 p.m. This was an opportunity for Dennis's friends on the island to gather and pay their respects, but surprisingly, some of those who had known him well, stayed away by making the excuse that although the service was a one-off occasion, they had to run the bars and restaurants for the lunchtime trade. Among those who attended were Edie Hamon, Regina Falle, Charles Falle, and David Le Feuvre, together with Dennis's brother and eldest daughter representing the family.

Once more, the family kept watch for the unwelcome presence of Wootton but were assured he would not be attending as he was still laid up in bed. A rumour circulated that his illness may not have been genuine and that he was 'lying low, too ashamed to show his face.' Whatever the reason, Marcus Wootton was criticised by Dennis's friends for not being present. Wootton had been a regular visitor during Dennis's long spell in hospital, though along with grieving for his friend and amusing associate, a damned good job had ended for him.

Among the congregation on Sark were some of the women who had befriended Dennis in his final years, hoping that their kindly gestures would be repaid by deeper affection. They had dreamed of becoming the next Mrs Price, but their fantasies of marrying a glamorous movie star were at odds with an alcoholic in declining health. Now the brutal reality faced them—that both the man and the movie star were beyond their reach. They wept openly for their shattered dreams. What compounded their distress was the Dennis they now saw in front of them, changed beyond all recognition. One of his lady admirers said 'I wanted so much to be there for Dennis, but it was hard to see him in that wooden box, like something I'd put my jewellery in. He used to be so tall and elegant, such an imposing figure, now reduced to dust.' Dennis's friend, David Le Feuvre, was also very disappointed that he was not buried whole and described his mortal remains as being 'just ashes'.

The service concluded with Dennis's casket being carried down the aisle by the priest and taken to the site where he was to be buried in Sark cemetery, to the right of the church. James Le Feuvre, having had the job of burying numerous islanders, knew the procedure and waited quietly in the doorway of the church while the service was in progress. James had dug a hole 12-inch square opposite the plot reserved for the seigneurs (Sark's rulers) and in view of the Dame of Sark's dislike of Dennis, the islanders remarked he was 'Too close for comfort!'

James lined the bottom and sides of the hole with ivy creepers, an old Sark tradition to make the grave look more attractive. Dennis's remains were carefully lowered into his final resting place, witnessed by the mourners while the vicar said a few words from his bible. James then filled the grave with care and respect, making sure he did a first-class job for his friend, and pushed a wooden stake in to mark the spot while his memorial was being prepared.

In due course, a headstone was erected, a simple wedge-shaped piece of stone with a bronze plaque, bearing the following inscription:

IN LOVING MEMORY OF
DENNIS PRICE
ACTOR
1915–1973
'So, we'll go no more a roving'
Lord Byron

In life, Dennis had been content to fritter his wealth away on idle pursuits without sparing a thought as to what would happen after his death, 'I take life as it comes' had always been his motto. It was through no malicious intent that he ended up with very little. Yet the Prices, despite all the publicity over his bankruptcy and other extravagances, were convinced he had a fortune stashed away somewhere, with valuable possessions, and were determined to find it. If they had bothered to spend more time on Sark and read the newspapers, it would have been clear his cash was all invested in the breweries, with the tax man, and the betting shops. Dennis had not felt it necessary to worry about his daughters, as he had always provided for them, and for Joan Schofield, in life. Over the years, they had all the privileges of a star's children and having both made good marriages, wanted for nothing.

Once Dennis had been laid to rest, the people of Sark gathered for a few drinks and hopefully exchange pleasantries with his relations, whom they were keen to meet informally. The locals were genuinely fond of Dennis, but if they hoped to find some of his warmth in his brother, they were in for a let-down. Casting a suspicious eye round the assembled group, Robin demanded to know 'where's the silver?' No one reacted, as they had as much idea as he did. The locals were shocked by his mercenary attitude and one of them said he was 'Glad Dennis didn't leave anything for him to grab.'

In further conversation, Robin boasted how he had made his fortune over the years by careful investments. During the war, he had rented out his home to American soldiers to use as their headquarters, and had been paid handsomely for his trouble. Once a high sherriff of Berkshire and a Lloyds underwriter, Colonel Robin had spent the past eight years at Tetworth Hall, a great white house set in acres of grounds, halfway between Ascot and Sunningdale. The grounds, incorporating a private tennis court, were large enough to build a housing estate. A former resident of Chelsea, he had more money than he knew what to do with. Dennis's friends were not sorry to see the back of him.

Having both offended and bored the islanders with his boasts and lack of remorse over his own brother's death, Robin and Susan headed for Dennis's house, Le Clos du Vivier, and seized the opportunity to go through Dennis's effects undisturbed, while Wootton lay in bed upstairs. They had brought some empty suitcases with them to take away whatever possessions they could find. Having obtained the key from his housekeeper, they were left in the house.

They had visualised an elegant abode in keeping with a film star's income, filled with luxurious trappings. When living in Chelsea, Dennis owned an impressive collection of glass and there were valuables passed down from his parents. The scene that greeted them was nothing like they expected. There was the guide rope attached to the wall, leading from the door to the unmade bed, which had crumpled, beer-stained sheets. The floor was liberally strewn with empty cigarette packets and Guinness bottles. The only furniture was the shabby kind found in cheap lodging houses and there was nothing of any value to be seen. The only indication this room belonged to an actor was the gallery of photos fastened to the walls. Then, there was the smell—a pungent mixture of stale cigarette smoke and strong beer. After taking in the squalor of their surroundings, his relatives began searching. They wanted to locate the Rose-Price family heirlooms they were sure he possessed—silver, jewellery, and antiques; instead, all that came to light was his clothing. In a state of exasperation, paranoid thoughts took hold as they assumed someone had raided his home. Was it Wootton, his housekeeper, or one of the islanders?

They quickly bundled anything worth taking into the suitcases and left in disgust. As Robin made his way along Sark's main high street, the locals were disappointed to see that this florid-faced, red-haired man looked nothing like his film star brother.

It was the last time the Prices visited Sark, but by no means the last time Wootton would hear from them. Brother Robin was not content to let the matter rest there, so he sent Wootton the bill for the funeral and for good measure, he included a copy of the death certificate as sarcastic proof he really was dead. Wootton showed he was the better man by paying the bill with quiet dignity, even though he was not obliged to. Whatever he had allegedly done was pure speculation, but Robin's actions were malicious.

Furthermore, Wootton received threats of legal action on behalf of the family. Perhaps a volatile argument was desired, but if the threats were intended to bait Wootton, he did not bite back. Speaking in 1987, Wootton described his feelings:

> I was hurt by the way I was treated when Dennis died. I would have very much liked to have attended both his funeral on Guernsey and the Sark service, but I was ill with a really bad cold that kept me in bed for over a week. Yes, I was very upset that Dennis died when he did, because I not only lost an employer, but a valued friend. They [the Price family] made threats trying to scare me, but I'm not afraid of anyone and I don't care who knows it.

Although he did not think they were half the person Dennis was, he never made contact with the Prices again and hoped they'd just leave him alone to get on with his life.

> I didn't stay living on Sark for long after he died, because there was nothing for me to do there. Without Dennis around, the islanders seemed to resent me, because Robin had made a lot of trouble, by bad-mouthing me at the funeral he'd arranged, but then he sent me the bill for it! I could have refused to pay, but I didn't want to give him the satisfaction of engaging me in legal battles, so I paid the bill for Dennis's sake, because I wanted him to have some dignity.

Dennis in conversation at a social event, with Marcus Wootton close by.

Having given Dennis a very low-key funeral, Susan then defied her father's request and organised a memorial service. This took place at the famous actors' church of St Paul's in Covent Garden, London, at noon on 27 November. Dennis never thought he was worthy of a big fuss, and suspected some of the congregation would be enemies and rivals, only there to gloat. Sure enough, a few of them proved he was right.

All his relations and many show business colleagues gathered to pay their respects. Reverend John Hester, parish priest of St Paul's, officiated and gave the introduction. Michael Caine read a passage from Ecclesiasticus; Bernard Lee read from the poems 'So, we'll go no more a roving' and 'When coldness wraps this suffering clay' by Byron, while Ian Carmichael gave the address. Music from *The Dancing Years* by Ivor Novello played during an interlude and three hymns were sung: 'The Lord my Pasture Shall Prepare', 'Immortal, Invisible, God Only Wise', and 'Jerusalem the Golden.' The service ended with prayers and a blessing.

Taking their seats in established order were Susan Mapp and husband Tom, Tessa and Hugh Burnett, Lt. Colonel Robert and the honourable Mrs Rose-Price, Dr John and Mary Wiseman (sister), Timothy (Robert's son), Maureen Burrell and husband (Timothy's sister), Vivian Taylor (his cousin) and husband George, Sir Rose-Price baronet, cousins Michael and David Verey, and other distant relations.

Among the friends and colleagues present were Lady Gardiner (formerly Muriel Box), Sir Alec Guinness (who had donated the flowers), Michael Wilding, Lionel Jeffries, Doreen Hawkins (widow of Jack), Stafford Byrne (Dennis's friend from Croydon rep), Aubrey Baring, Nigel Patrick, Patricia Roc, Madge Smith, Michael Thornton, Robert Coote, and Sheila Sim.

It seemed the perfect tribute to Dennis, but just like his funeral, the people closest to him were conspicuous by their absence. It was hardly surprising that Wootton was missing, but where was Joan Schofield? Although they had divorced some twenty-three years before, a memorial service is supposed to be a time of reflection, and by playing music from *The Dancing Years*, it summed up memories of the time long ago when he had first proposed marriage to Joan. It seemed Joan could not find the courage to face the painful memories of happy times they had shared, which had turned sour.

However much the Price family keep things to themselves, they cannot change the events in Dennis's life, nor block out other's memories of him. Whenever his films are shown, people will watch, discuss, and want to know more about him.

In St Paul's, Covent Garden, on the left-hand wall behind the pews, are a line of wooden tablets with the names and dates of actors who have passed into history. Dennis has one, which reads 'Dennis Price 1915–1973. Kind hearts are more than coronets'.

Dennis would not have been so contented in his life if he had not achieved his ambition to reach the top of his chosen profession, but he did and though the parts became smaller, he remained a star to the end. It must have been very satisfying for him to know he had been fortunate to have run the whole course of different roles, starting as a romantic lead, playing the villain, revelling in being sardonic, taking part in comedy, and ending as the victim of numerous horror yarns. He had made 100 films, of which the most popular and enduring is *Kind Hearts and Coronets*.

How different his life would have been if he had devoted it to the church as his family intended, but what the film world would have lost and how excruciatingly boring for the man who lived life to the full. It was his decision to act and he was a 'professional to his finger tips' as Wootton described him. He made some tragic mistakes in the pursuit of his ambition, so it is up to others to learn from his example—employ a good accountant and stick to a healthier lifestyle, for Dennis Price certainly paid the price of fame.

Postscript

Dennis Price was very much like Oscar Wilde's character Dorian Gray, a handsome, charming, refined young gentleman who was drawn into frequenting the roughest pubs in London where he was quickly initiated into a life of hedonism. He became fascinated by the mix of people he met in his favoured East End hostelries, from jovial cockney types to out-and-out gangsters; they were so different to his usual theatre and film industry companions and when drinking with them he said he felt truly classless. They in turn were fascinated by this posh actor who was willing to share his stories and adventures with them, along with his wallet. Though the excessive alcohol Dennis began consuming caused him to become addicted—especially to whisky, rum, and Guinness—and his increasingly regular drunken bouts were often at the cost of his family and professional life.

Dennis's generosity and willingness to always buy in a round of drinks meant he was soon spotted by the more unscrupulous characters who were only too keen to take advantage of a posh-talking man with cash in his pocket. The card sharps among them encouraged Dennis to play a hand, and Dennis often spent hours engrossed in various card games, always losing. He also regarded betting on horses as a particular thrill, and despite rarely backing a winner, he seemed strangely unconcerned. 'What is losing money compared to the excitement I feel every time I place a bet?' Dennis asked. 'There is nothing quite like it—not even sex'. He reasoned he could afford his new-found vices of drinking and gambling because there was always another acting role on the horizon. Yet his gambling debts lead to Dennis making career choices based more on financial rather than artistic merit, which sadly resulted in him appearing in some pretty bad films.

It soon became apparent, even to the most casual of observers, that Dennis was not very good at cards or picking horses, but such was the strength of his addiction that he became completely hooked. It was an addiction that very nearly brought him down on several occasions, and sadly, the addiction to alcohol did later kill him.

It was also in one of his favoured East End pubs he met Marcus Wootton, who became the greatest influence on his later life as we have read. I met Wootton in 1987 when he was living in Enfield. For some reason, ever to be unknown, he welcomed my enquiries whereas all other approaches made to him about Dennis Price had resulted in a swift 'F-off'. We chatted for hours, though sadly I never got to meet his wife Jenny as she was at work and I am sure I would have learned more about the man and what made him tick from her.

From what I saw myself, Wootton was certainly hypersensitive and a rather self-obsessed character. He was very concerned about his image and his talents, talents I had obviously not observed anywhere. I got on quite well with him until I made a light-hearted remark about a poem he had written; he got very annoyed very quickly. I can see why people found him hard to get on with as he was impossible to read, and turned prickly and very cold on the spin of a coin. For the life of me, I cannot understand what Dennis Price saw in him either as a friend or a manager. Of course, I was aware of the 'rumours' that he and Dennis were perhaps romantically involved because of their close and outwardly strange friendship. After all, no one could fathom what else would have attracted Dennis to the man let alone inviting him to occupy the flat above his in Mayfair and subsequently move into his house on Sark.

Though I could not really see what the physical attraction might be to Wootton, and despite my gentle questioning about his home and married life, he remained a total enigma, only ever telling me he was a stay-at-home husband and worked as a sometime ghostwriter; of what, he never said and I never found out. In the many hours we chatted, Wootton never spoke of children to me but years later, during a trip to Sark, I discovered he had three by his first wife Judith. They were all born when he was living on the island; sadly, one of them died, and the whereabouts of the two surviving children is unknown. It struck me as strange that a father would never mention his children, albeit from an earlier marriage.

Yet it was clear from the people I met and spoke with on Sark that Wootton was very much a lady's man and I genuinely think it was more a case of it suiting him living adjacent to, and with, Dennis merely to have his accommodation costs picked up. On Sark, Wootton lived upstairs with his wife Jenny in the six-bedroom house and they lead very separate lives to Dennis. I failed to uncover any proof, significant circumstantial evidence of, nor witnesses to any form of sexual relationship between the two men, nor could I find any semblance of proof that Dennis was being blackmailed towards the end of his life; seemingly, they were ill-founded rumours.

Marcus Wootton died in 1993, aged fifty-seven. He succumbed to cancer. I tried writing to his widow at the Enfield address quite recently, but she had moved away and has probably remarried by now. Wootton's first wife, Judith, now lives in Norfolk with her new husband and a lady on Sark gave me her address, but she never replied.

I was nineteen at the time I met Wootton. 'So why does a kid like you want to write a book about an old soak?' he asked. It struck me, that's what he thought of Dennis—a meal ticket and drinking chum—but they were certainly not the words of a lover. Wotton said: 'Dennis was a good friend—a big, upright man. He was a private man, he didn't tell me everything and I didn't ask. Now he's dead, I'm not interested in doing a book. And I haven't got any photographs.' Wootton's parting words to me were: 'If you write anything about me in your book that I don't like, I'll strangle you!'

In spite of claims that Wootton was only ever after Dennis's money, he did not sell his 'inside story' to the press or did he ever write a book himself. He preferred to leave him in the past.

News reports of Dennis's passing and subsequent internet biographies list the cause of his death as 'congestive heart failure'. The birth, marriage, and death records for Guernsey and Sark are held in the Channel Islands; they are not available on the mainland. In those records, it states Dennis died from 'cirrhosis of the liver'. Margaret Lockwood also died of cirrhosis, which is a strange and eerie coincidence.

I also contacted members of Dennis's family during my initial research, and although they replied, it was always to say they were not interested in talking:

Letter from Joan Schofield (Mrs Latto), 13 January 1989

> Thank you for your letter of 6th January in which you were good enough to refer to your literary project about my late husband with particular reference to his career. Your letter suggests that you are a sensitive person and if that is so you will readily understand that I find it difficult and distressful to try to recollect, with any certainty, those periods in my life that have become dimmed with the passage of time. These being the circumstances, I know that you will appreciate my reluctance to supply information that I cannot truly guarantee to be completely factual. Thank you for your consideration.

Robin Rose-Price (brother), 17 September 1986

> Thank you for your letter dated 16th and your kind thoughts with reference to my brother Dennis. I write this to tell you that very soon after his death 13 years ago I and other members of his family decided that we would never want any book written about him by an outsider, or collaborate with any such prospective author.

Further to this letter, I travelled to Ascot where Dennis's brother was living, as I really wanted to meet him face-to-face. I guess I was intrigued to find out if he bore any physical resemblance to Dennis. He was very polite to me and not hostile in any way, but confided in me how a journalist back in the 1970s had queered the pitch for anyone who considered writing a book with the family's help. We parted on amicable terms.

Mary Wiseman (sister), 20 January 1987

> Your letter arrived yesterday. It came as a surprise, as my brother Dennis died thirteen years ago! I can well understand your great admiration for his acting ability and your appreciation of his personality, although as you say you never met him.
>
> Shortly after his death, an author did make contact with various members of his family. He had met Dennis, he wished to write a book about him. After due consideration and consultations within the family, it was decided that the members concerned did not want a book written about Dennis by a stranger, outside the family.
>
> I was very fond of my brother and have of course, many happy memories of our shared childhood and youth together. However, you will I am sure understand why I cannot share them with you to help with the book you wish to write.

Tessa Burnett (daughter), date of letter unknown.

> The treasured memories that I have of my father are entirely private and will remain so.

Susan Mapp (daughter), in a phone call in 1986

> Susan spoke as if a book was being written with her collaboration, though it has never emerged. She said, 'Besides, I am a journalist myself'. She declined to give me an interview.

In these intervening years, I have added to my research, watched the majority of Dennis Price's previously unavailable films, and spoken to many of his friends and colleagues. Having gained a very wide series of opinions, anecdotes, and facts, I would like to think I have now presented an accurate and warm appreciation of this great British actor's life. His star will never diminish in my eyes.

APPENDIX I

Stage Plays

1937 *Behind Your Back*, Croydon Repertory Theatre
1937 *Richard II*, Queen's Theatre
1937 *The School for Scandal,* Queen's Theatre
1938 *Three Sisters,* Queen's Theatre
1938 *The Merchant of Venice,* Queen's Theatre
1938 *I Killed the Count,* Little Theatre, Hull
1938 *Hamlet,* Arts Theatre, London
1938 Plays at the Croydon Repertory Theatre:
Black Swans
Autumn
Housemaster
Whiteoaks
I Have Been Here Before
1938 *A Party for Christmas* Arts and Haymarket Theatres, London
1938 *I Killed the Count,* Croydon Repertory Theatre
1938 *1066 and All That,* Croydon Repertory Theatre
1939 Plays at the Croydon Repertory Theatre:
The Barratts of Wimpole Street
A Party for Christmas
Poison Pen
Gentleman Unknown
Thou Shalt Not
The Millionairess
Claudius and the Bee
Service
Sugar Plum
The Queen Was in the Parlour
1940 *The Scarlet Pimpernel,* The Playhouse Theatre, Oxford

1940 *September Rain,* Chanticleer Theatre, London
1942 *The Springtime of Others,* Arts Theatre, London
1942 *Blithe Spirit,* extensive UK tour
1942 *This Happy Breed,* extensive UK tour
1942 *Present Laughter,* extensive UK tour
1943 *Torn Banner,* Theatre Royal, Windsor
1943 *Present Laughter,* Haymarket Theatre, London
1943 *This Happy Breed,* Haymarket Theatre, London
1943 *Blithe Spirit,* Duchess Theatre, London
1944 *Hamlet,* New Theatre, London
1944 *A Scandal at Barchester,* The Lyric and Wyndham's Theatres, London
1945 *Blithe Spirit,* Duchess Theatre, London
1949 *The Last of Mrs Cheyney,* Connaught Theatre, Worthing
1949 *Gaslight,* The Opera House, Manchester
1950 *Rebecca,* The Playhouse Theatre, Oxford
1951 *Bell, Book and Candle,* Tour of the United States
1952 *The Man Upstairs,* The Grand Theatre, Blackpool
1952 *Husbands Don't Count,* Winter Gardens, London
1953 *Blind Man's Buff,* St. Martin's Theatre, London
1954 *Blithe Spirit,* extensive UK and Ireland tour.
1956 *To My Love,* Fortune Theatre, London
1956 *Not in the Book,* The Gate Theatre, Dublin
1957 *Be My Guest,* Winter Gardens, London
1957 *Separate Tables,* tour of South Africa
1959 *The Earrings of Madam De…,* Arts Theatre, London
1959 *Heartbreak House,* Billy Rose Theatre, New York and on tour in the United States
1965 *Any Wednesday,* Apollo and Wyndham's Theatres, London
1966 *Not in the Book,* Little Theatre, Guernsey
1966 *Any Wednesday,* Little Theatre, Guernsey
1966 *The Browning Version* and *Why Don't You Bring Her Home?* Little Theatre, Guernsey

APPENDIX II

Radio Broadcasts

All on BBC Radio:
1947 *Starstruck*
1947 *Navy Mixture*
1948 *Alhambra of the Air*
1954 *Top of the Town*
1954 *All Star Bill*
1954 *Happy Holiday* (his own radio series)
1956 *Desert Island Discs*
1959 *The Navy Lark* (series one of a very long running series)
1961 *It's a Deal* (a series in twelve episodes)
1961 *Movie Go Round*

APPENDIX III

Television Appearances

1938 *Lady Precious Stream* (as warden/Minister of Foreign Affairs)
1938 *Julius Caesar* (as Trebonius/Volumnius)
1939 *The Tempest* (as Ship's Master)
1939 *Rope* [as Kenneth Raglan]
1953 *The Cochran Story* [as Noël Coward]
1954 *Playhouse 90* ('The Jewels')
1954 *Crime on our Hands* (as Cecil Davenport—episodes: 2, 3, 4, and 6)
1954 *The Vise* ('Let Murder Be Done')
1955 *The Vise* ('The Serpent Beneath' and 'Account Closed')
1955 *Studio One in Hollywood* (as Julian Brimmer in 'Mrs Brimmer Did It')
1956 *ITV Play of the Week*: *The Last of Mrs Cheyney* (as Lord Dilling)
1956 *The Immortal Swan*
1956 *Alfred Marks Time*
1956 *Theatre Royal* ('The Gloves' as Bob Herrick)
1956 *Doctor Jekyll and Mr Hyde* (as Dr Jekyll and Mr Hyde)
1957 *ITV Play of the Week*: *Dear Brutus* (as Mr Dearth)
1957 *Chelsea at Nine* (as a comedy regular)
1957 *ITV Play of the Week*: *Rope* (as Rupert Cadell)
1957 *Assignment Foreign Legion* (as Major Louis De La Tour in 'The White Witch of Makala')
1957 *ITV Play of the Week*: *The Age of Abandon* (as Peter Conway)
1958 *Playhouse 90* ('Design for Murder' as Rex Berkely)
1958 *What Shall We Tell Caroline?* (as Tony Peters)
1958 *Myself When Young*
1958 *The Witching House*
1958 *Playhouse 90* ('Eden End' as Charles Appleby)
1958 *Playhouse 90* ('Lovers Leap' as Roger Storer)
1958 *The Fourposter* (as Michael)

1958 *On With the Show*
1959 *ITV Play of the Week: Skyline for Two* (as Steven Gaye)
1959 *Playhouse 90* ('Dark as the Night' as Percy)
1959 *H. G. Wells' The Invisible Man* (as Raphael Constantine in 'Behind the Mask')
1959 *The Locked Door* ('The Case of the Devil Girl' as Harry Price)
1959 *The Frankie Howerd Show*
1960 *Ladies and Gentlemen* (as a special guest)
1961 *The Seven Faces of Jim*
1961 *Theatre 70* ('Call for Mr Ariman' as Mr Ariman)
1961 *Armchair Theatre* ('The Picture of Dorian Gray' as Lord Henry Wotton)
1961 *Colonel Trumper's Private War* (as Colonel Trumper, episodes 1–5)
1961 *The Somerset Maugham Hour* ('The Lion's Skin')
1962 *ITV Play of the Week: Some Other Love* (as Michael Charlton)
1962 *No Hiding Place* (as Commander Adrian Falconer in 'Epitaph for Johnnie')
1962 *Make Room for Daddy* (as Sir Howard in 'The British Sense of Humour')
1962 *It Happened Like This* (as Sir James Hare in 'A Two to One Chance')
1963 *Drama 61-67* ('Drama 63: My Lords, Ladies and Gentlemen' as Percy Trouncer)
1963 *In Confidence* (as Colonel Edward Aplin)
1963 *The Sentimental Agent* (as Victor Frey in 'The Height of Fashion')
1963 *Hancock* (as a doctor in 'The Girl')
1963 *The Dave King Show*
1964 *Harry's Girls* (as Herbert Finchley in 'Bet it All')
1964 *ITV Play of the Week: Deep and Crisp and Stolen* (as William)
1964 *The Lady of the Camellias* (as De Varville)
1964 *Detective* (as Sir John Appleby in 'A Connoisseur's Case')
1964 *Spare the Tears for Happiness* (as Harry Debrett)
1964 *Story Parade* (as Lord Grabley in 'Bargains at Special Prices')
1964 *The Human Jungle* (as Major Falcon in 'Dual Control')
1965 *The Wednesday Play* ('The Confidence Course' as the director)
1965–1967 *The World of Wooster* (as Jeeves for four series)
1966 *Court Martial* (as Lawrence Creighton in 'Let Slip the Dogs of War')
1968 *Comedy Playhouse* ('The Gold Watch Club' as Edward Wilkins. This was a pilot episode for a TV series that was never made)
1968 *BBC Play of the Month: Hay Fever* (as David Bliss)
1968 *Sherlock Holmes* (as Lord Holdhurst in 'The Naval Treaty')
1968 *The Avengers* (as Jason in 'Whoever Shot Poor George Oblique Stroke XR40?')

1969 *Never Mind the Quality Feel the Width* (as Huntley in 'Situations Vacant, apply Saville Row')
1969 *Cribbins* (Episode 5)
1970 *W. Somerset Maugham* (as Admiral Frobisher in 'Jane')
1971 *Jason King* (as Sir Brian in 'A Deadly Line in Digits' and 'A Page Before Dying')
1972 *Callan* ('Charlie Says It's Goodbye')
1972 *Clochemerle* (as Alexis Luvelat in 'The Glorious Triumph of Barthelemey Piechut' and 'The Inexorable Power of the Third Republic')
1972–1973 *The Adventurer* (as Brandon in 'The Not So Merry Widow', 'The Case of the Poisoned Pawn', 'Nearly the End of the Picture')
1973 *The Tunnel*

APPENDIX IV

Film Appearances

1938

No Parking
Producer: Herbert Wilcox. Director: Jack Raymond. Writers: Gerald Elliott and Carol Reed. Cinematography: Francis Carver

Main cast: Hardcastle—Charles Carson; Orchestra leader—Geraldo; Walsh—Fred Groves; Albert—Gordon Harker; James Selby—George Hayes; Stanley—Cyril Smith; Extra—Dennis Price (uncredited)

1944

A Canterbury Tale
Producers/directors/writers: Michael Powell and Emeric Pressburger. Cinematography: Erwin Hillier

Main cast: Thomas Colpeper—Eric Portman; Alison Smith—Sheila Sim; Peter Gibbs—Dennis Price; Sergeant Bob Johnson—John Sweet; Narrator/village idiot/soldier—Esmond Knight; Thomas Duckett—Charles Hawtrey

1945

A Place of One's Own
Producer: R. J. Minney. Executive producer: Maurice Ostrer. Director: Bernard Knowles. Screenplay: Brock Williams, from the novel by Osbert Sitwell. Cinematography: Stephen Dade

Main cast: Annette—Margaret Lockwood; Mr Smedhurst—James Mason; Mrs Smedhurst—Barbara Mullen; Dr Robert Selbie—Dennis

Price; Mrs Manning Tutthorn—Helen Haye; Major Manning Tutthorn—Michael Shepley; Sarah—Dulcie Gray

The Echo Murders

Producer: Louis H. Jackson. Director: John Harlow. Writer: John Harlow. Cinematography: James Wilson.

Main cast: Sexton Blake—David Farrar; Dick Warren—Dennis Price; Stella Duncan—Pamela Stirling; James Duncan—Julien Mitchell; P. C. Smith—Cyril Smith; Rainsford—Dennis Arundell; Dacier—Ferdy Mayne

1946

Caravan

Producer: Harold Huth. Executive producer: Maurice Ostrer. Director: Arthur Crabtree. Writer: Eleanor Smith and Roland Pertwee (from the novel *Caravan* by Lady Eleanor Smith). Cinematography: Stephen Dade.

Main cast: Richard Darrell—Stewart Granger; Rosal—Jean Kent; Oriana Camperdine—Anne Crawford; Sir Francis Castleton—Dennis Price; Wycroft—Robert Helpmann; Don Carlos—Gerard Heinz; Bertha—Enid Stamp Taylor; Camperdine—David Horne; Juan—Pete Murray

The Magic Bow

Producer: R. J. Minney. Director: Bernard Knowles. Writers: Norman Ginsbury, Manuel Komroff (from his novel), and Roland Pertwee. Cinematography: Jack Asher and Jack E. Cox.

Main cast: Nicolo Paganini—Stewart Granger; Jeanne De Vermond—Phyllis Calvert; Bianchi—Jean Kent; Paul De La Rochelle—Dennis Price; Luigi Germi—Cecil Parker; Signor Fazzini—Felix Aylmer

1947

Hungry Hill

Producer: William Sistrom. Director: Brian Desmond Hurst. Writers: Daphne Du Maurier (from her novel), Terence Young, and Francis Crowdy. Cinematography: Desmond Dickinson.

Main cast: Fanny Rosa—Margaret Lockwood; Greyhound Johnny—Dennis Price; Copper John—Cecil Parker; Wild Johnnny Brodrick—Dermot Walsh; Henry Brodrick—Michael Denison; Jane Brodrick—Jean Simmons

Dear Murderer

Producers: Betty Box and Sydney Box (executive producer). Director: Arthur Crabtree. Writers: Muriel Box, Sydney Box, and Peter Rogers (from the play by St John Legh Clowes). Cinematography: Stephen Dade.

Main cast: Lee Warren—Eric Portman; Vivien Warren—Greta Gynt; Richard Fenton—Dennis Price; Inspector Pembury—Jack Warner; Jimmy Martin—Maxwell Reed; Avis Fenton—Hazel Court; Rita—Jane Hylton; Sergeant Fox—Andrew Crawford; Ernie—John Blyth

Holiday Camp

Producer: Sydney Box. Director: Ken Annakin. Writers: Godfrey Winn (original story), Sydney Box, Muriel Box, and Peter Rogers. Additional dialogue by Mabel Constanduros, Denis Constanduros, and Ted Willis. Cinematography: Jack E. Cox.

Main cast: Esther Harman—Flora Robson; Squadron Leader "Binkie" Hardwick/Geoffrey Baker—Dennis Price; Joe Huggett—Jack Warner; Joan Huggett—Hazel Court; Michael Halliday—Emrys Jones; Ethel Huggett—Kathleen Harrison; Angela Kirby—Yvonne Owen; Camp announcer—Esmond Knight; Jimmy Gardner—Jimmy Hanley.

Jassy

Producer: Sydney Box. Director: Bernard Knowles. Writers: Norah Lofts (from her novel), Dorothy Christie, Campbell Christie, and Geoffrey Kerr. Cinematography: Geoffrey Unsworth.

Main cast: Jassy Woodroffe—Margaret Lockwood; Dilys Helmar—Patricia Roc; Christopher Hatton—Dennis Price; Nick Helmar—Basil Sydney; Barney Hatton—Dermot Walsh; Lindy Wicks—Esma Cannon; Beatrice Helmar—Linden Travers; Tom Woodroffe—John Laurie.

The Master of Bankdam

Producers: Walter Forde, Edward Dryhurst, Culley Ford (associate producer), and Nat A. Bronstein (executive producer). Director: Walter Forde. Writers: Thomas Armstrong (from his novel), Edward Dryhurst, and Moie Charles. Cinematography: Basil Emmott.

Main cast: Annie Pickersgill—Anne Crawford; Joshua Crowther—Dennis Price; Simeon Crowther senior—Tom Walls; Zebediah Crowther—Stephen Murray; Clara Baker—Linden Travers; Simeon Crowther junior—Jimmy Hanley.

The White Unicorn

Producers: John Corfield and Harold Huth. Director: Bernard Knowles. Writers: Moie Charles, A. R. Rawlinson, and Robert Westerby (based on the novel *The Milk White Unicorn* by Flora Sandstrom). Cinematography: Reginald H. Wyer.

Main cast: Lucy—Margaret Lockwood; Lottie Smith—Joan Greenwood; Philip Templar—Ian Hunter; Richard Glover—Dennis Price; Joan—Eileen Peel; Fobey—Guy Middleton

1948

Easy Money

Producer: A. Frank Bundy. Director: Bernard Knowles. Writers: Arnold Ridley (from his play), Muriel Box, and Sydney Box. Cinematography: Jack Asher

Main cast: Philip Stafford—Jack Warner; Carol Stafford—Yvonne Owen; Jackie Stafford—Petula Clark; Martin Latham—David Tomlinson; Herbert Atkins—Mervyn Johns; Pat Parsons—Greta Gynt; Joe Henty—Dennis Price; Mr. Lee—Bill Owen

Snowbound

Producer: Aubrey Baring. Director: David Macdonald. Writers: Hammond Innes (from his novel *The Lonely Skiier*), David Evans, and Keith Campbell. Cinematography: Stephen Dade and Reg Johnson.

Main cast: Derek Engles—Robert Newton; Neil Blair—Dennis Price; Joe Wesson—Stanley Holloway; Von Kellerman/Keramikos—Herbert Lom

Good Time Girl

Producers: Sydney Box and Samuel Golwyn Jr (associate producer). Director: David Macdonald. Writers: Muriel Box, Sydney Box, Ted Willis, and Arthur La Bern (from his novel *Night Darkens the Streets*). Cinematography: Stephen Dade.

Main cast: Gwen Rawlings—Jean Kent; Michael "Red" Farrell—Dennis Price; Max Vine—Herbert Lom; Jimmy Rosso—Peter Glenville; Miss Thorpe—Flora Robson; Lyla Lawrence—Diana Dors.

1949

The Bad Lord Byron

Producers: Aubrey Baring and Alfred Roome (associate producer). Director: David Macdonald. Writers: Paul Holt, Laurence Kitchin, Anthony Thorne, Peter Quennell, and Terence Young. Cinematography: Stephen Dade

Main cast: Lord George Gordon Byron—Dennis Price; Teresa Guiccioli—Mai Zetterling; Lady Caroline Lamb—Joan Greenwood; Augusta Leigh—Linden Travers; Annabella Milbanke—Sonia Holm; John Hobhouse—Raymond Lovell; Fletcher—Leslie Dwyer; Mr. Hopton—Wilfrid Hyde-White.

Kind Hearts and Coronets
Producers: Michael Balcon, Michael Relph (associate producer), Director: Robert Hamer, Writers: Roy Horniman (from his novel "Oblese oblige"), Robert Hamer, John Dighton, Nancy Mitford. Cinematography - Douglas Slocombe
Main cast: Louis/Louis's father/Bishop of Matabililand—Dennis Price; Edith—Valerie Hobson; Sibella—Joan Greenwood; The D' Ascoyne family (all eight members)—Alec Guinness; The Hangman—Miles Malleson.

The Lost People
Producer: Gordon Wellesley. Directors: Muriel Box and Bernard Knowles. Writer: Bridget Boland (from her play *Cockpit*). Cinematography: Jack Asher.
Main cast: Captain Ridley—Dennis Price; Lily—Mai Zetterling; Jan—Richard Attenborough; Marie—Siobhan McKenna; Peter—Maxwell Reed; Sergeant Barnes—William Hartnell; Professor—Gerard Heinz

1950

The Dancing Years
Director: Harold French. Producer: Warwick Ward. Writers: Ivor Novello (play), Warwick Ward, and Jack Whittingham. Cinematography: Stephen Dade.
Main cast: Rudi Kleiber—Dennis Price; Gisèle Préville—Maria Zeitler; Grete—Patricia; Prince Reinaldt—Anthony Nicholls.

1951

Murder Without Crime
Producer: Victor Skutezky. Directorand writer (from his play): J. Lee Thompson. Cinematography: William McLeod.
Main cast: Matthew—Dennis Price; Stephen—Derek Farr; Jan—Patricia Plunkett; Grena—Joan Dowling

The Adventurers
Producers: Aubrey Baring, Alex Bryce (associate producer), and Maxwell Setton. Director: David MacDonald. Writer: Robert Westerby. Cinematography: Oswald Morris.

Main cast: Clive Hunter—Dennis Price; Pieter Brandt—Jack Hawkins; Anne Hunter—Siobhan McKenna; Jack O' Connell—Bernard Lee

The House in the Square

Producer: Sol C. Siegel. Director: Roy Ward Baker. Writers: John L. Balderston (from his play), Henry James, Joseph L. Mankiewicz, and Ranald MacDougall. Cinematography: Georges Perinal.

Main cast: Peter Standish—Tyrone Power; Helen Pettigrew/Martha Forsyth—Ann Blyth; Roger Forsyth—Michael Rennie; Tom Pettigrew—Dennis Price; Mr. Throstle—Raymond Huntley.

Lady Godiva Rides Again

Producer: Sidney Gilliat. Director: Frank Launder. Writers: Frank Launder and Val Valentine. Cinematography: Wilkie Cooper.

Main cast: Simon Abott—Dennis Price; Larry Burns—John McCallum; Mr. Clark—Stanley Holloway; Marjorie Clark—Pauline Stroud; Janie—Bernardette O' Farrell; Johnny—George Cole; Dolores August—Diana Dors; Sylvia—Kay Kendall.

The Magic Box

Producer: Ronald Neame. Director: John Boulting. Writers: Ray Allister (from the biography *Friese-Greene, Close-Up of an Inventor*) and Eric Ambler. Cinematography: Jack Cardiff.

Main cast: Miss Tagg—Renee Asherson; Jack Carter—Richard Attenborough; Lord Beaverbrook—Robert Beatty; Reporter—Michael Denison; William Friese-Greene—Robert Donat; Police constable 94-B—Laurence Olivier; Harold the photographer—Dennis Price (many other well-known actors appear in very minor roles).

1952

Song of Paris

Producers: Roger Proudlock and Nigel Proudlock (associate producer). Director: John Guillermin. Writers: Allan MacKinnon, Frank Muir, Denis Norden, and William Rose. Cinematography: Ray Elton.

Main cast: Matthew Ibbetson—Dennis Price; Clementine—Anne Vernon; Count Marcel De Sarliac—Mischa Auer; Mrs. Ibbetson—Hermione Baddeley

Tall Headlines

Producer: Raymond Stross. Director: Terence Young. Writers: Audrey Erskine-Lindop (from her novel) and Dudley Leslie. Cinematography: C. M. Pennington-Richards.

Main cast: Doris Richardson—Mai Zetterling; Philip Rackham—Michael Denison; Mary Rackham—Flora Robson; Maurice Fletcher—Dennis Price; Mr. Spencer—Sidney James

1953

Noose for a Lady

Producer: Victor Hanbury. Director: Wolf Rilla. Writers: Rex Rienits and Gerald Verner (from his novel). Cinematography: Walter J. Harvey.

Main cast: Simon Gale—Dennis Price; Jill Hallam—Rona Anderson; Doctor Evershed—Ronald Howard; Margaret Allan—Pamela Alan; Vanessa Lane—Melissa Stribling; Miss Ginch—Esma Cannon; Robert Upcott—Charles Lloyd Pack

Murder at 3am

Producers: John Ainsworth and David Henley. Director: Francis Searle. Writers: John Ainsworth and Moie Charles. Cinematography: S. D. Onions.

Main cast: Inspector Peter Lawton—Dennis Price; Joan Lawton—Peggy Evans; Edward King/Jim King—Philip Saville; Lena—Greta Mayaro; Sergeant Bill Todd—Rex Garner; Old Skip—Leonard Sharp

The Intruder

Producer: Ivan Foxwell. Director: Guy Hamilton. Writers: Robin Maugham (from his book, *Line on Ginger*), John Hunter, and Anthony Squire. Cinematography: Edward Scaife.

Main cast: Wolf Merton—Jack Hawkins; Tim—Hugh Williams; Ginger Edwards—Michael Medwin; John Summers—George Cole; Leonard Pirry—Dennis Price; Don Cope—Duncan Lamont

1954

Time Is My Enemy

Director: Don Chaffey. Writers: Ella Adkins (based on her play *Second Chance*) and Allan MacKinnon. Cinematography: Geoffrey Faithfull.

Main cast: Martin Radley—Dennis Price; Barbara Everton—Renee Asherson; John Everton—Patrick Barr; Charles Wayne—Duncan Lamont; Evelyn Gower—Susan Shaw

Eight Witnesses

Producers: Gene Martel and Burt Balaban (executive producer). Director: Lawrence Huntington. Writer: Halstead Welles (story and screenplay). Cinematography: Bruno Stephan.

Main cast: Helen Hildebrand—Peggy Ann Garner; Allan—Dennis Price; Hildebrand—Charles Jacquemar; the killer—Wolfgang Buttner

For Better, For Worse

Producer: Kenneth Harper. Director: J. Lee Thompson. Writers: Alec Grahame, J. Lee Thompson, Peter Myers, and Arthur Watkyn (from his play). Cinematography: Guy Green.

Main cast: Tony Howard—Dirk Bogarde; Anne Purves—Susan Stephen; Anne's father—Cecil Parker; Anne's mother—Eileen Herlie; Miss Mainbrace—Athene Seyler

1955

That Lady

Producers: Sy Bartlett and Ronald Kinnoch (associate producer). Director: Terence Youngsters. Writers: Kate O' Brien (from her play), Sy Bartlett, and Anthony Veiller. Cinematography: Robert Krasker,

Main cast: Ana De Mendoza—Olivia de Havilland; Antonio Perez—Gilbert Roland; King Philip II of Spain—Paul Scofield; Mateo Vasquez—Dennis Price; Captain—Christopher Lee

Oh, Rosalinda!!!

Producers: Michael Powell, Emeric Pressburger, and Sydney Streeter (associate producer). Directors and writers: Michael Powell and Emeric Pressburger. Cinematography: Christopher Challis.

Main cast: General Orlovsky—Anthony Quayle; Doctor Falke 'The Bat'—Anton Walbrook; Major Frank—Dennis Price; Rosalinda—Ludmilla Tcherina; Colonel Eisenstein—Michael Redgrave

1956

Private's Progress

Producers: Roy Boulting and Ernest Holding (associate producer). Director: John Boulting. Writers: Alan Hackney (based on his story), Frank Harvey, and John Boulting. Cinematography: Eric Cross.

Main cast: Private Stanley Windrush—Ian Carmichael; Brigadier Bertram Tracepurcel—Dennis Price; Private Cox—Richard Attenborough;

Major Hitchcock—Terry-Thomas; Arthur Egan—Peter Jones; Private Horrocks—Ian Bannen; Private George Blake—Victor Maddern; Private Dai Jones—Kenneth Griffith; Captain Bootle—Thorley Walters; Prudence Greenslade—Jill Adams; Psychiatrist—John Le Mesurier

Charley Moon

Producers: Aubrey Baring and Colin Lesslie. Director: Guy Hamilton. Writers: Reginald Arkell (from his novel), Leslie Bricusse, and John Cresswell. Cinematography: Jack Hildyard.

Main cast: Charley Moon—Max Bygraves; Harold Armytage—Dennis Price; Alf Higgins—Michael Medwin; Mary Minton—Florence Desmond; Angel Dream—Shirley Eaton; Charley moon at 8 years old—Anthony Bygraves (uncredited)

Port Afrique

Producers: David E. Rose (executive producer) and John R. Sloan. Director: Rudolph Mate. Writers: Bernard Victor Dryer (from his novel), Frank Partos, and John Cresswell. Cinematography: Wilkie Cooper.

Main cast: Ynez—Pier Angeli; Rip Reardon—Philip Carey; Robert Blackton—Dennis Price. Colonel Moussac—Eugene Deckers; Franz Vermes—Christopher Lee

A Touch of the Sun

Producer: Raymond Stross. Director: Gordon Parry. Writer: Alfred Shaughnessy (original story and screenplay). Cinematography: Arthur Grant.

Main cast: William Darling—Frankie Howerd; Ruby—Ruby Murray; Digby Hatchard—Dennis Price; Rose Blake—Dorothy Bromiley. Lucienne—Katherine Kath; Sid—Gordon Harker; Herbert Hardcastle—Reginald Beckwith; Purchase—Richard Wattis; May—Alfie Bass; Alice Kann—Miriam Karlin; Miss Tickle—Esma Cannon; Honeymooner (uncredited)—Pete Murray.

1957

Fortune is a Woman

Producers: Sidney Gilliat, Frank Launder, Leslie Gilliat (associate producer), and John Harvel (executive producer). Director: Sidney Gilliat. Writers: Sidney Gilliat, Winston Graham (from his novel), Frank Launder, and Val Valentine. Cinematography: Gerald Gibbs.

Main cast: Oliver Branwell—Jack Hawkins; Sarah Morton/Branwell—Arlene Dahl; Tracey Moreton—Dennis Price; Mrs. Moreton—Violet

Farebrother; Clive Fisher—Ian Hunter; Old Abercrombie—Malcolm Keen; Michael Abercrombie—Geoffrey Keen; Detective Inspector Barnes—Michael Goodliffe

The Naked Truth

Producers: Giulio Zampi (associate producer) and Mario Zampi, Director: Mario Zampi. Writer: Michael Pertwee. Cinematography: Stanley Pavey.

Main cast: Lord Mayley—Terry-Thomas; Wee Sonny MacGregor—Peter Sellers; Flora Ransom—Peggy Mount; Melissa Right—Shirley Eaton; Nigel Dennis—Dennis Price

1958

Hello London

Producers: George Fowler, Sonja Henie, and Alan Neuman (executive producer). Writers: Guy Elmes, Ken Englund, George Fowler, and Herbert Sargent. No director credit is given. Cinematography: Otto Heller.

Main cast (nearly all the actors play themselves): Sonja Henie, Michael Wilding, Dora Bryan, Roy Castle, Robert Coote, Lisa Gastoni, Eunice Gayson, Ronny Graham, Charles Heslop, Stanley Holloway, Oliver Johnston, Trefor Jones, Dennis Price, Oliver Reed (film debut), Joan Regan.

1959

Danger Within

Producers: Colin Lesslie and Adrian D. Worker (associate producer). Director: Don Chaffey. Writers: Bryan Forbes, Frank Harvey, and Michael Gilbert (from his novel). Cinematography: Arthur Grant.

Main cast: Lieutenant Colonel Baird - Richard Todd; Lieutenant Colonel Huxley—Bernard Lee; Major Charles Marquand—Michael Wilding; Captain 'Bunter' Phillips—Richard Attenborough; Captain Rupert Callender—Dennis Price; Captain Roger Byfold—Donald Houston; Captain Tony Long—William Franklyn; Prisoner with pin-up (uncredited)—Michael Caine

I'm Alright, Jack

Producer: Roy Boulting. Director: John Boulting. Writers: Alan Hackney (from his novel), Frank Harvey, and John Boulting. Cinematography: Mutz Greenbaum.

Main cast: Stanley Windrush—Ian Carmichael; Major Hitchcock—Terry-Thomas; Fred Kite/Sir John Kennaway—Peter Sellers; Sidney De Vere Cox—Richard Attenborough; Bertram Tracepurcel—Dennis Price; Aunt Dolly—Margaret Rutherford; Mrs. Kite—Irene Handl

Don't Panic, Chaps

Producer: Teddy Baird. Director: George Pollock. Writers: Michael Corston, Jack Davies, and Ronald Holroyd. Cinematography: Arthur Graham.

Main cast: Captain Von Krisling—Dennis Price; Finch—George Cole; Brown—Thorley Walters; Elsa—Nadja Regin; Ackroyd—Harry Fowler.

1960

Five Golden Hours

Producers: Giulio Zampi and Mario Zampi. Director: Mario Zampi. Writer: Hans Wilhelm.
Cinematography: Christopher Challis.

Main cast: Aldo Bondi—Ernie Kovacs; Baroness Sandra—Cyd Charisse; Mr. Bing—George Sanders; Raphael—Dennis Price; Doctor Alfieri—John Le Mesurier; Father Superior—Finlay Currie; Gabrielle—Ron Moody.

School for Scoundrels

Producers: Hal E. Chester (executive producer), Douglas Rankin, and Cyril Frankel. Directors: Robert Hamer and Hal E. Chester. Writers: Stephen Potter (from his novels), Patricia Moyes, and Hal E. Chester. Cinematography: Erwin Hillier.

Main cast: Henry Palfrey—Ian Carmichael; Raymond Delauney—Terry-Thomas; Mr. Stephen Potter—Alastair Sim; April Smith—Janette Scott; Dunstan Dorchester—Dennis Price; Dudley Dorchester—Peter Jones.

Oscar Wilde

Producers: Gregory Ratoff, David Middlemas, William Kirby, amd Jo Eisinger. Director: Gregory Ratoff. Writers: Jo Eisinger, Frank Harris, Leslie Stokes, and Sewell Stokes. Cinematography: Georges Perinal.

Main cast: Oscar Wilde—Robert Morley; Sir Edward Carson—Ralph Richardson; Constance Wilde—Phyllis Calvert; Lord Alfred Douglas—John Neville; Robert Ross—Dennis Price.

Tunes of Glory

Producers: Albert Fennell (executive producer) and Colin Lesslie. Director: Ronald Neame. Writer: James Kennaway (from his novel). Cinematography: Arthur Ibbetson.

Main cast: Major Jock Sinclair—Alec Guinness; Lieutenant Colonel Basil Barrow—John Mills; Major Charlie Scott—Dennis Price; Mary Titterington—Kay Walsh; Corporal Piper Ian Fraser—John Fraser; Morag Sinclair—Susannah York; Captain Jimmy Cairns—Gordon Jackson.

Piccadilly Third Stop

Producers: Norman Williams and Sydney Box (executive producer). Director: Wolf Rilla. Writer: Leigh Vance. Cinematography: Ernest Steward.

Main cast: Dominic Colpoys-Owen—Terence Morgan; Seraphina Yokami—Yoko Tani; Joe Preedy—John Crawford; Christine Preedy—Mai Zetterling; Colonel—William Hartnell; Edward—Dennis Price.

The Millionairess

Producers: Pierre Rouve and Dimitri De Grunwald (executive producer), Director: Anthony Asquith. Writers: George Bernard Shaw (from his play), Ricardo Aragno, and Wolf Mankowitz. Cinematography: Jack Hildyard.

Main cast: Epifania Parerga—Sophia Loren; Dr. Ahmed El Kabir—Peter Sellers; Julius Sagamore—Alastair Sim; Joe—Vittorio De Sica; Doctor Adrian Bland—Dennis Price; Alastair—Gary Raymond.

The Pure Hell of St. Trinian's

Producers: Sidney Gilliat, Frank Launder, and Leslie Gilliat (associate producer). Director: Frank Launder. Writers: Sidney Gilliat, Frank Launder, and Val Valentine. Cinematography: Gerald Gibbs.

Main cast: Professor Canford—Cecil Parker; 'Flash' Harry—George Cole; Sergeant Ruby Gates—Joyce Grenfell; Culpepper-Brown—Eric Barker; Butters—Thorley Walters; Miss Harker-Parker—Irene Handl; Gore Blackwood—Dennis Price; Alphonse O' Reilly—Sidney James; Minister of Education—John Le Mesurier.

1961

No Love for Johnnie

Producers: Betty Box and Earl St John (executive producer). Director: Ralph Thomas. Writers: Wilfred Fienburgh (from his novel), Nicholas Phipps, and Mordecai Richler. Cinematography: Ernest Steward.

Main cast: Johnnie Byrne—Peter Finch; Fred Andrews—Stanley Holloway; Pauline—Mary Peach; Roger Renfrew—Donald Pleasence; Mary—Billie Whitelaw; Flagg—Dennis Price.

The Rebel

Producer: W. A. Whittaker. Director: Robert Day. Writers: Ray Galton, Alan Simpson, and Tony Hancock. Cinematography: Gilbert Taylor.

Main cast: Anthony Hancock—Tony Hancock; Sir Charles Broward—George Sanders; Paul—Paul Massie; Margot—Margit Saad; Jim Smith—Dennis Price; Mrs. Crevatte—Irene Handl.

Double Bunk

Producers: George H. Brown and Jan Darnley-Smith (associate producer). Director and writer: C. M. Pennington-Richards. Cinematography: Stephen Dade.

Main cast: Jack—Ian Carmichael; Peggy—Janette Scott; Sid—Sidney James; Sandra—Liz Fraser; Leonard Watson—Dennis Price; Harper—Reginald Beckwith; Mrs. Harper—Irene Handl; O' Malley—Noel Purcell; Flower man—Graham Stark.

Watch It, Sailor!

Producers: Maurice Cowan, Michael Carreras (executive producer), and Anthony Nelson Keys (associate producer). Director: Wolf Rilla. Writers: Faulkland L. Cary and Philip King. Cinematography: Arthur Grant.

Main cast: Lieutenant Commander Hardcastle—Dennis Price; Daphne Pink—Liz Fraser; Edie Hornett—Irene Handl; Shirley Hornett—Vera Day; Carnoustie Bligh—Graham Stark; Albert Tufnell—John Meillon; Emma Hornett—Marjorie Rhodes.

Victim

Producer: Michael Relph. Director: Basil Dearden. Writers: Janet Green and John McCormack. Cinematography: Otto Heller.

Main cast: Melville Farr—Dirk Bogarde; Laura Farr—Sylvia Syms; Calloway—Dennis Price; Lord Fullbrook—Anthony Nicholls; Paul Mandrake—Peter Copley; Sandy Youth (the blackmailer)—Derren Nesbitt.

What a Carve Up!

Producers: Robert S. Baker and Monty Berman. Director: Pat Jackson. Writers: Ray Cooney, Tony Hilton, and Frank King. Cinematography: Monty Berman.

Main cast: Syd Butler—Sidney James; Ernie Broughton—Kenneth Connor; Linda Dickson—Shirley Eaton; Guy Broughton—Dennis Price;

Everett Sloane—Donald Pleasence; Fisk—Michael Gough; Aunt Emily—Esma Cannon.

1962

Behave Yourself (short film)

Producers: Harold Baim. Director: Michael Winner. Writers: Emily Post and Michael Winner. Cinematography: Eric Owen.

Main cast: Dennis Price—Mr Dennis Price; Jack Jackson—Mr Jack Jackson; Pete Murray—Mr Pete Murray.

Play it Cool

Producers: David Deutsch, Julian Wintle, Leslie Parkin, and Denis Holt (associate producer). Director: Michael Winner. Writer: Jack Henry. Cinematography: Reginald H. Wyer.

Main cast: Billy Universe—Billy Fury; Alvin—Michael Anderson Jr; Sir Charles Bryant—Dennis Price; Ring-a-ding—Keith Hamshere; Freddy—Ray Brooks; Joey—Jeremy Bulloch; Larry Granger—Maurice Kaufmann; Herself—Helen Shapiro; Himself—Bobby Vee; Himself—Alvin Stardust.

Go to Blazes

Producer: Kenneth Harper. Director: Michael Truman. Writers: Patrick Campbell, Ronald Cass (story adaptation), Vivienne Knight, and Peter Myers. Cinematography: Erwin Hillier.

Main cast: Bernard—Dave King; Arson Eddie—Robert Morley; Harry—Daniel Massey; Fire Chief Withers—Dennis Price; Colette—Coral Browne; Alfie—Norman Rossington; Chantal—Maggie Smith; Scrap dealer—Wilfrid Lawson.

The Pot Carriers

Producer: Gordon Scott. Director: Peter Graham Scott. Writers: T. J. Morrison and Mike Watts. Cinematography: Erwin Hillier.

Main cast: Red Band—Ronald Fraser; Rainbow—Paul Massie; Wendy—Carole Lesley; Smooth Tongue Bertie—Dennis Price; Governor—Paul Rogers; Mouse—Davy Kaye; Chief Officer Bailey—Eddie Byrne; Lang—Alfred Burke; Mrs. Red Band—Vanda Godsell.

Kill or Cure

Producers: Lawrence P. Bachmann and George H. Brown. Director: George Pollock. Writers: David Pursall and Jack Seddon. Cinematography: Geoffrey Faithfull.

Main cast: Captain Jeroboam Barker-Rynde—Terry-Thomas; Rumbelow—Eric Sykes; Doctor Julian Crossley—Dennis Price; Detective Inspector Hook—Lionel Jeffries; Frances Roitman—Moira Redmond.

The Amorous Prawn
Producer: Leslie Gilliat. Director: Anthony Kimmins. Writers: Anthony Kimmins (from his play) and Nicholas Phipps. Cinematography: Wilkie Cooper.

Main cast: Corporal Sidney Green—Ian Carmichael; Lady Dodo Fitzadam—Joan Greenwood; General Sir Hamish Fitzadam—Cecil Parker; Prawn (Mr. Vernon)—Dennis Price; Larry Hoffman—Robert Beatty; Private Suzie Tidmarsh—Liz Fraser.

1963

The Cool Mikado
Producer: Harold Baim. Director: Michael Winner. Writers: Michael Winner, Lew Schwarz, Phyllis White, and Maurice Browning (adapted from the Gilbert and Sullivan opera). Cinematography: Dennis Ayling and Martin Curtis.

Main cast: Ko-Ko Flintridge—Frankie Howerd; Judge Herbert Mikado/ Charlie Hotfleisch—Stubby Kaye; Mike—Mike Winters; Bernie—Bernie Winters; Pooh-Bah Private Detective—Tommy Cooper; Ronald Fortescue—Dennis Price; Nanki—Lionel Blair.

The Wrong Arm of the Law
Producers: Robert Velaise (executive producer), Aubrey Baring, E. M. Smedley-Aston, and Cecil F. Ford (associate producer). Director: Cliff Owen. Writers: Ray Galton, Alan Simpson, Ivor Jay, William Whistance Smith, Len Heath, John Antrobus, and John Warren. Cinematography: Ernest Steward.

Main cast: Pearly Gates—Peter Sellers; Inspector Fred 'Nosey' Parker—Lionel Jeffries; Nervous O'Toole—Bernard Cribbins; Trainer King—Davy Kaye; Valerie—Nanette Newman; Jack Coombes—Bill Kerr; Bluey May—Ed Devereaux; Educated Ernest (uncredited guest appearance)—Dennis Price.

The V.I.P.s
Producers: Anatole De Grunwald and Roy Parkinson (associate producer). Director: Anthony Asquith. Writer: Terence Rattigan. Cinematography: Jack Hildyard.

Main cast: Frances Andros—Elizabeth Taylor; Paul Andros—Richard Burton; Marc Champselle—Louis Jordan; Gloria Gritti—Elsa Martinelli; The Duchess of Brighton—Margaret Rutherford; Miss Mead—Maggie Smith; Les Magnum—Rod Taylor; Max Buda—Orson Welles; Commander Millbank—Dennis Price.

Tamahine

Producers: John Bryan and Michael Forlong (associate producer). Director: Philip Leacock. Writers: Denis Cannan and Thelma Niklaus (from her novel). Cinematography: Geoffrey Unsworth.

Main cast: Tamahine—Nancy Kwan; Richard Poole—John Fraser; Charles Poole—Dennis Price; Madam Becque—Coral Browne; Tim Clove—Derek Nimmo.

The Cracksman

Producer: W. A. Whittaker. Director: Peter Graham-Scott. Writers: Lew Schwarz, Charlie Drake, and Mike Watts. Cinematography: Harry Waxman.

Main cast: Ernest Wright—Charlie Drake; Muriel—Nyree Dawn-Porter; Guvnor—George Sanders; Grantley—Dennis Price; Nosher—Percy Herbert; Domino—Eddie Byrne; Feathers—Finlay Currie.

Doctor in Distress

Producers: Betty Box and Earl St John (executive producer). Director: Ralph Thomas. Writers: Nicholas Phipps, Ronald Scott Thorn, and Richard Gordon (from his Doctor novels). Cinematography: Ernest Steward.

Main cast: Doctor Simon Sparrow—Dirk Bogarde; Sir Lancelot Spratt—James Robertson Justice; Delia Mallory—Samantha Eggar; Iris Marchant—Barbara Murray; Sonia/Helga—Mylene Demongeot; Major Tommy Ffrench—Donald Houston; Harry Heilbronn—Leo McKern; Doctor Blacker—Dennis Price.

1964

Murder Most Foul

Producers: Ben Arbeid and Lawrence P. Bachmann (executive producer). Director: George Pollock. Writers: David Pursall and Jack Seddon (adapted from Agatha Christie's novel). Cinematography: Desmond Dickinson.

Main cast: Miss Jane Marple—Margaret Rutherford; H. Driffold Cosgood—Ron Moody; Inspector Craddock—Charles Tingwell; Justice

Crosby—Andrew Cruickshank; Mrs. Gladys Thomas—Megs Jenkins; Ralph Summers—Ralph Michael; Bill Hanson—James Bolam; Sheila Upward—Francesca Annis; Harris Tumbrill—Dennis Price.

A Jolly Bad Fellow

Producer: Donald Taylor. Director: Don Chaffey. Writer: Robert Hamer. Cinematography: Gerald Gibbs.

Main cast: Professor Kerris Bowles-Ottery—Leo McKern; Delia Brooks—Janet Munro; Clarinda Bowles-Ottery—Maxine Audley; Doctor John Hughes—Dennis Price; Doctor Woolley—Miles Malleson; Willie Pugh-Smith—Mervyn Johns; Mrs. Pugh-Smith—Patricia Jessel.

The Horror of It All

Producers: Margia Dean and Robert L. Lippert (executive producer). Director: Terence Fisher. Writer: Ray Russell. Cinematography: Arthur Lavis.

Main cast: Jack Robinson—Pat Boone; Cynthia Marley—Erica Rogers; Cornwallis Marley—Dennis Price; Natalia Marley—Andree Melly; Reginald Marley—Valentine Dyall.

The Comedy Man

Producers: David Henley and Jon Penington. Director: Alvin Rakoff. Writers: Douglas Hayes (from his novel) and Peter Yeldham. Cinematography: Ken Hodges.

Main cast: Chick Byrd—Kenneth More; Thomas Rutherford—Cecil Parker; Tommy Morris—Dennis Price; Judy—Billie Whitelaw; Theodore Littleton—Norman Rossington; Fay Trubshaw—Angela Douglas; Julian Baxter—Edmund Purdom.

The Earth Dies Screaming

Producers: Robert L. Lippert and Jack Parsons. Director: Terence Fisher. Writer: Harry Spalding. Cinematography: Arthur Lavis.

Main cast: Jeff Nolan—Willard Parker; Peggy Hatton—Virginia Field; Quinn Taggart—Dennis Price; Edgar Otis—Thorley Walters; Violet Courtland—Vanda Godsell; Mel Brenard—David Spenser.

1965

A High Wind in Jamaica

Producers: John Croydon, Clifford Parkes (associate producer), and Tom Pevsner (associate producer). Director: Alexander MacKendrick. Writers:

Stanley Mann, Ronald Harwood, Denis Cannan, and Richard Hughes (from his novel). Cinematography: Douglas Slocombe.

Main cast: Chavez—Anthony Quinn; Zac—James Coburn; Mathias—Dennis Price; Rosa—Lila Kedrova; Frederick Thornton—Nigel Davenport; Alice Thornton—Isabel Dean; Captain Marpole—Kenneth Warren.

The Curse of Simba

Producers: Richard Gordon, Kenneth Rive, and Gerald A. Fernback (executive producer). Director: Lindsay Shonteff. Writers: Brian Clemens and Leigh Vance. Cinematography: Gerald Gibbs.

Main cast: Mike Stacey—Bryant Halliday; Major Lomas—Dennis Price; Janet Stacey—Lisa Daniely; Janet's mother—Mary Kerridge; Police Inspector—John Witty; Mrs. Lomas—Jean Lodge; African expert—Louis Mahoney.

Ten Little Indians

Producers: Harry M. Popkin, Harry Alan Towers, and Oliver A. Unger (executive producer). Director: George Pollock. Writers: Peter Yeldham and Harry Alan Towers (based on the novel by Agatha Christie). Cinematography - Ernest Steward.

Main cast: Hugh Lombard—Hugh O' Brian; Ann Clyde—Shirley Eaton; Mike Raven—Fabian;
General Mandrake—Leo Genn; William Blore—Stanley Holloway; Judge Cannon—Wilfrid Hyde-White
Ilona Bergen—Dahlia Lavi; Doctor Armstrong—Dennis Price.

1967

Just Like a Woman

Producers: Bob Kellett and Stuart Ford Marchant (associate producer). Director and writer: Robert Fuest. Cinematography: Billy Williams.

Main cast: Scilla McKenzie—Wendy Craig; Lewis McKenzie—Francis Matthews; John Martin—John Wood; Bathroom salesman—Dennis Price; Saul Alexander—Peter Jones; Graff Von Fischer—Clive Dunn.

Jules Verne's Rocket to the Moon

Producers: Harry Alan Towers and Louis M. Heyward. Director: Don Sharp. Writers: Harry Alan Towers and Dave Freeman (inspired by the novels of Jules Verne). Cinematography: Reginald H. Wyer.

Main cast: Phineas T. Barnum—Burl Ives; General Tom Thumb—Jimmy Clitheroe; Captain Sir Harry Washington Smythe - Terry-Thomas;

Professor Von Bulow—Gert Frobe; Sir Charles Dillworthy—Lionel Jeffries; The Duke of Barset—Dennis Price; Gaylord Sullivan—Troy Donahue; Madelaine—Dahlia Lavi; Electra—Judy Cornwell.

1969

The Haunted House of Horror

Producers: Tony Tenser and Louis B. Heyward. Director: Michael Armstrong. Writers: Michael Armstrong and Gerry Levy. Cinematography: Jack Atcheler.

Main cast: Chris—Frankie Avalon; Sheila—Jill Haworth; Inspector Bill Bradley—Dennis Price; Gary Scott—Mark Wynter; Bob Kellett—George Sewell; Sylvia Fuller—Gina Warwick; Peter—Richard O'Sullivan.

Venus in Furs

Producer: Harry Alan Towers. Director: Jesus Franco. Writers: Jesus Franco, Malvin Ward, Milo G. Cuccia, Carlo Fadda, and Bruno Leder. Cinematography: Angelo Lotti.

Main cast: Jimmy Logan—James Darren; Rita—Barbara McNair; Wanda Reed—Maria Rohm; Ahmed Kortobawi—Klaus Kinski; Percival Kapp—Dennis Price.

The Magic Christian

Producers: Denis O'Dell, Anthony B. Unger (executive producer), and Henry T. Weinstein (executive producer). Director: Joseph McGrath. Writers: Terry Southern (from his novel), Joseph McGrath, Graham Chapman, John Cleese, and Peter Sellers. Cinematography: Geoffrey Unsworth.

Main cast: Sir Guy Grand—Peter Sellers; Youngman Grand—Ringo Starr; Hamlet—Laurence Harvey; Ship's (on board the Magic Christian) Vampire—Christopher Lee; Traffic warden—Spike Milligan; Solitary drinker—Roman Polanski; Priestess of the whip—Raquel Welch; Winthrop—Dennis Price; Transvestite cabaret singer—Yul Brynner.

1970

Some Will, Some Won't

Producer: Giulio Zampi. Director: Duncan Wood. Writers: Jack Davies, Michael Pertwee, and Lew Schwarz. Cinematography: Harry Waxman.

Main cast: Herbert Russell—Ronnie Corbett; Agnes Russell—Thora Hird; Deniston Russell—Michael Hordern; Lucille—Barbara Murray;

Simon Russell—Leslie Phillips; Henry Russell—Wilfrid Brambell; Benson—Dennis Price.

The Horror of Frankenstein

Producer and director: Jimmy Sangster. Writers: Jimmy Sangster and Jeremy Burnham (based on Mary Shelley's novel). Cinematography: Moray Grant.

Main cast: Baron Victor Frankenstein—Ralph Bates; Alys—Kate O' Mara; Elizabeth Heiss—Veronica Carlson; The Graverobber—Dennis Price; Lieutenant Henry Becker—Jon Finch; Professor Heiss—Bernard Archard

Graverobber's wife—Joan Rice; The Monster—Dave Prowse.

The Rise and Rise of Michael Rimmer

Producers: Harry Fine and David Frost (executive producer). Director: Kevin Billington. Writers: Peter Cook, John Cleese, Graham Chapman, and Kevin Billington. Cinematography: Alex Thomson.

Main cast: Michael Rimmer—Peter Cook; Peter Niss—Denholm Elliott; Tom Hutchinson—Ronald Fraser; Patricia Cartwright—Vanessa Howard; Ferret—Arthur Lowe; Colonel Moffat—Julian Glover; Steven Hench—Harold Pinter; Mr. Fairburn—Dennis Price; Fromage—Graham Chapman; Pumer—John Cleese.

1971

Vampyros Lesbos

Producers: Artur Brauner and Karl Heinz Mannchen (executive producer). Director: Jesus Franco. Writers: Jesus Franco, Jaime Chavarri, and Anne Settimo (based on the novel by Bram Stoker). Cinematography: Manuel Merino.

Main cast: Countess Nadine Carody—Soledad Miranda; Doctor Alwin Seward—Dennis Price; Linda Westinghouse—Ewa Stromberg; Agra—Heidrun Kussin; Morpho—Jose Martinez Blanco.

Twins of Evil

Producers: Harry Fine and Michael Style. Director: John Hough. Writer: Tudor Gates (based on the novel by Sheridan Le Fanu). Cinematography: Dick Bush.

Main cast: Gustav Weil—Peter Cushing; Dietrich—Dennis Price; Maria Gellhorn—Mary Collinson; Frieda Gellhorn—Madeleine Collinson; Katy Weil—Kathleen Byron; Count Karnstein—Damien Thomas.

1972

Pulp

Producers: Michael Klinger and Michael Caine. Director and Writer: Mike Hodges. Cinematography: Ousama Rawi.

Main cast: Mickey King—Michael Caine; Preston Gilbert—Mickey Rooney; Ben Dinuccio—Lionel Stander; Betty Cippola—Lizabeth Scott; Liz—Nadia Cassini; Mysterious Englishman—Dennis Price; Miller—Al Lettieri; Prince Cippola—Victor Mercieca

Tower of Evil

Producers: Richard Gordon, John Pellatt (associate producer), and Joe Solomon (executive producer). Director: Jim O' Connolly. Writers: George Baxt and Jim O' Connolly. Cinematography: Desmond Dickinson.

Main cast: Brent—Bryant Haliday; Mason—Jill Haworth; Adam—Mark Edwards; Hamp—Jack Watson; Nora—Anna Palk; Dan—Derek Fowlds; Bakewell—Dennis Price; Doctor Simpson—Anthony Valentine; Des—Robin Askwith.

Dracula, Prisoner of Frankenstein

Producer: Arturo Marcos. Director: Jesus Franco. Writers: Paul D' Ales and Jesus Franco (based on the novels of Mary Shelley and Bram Stoker). Cinematography: Jose Climent.

Main cast: Doctor Frankenstein—Dennis Price; Dracula—Howard Vernon; Maria—Paca Gabaldon; Doctor Jonathan Seward—Alberto Dalbes; Chica Vampira—Britt Nichols; Amira—Genevieve Deloir Morpho—Luis Barboo; The Monster—Fernando Bilbao.

The Adventures of Barry McKenzie

Producer: Phillip Adams. Director: Bruce Beresford. Writers: Bruce Beresford and Barry Humphries.
Cinematography: Donald McAlpine.

Main cast: Barry McKenzie—Barry Crocker; Aunt Edna Everage/Hoot/Doctor De Lamphrey—Barry Humphries; Dominic—Peter Cook; Curly—Paul Bertram; Mr. Gort—Dennis Price; Mrs Gort—Avice Landone.

Alice's Adventures in Wonderland

Producers: Rene Dupont (associate producer), Derek Horne, and Josef Shaftel (executive producer).
Director: William Sterling. Writer: William Sterling (adapted from the novel by Lewis Carroll).
Cinematography: Geoffrey Unsworth.

Main cast: Alice—Fiona Fullerton; Lewis Carroll—Michael Jayston; White Rabbit—Michael Crawford; The Caterpillar - Ralph Richardson; The Duchess—Peter Bull; The Mad Hatter—Robert Helpmann; The March Hare—Peter Sellers; King of Hearts—Dennis Price; Queen of Hearts—Flora Robson.

Go For A Take

Producer: Roy Simpson. Director: Harry Booth. Writers: Harry Booth and Alan Hackney. Cinematography: Mark McDonald.

Main cast: Wilfrid Stone—Reg Varney; Jack Foster—Norman Rossington; Generous Jim—Patrick Newell; Suzi Eckmann—Anouska Hempel; Angel Montgomery—Sue Lloyd; Dracula/Himself—Dennis Price.

That's Your Funeral

Producer: Michael Carreras. Director: John Robins. Writer: Peter Lewis. Cinematography: David Holmes.

Main cast: Basil Bulstrode—Bill Fraser; Emmanuel Holroyd—Raymond Huntley; Percy—David Battley; Eugene Soul—Dennis Price; Roland Smallbody—John Ronane; Miss Peach—Sue Lloyd.

1973

Theatre of Blood

Producers: Gustave M. Berne (executive producer), Sam Jaffe (executive producer), John Kohn, and Stanley Mann. Director: Douglas Hickox. Writers: Anthony Greville-Bell, Stanley Mann, and John Kohn (inspired by the plays of William Shakespeare). Cinematography: Wolfgang Suschitzky.

Main cast: Edward Lionheart—Vincent Price; Edwina Lionheart—Diana Rigg; Peregrine Devlin—Ian Hendry; (The 'critics' in alphabetical order) Trevor Dickman—Harry Andrews; Chloe Moon—Coral Browne; Oliver Larding—Robert Coote; Solomon Psaltery—Jack Hawkins; George Maxwell—Michael Hordern; Horace Sprout—Arthur Lowe; Meredith Meredew—Robert Morley; Hector Snipe—Dennis Price.

Horror Hospital

Producers: Richard Gordon and Ray Corbett (associate producer). Director: Antony Balch. Writers: Antony Balch and Alan Watson. Cinematography: David McDonald.

Main cast: Doctor Christian Storm—Michael Gough; Jason Jones—Robin Askwith; Judy Peters—Vanessa Shaw; Aunt Harris—Ellen Pollock; Mr Pollack—Dennis Price; Frederick—Skip Martin.

The Erotic Experience of Frankenstein

Producer: Arturo Marcos. Director and writer: Jesus Franco. Cinematography: Raul Artigot.

Main cast: Doctor Seward—Alberto Dalbes; Doctor Frankenstein—Dennis Price; Cagliostro—Howard Vernon; Vera Frankenstein—Beatriz Savon; Melisa—Anne Libert; Monstruo—Fernando Bilbao; Madam Orloff—Britt Nichols; Morpho—Jesus Franco.

The Lovers of Devil's Island

Producer: Arturo Marcos. Director and writer: Jesus Franco. Cinematography: Jose Climent.

Main cast: Raymond Franval—Andres Resino; Beatriz Coblan—Genevieve Robert; The Lawyer—Dennis Price; Senora Cardel—Rosa Palomar; Rosa—Josyane Gibert; Emilia Franval—Danielle Godet; Lola—Gogo Rojo; Colonel Ford—Howard Vernon; Colonel Mendoza—Jean Guedes.

1974

Son of Dracula

Producers: Ringo Starr and Jerry Gross. Director: Freddie Francis. Writer: Jennifer Jayne. Cinematography: Norman Warwick.

Main cast: Count Downe/Musician—Harry Nilsson; Merlin the Magician—Ringo Starr; Baron Frankenstein—Freddie Jones; Amber—Suzanna Leigh; Van Helsing—Dennis Price; Igor—Skip Martin.

Excerpts

Helter Skelter (1949)

Although this is listed as being one of his films, Dennis Price's scene was actually taken from *The Bad Lord Byron* and lasted just a few seconds.

Producers: Antony Darnborough and Alfred Roome (associate producer). Director: Ralph Thomas. Writers: Gerard Bryant, Patrick Campbell, and Jan Read. Cinematography: Jack Asher.

Main cast: Susan Graham—Carol Marsh; Nick Martin—David Tomlinson; Ernest Bennett—Mervyn Johns; Spencer Stone—Peter Hammond; Giselle—Zena Marshall; Himself—Terry-Thomas; Lord Byron—Dennis Price